ARMING

without

AIMING

ARMING *without* AIMING

INDIA'S MILITARY MODERNIZATION

STEPHEN P. COHEN

and

SUNIL DASGUPTA

BROOKINGS INSTITUTION PRESS

Washington, D.C.

Copyright © 2010
THE BROOKINGS INSTITUTION
1775 Massachusetts Avenue, N.W., Washington, DC 20036
www.brookings.edu

Library of Congress Cataloging-in-Publication data

Cohen, Stephen P., 1936–
   Arming without aiming : India's military modernization / Stephen P. Cohen and
Sunil Dasgupta.
     p. cm.
   Includes bibliographical references and index.
   Summary: "India, a leading importer of advanced conventional weaponry, has
not planned strategically for its military needs, although the haphazard approach,
due to competing elements within the military and a restraint policy in place since
the Nehru era, may be the right one in seeking accommodation with others in the
region"—Provided by publisher.
   ISBN 978-0-8157-0402-7 (hardcover : alk. paper)
   1. India—Armed Forces—Weapons systems. 2. India—Armed Forces—
Operational readiness. 3. India—Defenses. 4. India—Military policy.
I. Dasgupta, Sunil. II. Title.
   UA840.C628 2010
   355.80954—dc22   2010024055

9 8 7 6 5 4 3 2 1

Printed on acid-free paper

Typeset in Minion

Composition by Cynthia Stock
Silver Spring, Maryland

Printed by R. R. Donnelley
Harrisonburg, Virginia

To Pabitra Kumar Dasgupta
who has walked long and far from his childhood
in the mica mining outpost of Koderma
in pre-independence Bihar

CONTENTS

PREFACE

There is widespread acknowledgment that India is newly important. Whether emerging, rising, or an Asian "giant," there is some expectation that India's new affluence will enable it to deploy vastly improved armed forces. This expanded military capability will enable it, then, to play a larger role in world affairs, notably in Asia, and to more effectively address military challenges both abroad and at home.

While India's historical poverty would seem to explain why it has not developed its military power, several studies have suggested reasons for why this is not the case, and why India has not been able to alter its strategic condition. In a very influential analysis in the 1990s, American strategist George Tanham argued that India had problems developing a robust security policy, including a strong military force, because the country was bereft of coherent strategic thought.[1] Tanham attributed this missing piece to internal divisions in Indian society, which left a small elite responsible for strategic matters. Cut off from the rest of society, this elite was unable to mobilize available resources into military power. The result was repeated invasions of India over the last millennium. Stephen Peter Rosen argued that internal social divisions in India prevented collective action necessary for strong defense.[2] He argued that the British had been able to raise an extraordinarily effective Indian Army by isolating the armed forces from the divisions of society. While it was possible for an independent government in India to do the same, a democratic India committed to egalitarian values and proper representation in the services would be hard-pressed to maintain a military set apart from the rest of society. In contrast, the Indian scholar Rajesh M.

Basrur has emphasized political choices and ideological preferences.[3] Indian leaders, he says, preferred to view security as a political rather than a military matter and consistently made choices that downplayed military aspects such as nuclear weapons in favor of political management of security issues.

Recent writing on India, drawing on the first period of sustained economic growth in the history of independent India, expects dramatic changes in how the country demonstrates its national power.[4] Ashley Tellis, an American strategist who has been central to the reordering of U.S.-India ties, writes, "The record thus far amply substantiates the claim that India will be one of Asia's two major ascending powers. It is expected that the Indian economy could grow at a rate of 7 to 8 percent for the next two decades. If these expectations are borne out, there is little doubt that India will overtake current giants."[5] Tellis has concurred with Central Intelligence Agency assessments that India will be the fourth most "capable concentration of power" after the United States, the European Union, and China.[6] The assumption here is that India will continue to grow rapidly and that fast growth, which will give the country the wherewithal to function as a great power, reiterates the traditionally realist affluence theory that wealth and military power go hand-in-hand. Rodney Jones, for example, finds that between 1990 and 2003 India's ability to conduct combined arms operations against Pakistan improved dramatically, giving India a 3:1 advantage in military capacity.[7] Several observers, from Singapore diplomat Kishore Mahbubani to American strategic thinker and journalist Fareed Zakaria, see India as part of the gravitational shift eastward to Asia.[8] Ambassador Teresita Schaffer notes that India is dramatically changing its outlook toward the world and is envisioning itself as a world power, with an expanding economy and greater engagement in global governance.[9]

In contrast, neorealists such as Kenneth Waltz have emphasized threat over resources.[10] States reorder their priorities when threatened, irrespective of their economic condition. Poor societies are quite capable of generating military power sufficient to frustrate and even defeat wealthier nations with bigger and better-equipped armies. In this view, India's 1998 nuclear tests were driven by its security concerns about the rising threats from Pakistan and China and established that India was willing to pay for the ability to secure its interests. On the other hand, richer societies may hold back their military spending to curb arms races; here politicians pursue political security rather than military power alone. Both India's nonalignment and nuclear weapons programs, for example, have deviated from the predictions of the affluence theory. Its nonalignment during the cold war was the legacy of its colonial history and defined by its ability to play off the United States and the Soviet Union. Further, its nuclear program sought to preserve its nuclear options while trying not to antagonize other great powers. When the tests occurred in 1974 and 1998, the circumstances were extraordinary. Certainly, the testing decisions had little to do with India's affluence at the time.

The preeminence of threat in determining the direction and content of military modernization is subject to debate as well. Over the last two decades, the military threat to India has changed dramatically toward unconventional war, but the nation's armed forces and national security decisionmaking structure appear not to have made insurgency and terrorism the centerpiece of the military modernization effort. Advanced conventional weapons such as fighter aircraft, tanks, and aircraft carriers heavily dominate India's wish list even though they have tenuous influence on the problems of insurgency and terrorism. Doctrinal changes have sought to extend conventional deterrence to subconventional conflict. However, the prospects of extending deterrence to insurgency and terrorism and especially the difficulty the Indian Army has had in going from conventional war preparation to counterinsurgency and back demonstrates the difficulties of moving large organizations, especially without strong direction from the political leadership. Juli MacDonald has taken a critical view of the Indian military establishment, especially of the ability of the armed forces to modernize meaningfully.[11]

The American scholar Amit Gupta argues that the structural context of India's modernization efforts is critical.[12] He argues that regional powers such as India suffer from uneven development because they live on a feast or famine cycle of funding and access to foreign technology and weapons. Doctrinal development is erratic as the services scramble to fit their strategies to available weapons; their armed forces do not have the balance of the great powers. Meanwhile, at home regional powers have focused energies on unconventional technologies such as nuclear weapons to minimize the consequences of their weak conventional militaries.

Others have written mournfully or scornfully of the absence of creative Indian strategic thought, especially among civilians, returning to the theme explored by Tanham earlier.[13] Former Indian defense and foreign minister Jaswant Singh says that unless India as a society comes together more effectively, it is unlikely to generate the requisite military power to pursue an active security policy.[14] Indian scholar Harsh Pant argues that in the absence of strategic thinking, economic growth has become a surrogate for national strategy.[15]

All of these explanations with their separate focuses—culture, society, political will, poverty, strategic environment—capture some of the truth. In our view India's deeply ingrained tradition of strategic restraint most powerfully explains the puzzling inability of the Indian state to generate sufficient military power to alter its strategic position vis-à-vis Pakistan or China. We see the restraint as deliberate, the result of Indian political leaders deciding that (1) the international environment was at least somewhat benign, or put another way, that India had the possibility of politically managing its threat; (2) the balance of resource allocation between defense and development had to favor the latter; and (3) there must be an ideological rejection of armed force as an instrument of state policy, a view stemming from the colonial experience and the great-power politics in which India became independent in 1947.

While expensive and redundant, India's approach of arming without strategic purpose is not without wisdom. The political preference of restraint has wisely sought to escape the security dilemma rather than embrace it. It is because of strategic restraint that other great powers in the world are facilitating, rather than fretting over, India's current rearmament, which is one of the biggest peacetime efforts by any developing country in recent history. But strategic restraint also contributes to the astounding lack of political direction in Indian efforts at military modernization. India's most eminent strategic thinker, K. Subrahmanyam, has spent most of his career pleading for modernization of the defense and strategic policy process. While Subrahmanyam has strong interests in weapons modernization (he was the leading advocate for many years of going nuclear), much of his wrath has been directed at the antiquated system by which India formulates strategic policy, makes weapons decisions, and manages the entire defense policy process.[16]

India's armed forces have long disagreed with strategic restraint as a viable position in defense policy. The country's rapidly growing strategic community would like to use India's newfound affluence and access to technology to achieve military transformation, but there is tension here and it is not clear that the new forces of change will prevail. On the one hand, India's new affluence and the nuclear tests of 1998 raise hopes that the country will break out of its strategic restraint—and assume its place as a great power.[17] On the other, India's military modernization has lacked political direction and has suffered from weak prospective planning, individual service-centered doctrines, and a disconnect between strategic objectives and the pursuit of new technology. The haphazard character of military change in India suggests that the country's historical preference for strategic restraint remains firmly in place.

No country in the world succeeds in all dimensions of military power all of the time. However, it is not so much the standard that is important, but the capability of a country compared to others, especially those with whom it could fight wars. In India's case the most likely state is Pakistan, followed by China, but there is also the possibility of military use elsewhere in the region, especially against nonstate actors. India's military power must be understood in the context of these potential calls to armed service.

THE STRUCTURE OF THIS BOOK

In chapter 1 we examine the key factors shaping India's military modernization, the deeply embedded tradition of strategic restraint, the new affluence that is driving increases in defense spending, and the growing access to advanced technology. We try to answer the question of whether affluence and technology will overcome historical restraint and lead to a new Indian assertiveness in strategic matters. In other words, will India act as a military great power? Chapter 2 offers an overview of reform efforts. Chapters 3 and 4 examine the way in which the Indian armed forces have tried to modernize, especially in marrying threats, doctrines, and equipment. Chapters 5 and 6 examine the modernization of India's capacities at the highest and lowest levels of violence, the nuclear program and the police. Our approach in these chapters is to see India's growing affluence as a starting point and examine the behavior of different institutions and actors in India's defense establishment, especially in the context of its historical strategic restraint. Chapter 7 provides a summary and conclusions regarding India's military modernization. Chapter 8 identifies some implications of our analysis for the United States.

Acknowledgments

The modernization of India's defense and military establishment is very much a work in progress. The dramatic changes in India over the last five years prolonged the writing of this book.

We warmly thank our research assistants, interns, and others who stuck with this project and made their own important contributions. First and foremost, Dhruva Jaishankar, now of the German Marshall Fund and Georgetown University, who contributed much to our understanding of India's approach to strategic affairs. We were ably assisted by four interns from the University of Chicago, Tara Chandra, Jacob Friedman, Ryan Kaminski, and Rohan Sandhu. While not formally associated with this project, Anit Mukherjee (now of Johns Hopkins School of Advanced International Studies) and Tanvi Madan (of the Lyndon B. Johnson School of Public Affairs, University of Texas) offered their valuable insights, and in Mukherjee's case, shared his work on post-Kargil military reforms.

We are indebted to many serving Indian military officers and civilian officials, who provided their understanding of India's defense modernization processes, and to others with deep understanding of the problem and processes, notably Dipankar Banerjee, P. R. Chari, Shekhar Gupta, Gurmeet Kanwal, Verghese Koithara, Raja Menon, C. Raja Mohan, Arun Sahgal, Arun Singh, Jaswant Singh, and Narendra Sisodia.

Ned Bagley, Jack Gill, Woolf Gross, Tim Hoyt, and Rajesh Kadian made up an informal sounding board in the early stages of this project. We are grateful to the anonymous readers and to Michael O'Hanlon for helping us turn a manuscript about everything into a book about something. While we received unstinting help from many individuals and organizations, the responsibility for all errors of fact and argument is ours alone.

Writing this book was partly supported by the MacArthur Foundation.

We are grateful to our children and to our wives, Roberta and Elana, for their support, patience, and humor.

CHAPTER ONE

RESTRAINT
AND AFFLUENCE

One of the most remarkable attributes of India as an independent nation has been its longstanding restraint in military strategy. Reticence in the use of force as an instrument of state policy has been the dominant political condition for Indian thinking on the military, including military modernization. From the initial delay in sending troops to defend Kashmir in 1948 to the twenty-four-year hiatus in testing nuclear weapons, India has used force mainly in response to grave provocation and as an unwelcome last resort. The country's greatest strategic success, the victory of 1971, occurred in response to a Pakistan Army crackdown on rebel Bengalis, which killed tens of thousands and forced millions of refugees to flee to India. It is notable that New Delhi did not press its military advantage in the west to resolve the Kashmir problem. Similarly, India's nuclear weapons program, the military capacity that could have transformed India's strategic position, remained in limbo for twenty-four years after India tested its first atomic device in 1974. There are exceptions to Indian restraint as well as questions about whether it was driven by capacity or intention. Of course, Pakistan has never been persuaded of Indian restraint. We discuss these issues below as part of our investigation in this chapter into whether India's new affluence and access to advanced weapons technology will end the pattern of strategic restraint, turning India into a traditional great power with clear strategic objectives and the military means to achieve them.

The answer is not self-evident. India's burgeoning resources will go a long way in reducing the most apparent obstacle to India's strategic ambition: lack of resources. Equally, India's access to Western technology—most importantly from the United States—could transform the Indian armed forces in unprecedented ways, giving the country new instruments of strategic assertion. While there are good reasons to expect a breakthrough, we do not believe it is likely. Military preparation just does not receive the kind of political attention that is necessary to marry military modernization and strategy. India's military modernization suffers from weak planning, individual service-centered doctrines, and disconnect between strategic objectives and the pursuit of new technology. In comparison, other modern states, especially India's primary rivals, Pakistan and China, focus more steadily on developing the military means to deal with their own security concerns.

The bar for change in India is so high that any talk of imminent military transformation is highly premature. Since armed force has not been a central instrument of state policy, the country has not developed the institutional structures necessary to overhaul the mechanisms for generating military power. Notwithstanding India's newfound affluence or new access to military technology, we do not see good reasons to expect dramatic change. Contrary to conventional realist wisdom, wherein threat and affluence drive military posture, we believe that military change in India will be evolutionary, driven by the slow pace of institutional change in the Indian military system. Consequently, India's strategic choices will remain limited. The Indian military system can expand in size; create new agencies, commands, and positions; and purchase new advanced weaponry, but it cannot address the contested demands over retrenchment, coordination, and reconciliation of competing interests.

It is important to emphasize that strategic restraint has not served India poorly thus far, nor will it be an ill-conceived choice for the future. In a region characterized by many conflicts and an uneasy nuclear standoff, restraint is a positive attribute. However, restraint is not seen as a virtue by those who want India to be a great power, a counterbalance to a rising China, and a provider of security in the international system rather than a passive recipient of the order created and managed by others They strongly criticize the lack of political direction, confused military doctrines, dysfunctional civil-military relations, and lack of interest in reforming defense acquisition and policymaking processes. Below, we examine the roots and trajectory of Indian strategic restraint and then the challenges to restraint brought on by the advent of affluence and new technology.

THE DEVELOPMENT OF RESTRAINT

India's weak military policy from independence in 1947 to the war with China in 1962 is evidence of the lower priority given to military matters than to other national concerns. The country was unable to afford ambitious strategic objectives and robust military rearmament. Instead, as the cold war intensified, the national leadership sought gains in the political arena through its policy of nonalignment. As has often been noted, India's position resembled America's strategy of distancing itself from European wars, and Nehru's speeches of the day resembled George Washington's Farewell Address, which cautioned against entangling alliances.

The primary military assignment in the 1950s was international peacekeeping, a function in which the Indian Army excelled. In Korea and later in the Congo, the Indian Army's performance was professional and measured. In the peacekeeping roles of the time—as opposed to contemporary UN Chapter 7 peace enforcement—the Indian Army found the perfect canvas for the expression of its quiet capacity. In national defense, however, the civil-military system, and particularly the political leadership, fell short.

The British Empire had raised a powerful Indian Army, which had fought creditably in the world wars in Europe, North Africa, and Burma, and secured possessions from Hong Kong to Aden; but India's nationalists saw military power as an instrument of oppression, imperialism, and undue financial burden, and most were strongly critical of India's armed forces.[1] The struggle against the British had focused in part on the Raj's use of military power. The success of the nonviolent independence movement buttressed the view that India did not have to raise a strong military to develop effective means of international influence.

Though early Indian nationalists such as Bal Gangadhar Tilak and Gopal Krishna Gokhale saw military service as a means to secure home rule; Mahatma Gandhi and Jawaharlal Nehru, the two Indian leaders with the greatest influence on the direction of independent India, saw military spending as a burden imposed by the British in defense of their empire. In 1938 Nehru wrote that India did not face any significant military challenge; the only military role he saw for the Indian Army was in suppressing the tribes of the North-West Frontier Province, who were, in any case, too primitive in his view to fight a modern military outside the tribal areas.[2] In general, Nehru agreed with Gandhi that the use of force in political life was inappropriate. The mainstream in the Indian independence struggle was committed to nonviolent strategies. Nehru, in particular, believed that high principles trumped the use of force as an instrument of Indian foreign policy. This thinking was in sharp contrast to that of Nehru's greatest political rival, Subhas Chandra Bose, who had a very different view about the use of force as an instrument of politics. Bose turned to the Germans and Japanese to support his Indian National Army that fought the British during World War II. Had Bose survived the war (he was killed in a 1945 plane crash), India's history would have been very different. There were others who remained in the Congress but expressed strong interest in strategic and military matters, most exceptionally, K. M. Panikkar, the eminent diplomat-scholar, who wrote an important treatise on India's new security situation, especially regarding China and the Indian Ocean.[3]

Despite the ideological preference, the new government did use force repeatedly in the early years. The Indian Army put up a rearguard action to defend Kashmir in 1948–49. The First Kashmir War remains one of India's most intense conflicts; the Indian Army won more Param Vir Chakra medals, the highest military honor in India, in that war than in any other conflict since. Earlier the Indian Army had contributed units to the binational Punjab Boundary Force deployed along the India-Pakistan border in the Punjab. The campaign was unable to stop the ethnic carnage that accompanied partition, and it went down in history as an early example of a catastrophically failed peacekeeping force.

The army deployed at home on three other occasions. In 1948 Nehru ordered the Indian Army to annex the princely states of Hyderabad and Junagadh. In 1955 he asked the Indian Army to conduct a counterinsurgency campaign against the rebel Naga tribesmen in Northeast India, a campaign that has since haunted the region. In 1961 he pushed for the military liberation of Goa from continued Portuguese colonization.

Civil-Military Relations

India's nationalist leaders preserved much of the colonial state and its institutions, including the armed forces, police, and civilian bureaucracy. They sought to maintain continuity despite imperfections and contradictions in how the colonial institutions served a new democracy. With respect to the armed forces, the new government allowed continuity within the institution but brought strong political and, in time, bureaucratic supervision. The role of the armed forces in the new nation was limited sharply, control over the armed forces was lodged in the civilian cabinet, and after independence the status of the army was reduced by making the uniformed heads of the navy and air force "commanders in chief." Then in 1955 all three positions of commander in chief were abolished, and the chiefs assumed leadership of their respective staffs.

Continuity in military institutions also meant that the Indian Army remained caste- and ethnolinguistic-based in contradiction to the egalitarian principles of the Indian Constitution. It also meant that the Indian officer corps preserved the tenets of British military professionalism, which, especially since the interwar period, emphasized technology-driven doctrinal innovation. The British inventions of tank warfare and air power revolutionized war. Similarly, India's officer corps sought the best technology available, which in the early decades of independence meant importing from the United Kingdom. In keeping with Western traditions, Indian military officers prioritized security objectives and, unlike Pakistan, avoided involvement in domestic politics.

A three-tiered structure from the colonial period continued to be used in higher defense policymaking. The Cabinet Committee on Political Affairs (CCPA) was the foremost national security authority. The CCPA comprised all senior ministers of the prime minister's cabinet and was responsible for policymaking on a variety of subjects including foreign affairs and defense. The next tier below the CCPA, the Defence Planning Committee (DPC)—previously the Defence Minister Committee—consisted of the cabinet secretary; the prime minister's special secretary; the secretaries of finance, external affairs, planning, defense, defense production, and defense research and development; and the three service chiefs. The Chief of Staff Committee (CSC) was the military component of the third tier. The other half was the Ministry of Defence's (MoD) Defence Coordination and Implementation Committee (DCIC) chaired by the defence secretary. The DCIC coordinated defense production, defense research and development, finances, and the requirements of the services.[4] A version of this arrangement continues to this day.

Despite production, release, and updating of official documents to facilitate the acquisition process (the Defence Procurement Manual and Defence Procurement Procedure), the system continues to be plagued by fundamental structural problems. The Ministry of Finance, which has its own defense wing, has the authority to intervene in specific spending decisions of the Ministry of Defence, often with an eye toward limiting costs. One of the key unresolved problems in the acquisition process, which is almost entirely about importing weapons from advanced industrial societies (the West and the Soviet Union), is an unrealistic and ambiguous policy of offsets (where foreign companies, as part of their bids, commit to source a percentage of the contract in India). However, any leader or bureaucrat advocating lower offsets becomes vulnerable to charges of corruption. India simply lacks civilian expertise in military matters. Few politicians are interested in defense until forced by events. The bureaucracy that functions as the secretariat for the political leaders comprises generalists with little practical knowledge of military matters, but this group lobbies powerfully to preserve its position against military encroachment. Even the Ministry of External Affairs, with the greatest institutional capacity for international relations, has very few people with sound knowledge of military matters. Although the armed services are highly professional and have the necessary expertise, they remain excluded from the high table.

A Fresh Start on Strategy

In military planning, the Indian government initially retained most of the defense plan proposed by Field Marshall Sir Claude Auchinleck, the last British commander in chief of the Indian Army. The plan envisaged a regular army of 200,000 backed by reserve and territorial forces, a twenty-squadron air force, and a naval task force with two aircraft carriers. However, the new strategic reality, the main threat coming overland from Pakistan, intruded once the Kashmir War started, and the Indian government reduced its ambitious plans for the air force and the navy.

To make a fresh start on military and defense affairs, Nehru hired British scientist and Nobel Prize–winning physicist P. M. S. Blackett to advise him on how the Indian state could leverage science for defense.[5] Blackett had been at the center of the Allied war effort. He was privy to Ultra codebreaking, the development of nuclear weapons, and other major military technology programs. In 1946 the United States gave him the Medal of Honor for his service during the war, and in 1948 he won the Nobel Prize for physics for his prewar work. Blackett's 1948 report went beyond the role of science in military affairs to address both India's strategic position and its military spending. It recommended that India limit its military ambitions and pursue a policy of nonalignment with both superpowers to escape a potentially debilitating arms race. He proposed that military spending should not exceed 2 percent of Indian GDP. Blackett also argued against India's acquisition of nuclear and chemical weapons. Instead, he emphasized India's need to develop an industrial and technological base.

Blackett's report resonated in the Indian government and especially with Nehru, a secular modernist who believed entirely in the ability of science to deliver not only economic progress but also social change. He called India's first large dam project, the Bhakra Nangal in Punjab, "a temple of modernity." The Indian government shifted spending priorities and pushed infrastructure for technology development over military readiness. Nehru charged a number of scientists to develop institutions to alter the defense landscape in India. The Cambridge-educated physicist Homi Bhabha was the father of India's nuclear program, and a close friend of Nehru's. Bhabha's home was one of the few places Nehru visited regularly. Daulat Singh Kothari, a Blackett protégé, became the head of the Defence Science Organisation, the precursor to the Defence Research and Development Organisation (DRDO). While Indian defense research gathered momentum, India did make some procurement decisions. In the 1950s the Indian Air Force (IAF) ordered Canberra bombers and transport aircraft. The Indian Army's purchase of jeeps precipitated India's first major defense corruption scandal in 1955. British debt, held by the Indian government from the colonial period, paid for the purchases. India also struck its first nuclear deal, buying a nuclear reactor from Canada.

On the conventional front, Indian capacity declined. Through the 1950s defense budgets fell below what they had been under the British and were less than those of other countries such as Pakistan and China as well as those of the United States and the Soviet Union.[6] At this time, the Indian Army was clamoring for greater preparation against the Chinese, especially as the Indian government had adopted a dangerous forward policy of setting up small, unsupported positions in the disputed territory to serve as a tripwire for a general war that New Delhi believed China did not want. Nehru worked through close confidant V. K. Krishna Menon, the defense minister, to overrule military objections to the forward policy. Menon's promotion of officers who supported the forward policy led to India's first civil-military crisis in 1958 when army chief General K. S. Thimayya resigned in protest. Nehru persuaded him to stay, but was severely weakened thereafter. In contrast, B. M. Kaul, one of Nehru's and Menon's handpicked generals, made a spectacular rise to chief of general staff in New Delhi. His relentless push for a forward policy against the better judgment of his colleagues in the army brought the charge by Neville Maxwell, author of the definitive book on India's 1962 defeat, that he had led a putsch in the army headquarters.[7]

The forward policy angered the Chinese; they were further upset in 1959 when the Dalai Lama was granted asylum in India after the Chinese had crushed the Tibetan uprising. In October 1962, after three years of Sino-Indian confrontation, the better-prepared People's Liberation Army routed the Indian Army. China retained all of the disputed territory it claimed in the northwest (including a sizable chunk of Kashmir); but more shockingly, it invaded and occupied most of the North East Frontier Agency (NEFA—later renamed Arunachal Pradesh). The Henderson Brooks Report, which was prepared in the aftermath of the defeat and remains secret even today, reported that Kaul's general staff conducted the war from New Delhi, ordering thousand-yard movements when local commanders reported their inability to gain and hold ground.[8] The official history of this war remains unpublished.[9]

Consolidation

After the shock of defeat in 1962, the Indian government moved quickly to redress the military retrenchment of the previous decade. Over the next two years, the country doubled its military manpower, raised a fighting air force (as opposed to a transport fleet), and reversed its position on forging relationships with foreign powers. Both the United States and the Soviet Union stepped in to fill the breach in Indian defenses. Moscow supplied MiG-21 fighters and also built a number of factories in India to assemble advanced weapons.[10] The U.S. equipped eight new infantry divisions for mountain defense against the Chinese and rebuilt some defense production facilities. The United States stopped the aid program during the 1965 India-Pakistan war, embittering Indian security managers who marked the United States as an unreliable military supplier. The navy, which had enjoyed a boost from the Nehru-Panikkar vision of Indian maritime renewal, went into decline as the country refocused on its land borders.

The 1965 war, political unrest, and economic decline in the late 1960s stalled military rearmament. The United States stopped military supplies to both India and Pakistan; the Soviet Union, to forestall escalation in the regional conflict, mediated a cease-fire agreement in Tashkent. The war itself was short and ended in a draw. The Indian Army committed most of its forces in the early days of the armored confrontation with Pakistan, taking the risk of not leaving any reserves. Had Pakistani forces managed to break through to the Beas River on the Grand Trunk Road, Delhi would have been a day away. In the event, Pakistan's first armored division disintegrated at Khem Karan in the Battle of Assal Uttar. India did not press the advantage and soon after suffered its own debacle in the Battle of Chawinda. When the Soviets offered mediation, New Delhi accepted, and India's strategic condition remained unchanged. Nehru's death in 1964 began a political battle for succession that lasted until 1969, and split the Indian National Congress—the movement that had won the country's independence and held uninterrupted power as the preeminent political party for two decades. Concomitant with the political unrest, the Indian economy nosedived due to growing international and domestic pressures. This period saw the large-scale delivery of American food supplies under Public Law 480, which both saved millions of Indian lives and made Indian leaders bitterly aware of their dependency on the United States.

The 1970 Pakistan Army crackdown on Bengali dissidence in East Pakistan offered Prime Minister Indira Gandhi the chance at redemption after a decade of uncertainty. As tens of thousands of Bengalis died and millions escaped into India, New Delhi saw a clear opportunity to eliminate the two-front threat from Pakistan in the east and in the west. But India did not rush headlong into conflict. In early 1971, the Indian Army chief, General Sam Manekshaw, told Indira Gandhi that he needed nine months to prepare for war; she accepted this advice. Before starting the war, New Delhi also signed the Indo-Soviet Treaty of Peace, Friendship and Cooperation to ensure international balance and continued military supplies. The United States was all but certain to back Pakistan. The war in December 1971 lasted fourteen days and brought India its most spectacular military victory. The Indian Army attacked along three axes and easily took East Pakistan's capital, Dacca. Pakistani forces were unable to put up resistance, and the Bengali uprising that had occasioned the invasion helped the Indian Army in no small measure. The western front, however, remained in another 1965-like draw. The Indian Army did not swing west to assert its dominance on West Pakistan, the true source of the "Pakistani threat." Nor did India use the 90,000 Pakistani prisoners of war, held in liberated Bangladesh, to coerce Pakistan into relinquishing all claims over Kashmir. India and Pakistan did, however, agree to settle future disputes, including Kashmir, peacefully at Simla in 1972. Clearly, this did not happen, and the two countries have been embroiled in several major crises and a mini-war.

Why did India not pursue its strategic goals more completely? The conventional answer is that India was under international pressure. President Nixon had ordered the USS *Enterprise* carrier group into the Bay of Bengal to coerce New Delhi. Even India's Soviet allies wanted a quick cessation of hostilities. There was also the military reality that Pakistani defenses in the west were much stronger than in the east. The irrigation ditches in the Punjab, which had proved to be a considerable obstacle in 1965, continued to present a serious challenge. No popular insurrection welcomed the invaders. Additionally, there is the view that India had concentrated its military capacity so overwhelmingly in the east that a change of theater to the west was not even feasible. Further, Indian military stocks were low and needed replenishment. While all these arguments are valid, it is also the case that these problems were surmountable. New Delhi could have prevailed on Moscow to undertake a serious resupply effort and even asked for Soviet submarines to enter the Bay of Bengal to counter the threat from the USS *Enterprise* task force. Had Indian leaders been ambitious, they might have taken these risks. The decision to keep war goals in check, we believe, is evidence of strategic restraint. New Delhi saw advantage in breaking up Pakistan, but it did not want to prolong the war.

India followed the military victory of 1971 with a dramatic demonstration of its unconventional capabilities. New Delhi tested a nuclear device in 1974, calling it a peaceful nuclear explosion. There are many competing theories of the timing of India's 1974 nuclear test—chief among these is Indira Gandhi's own domestic political concerns—however, it is equally noteworthy that the Indian nuclear weapons program slowed down, if not froze altogether, for at least the next decade. In fact the country did not think it necessary to conduct another nuclear test for twenty-four years—a period during which India's strategic resolve was tested by repeated provocations, and India was shielded from international sanctions by the Soviet veto.

Why did India go this far and no further? Nuclear weapons offered India the only viable deterrent against China and even against the possibility of another American effort at gunboat diplomacy. If India had conducted more tests and built a nuclear arsenal, it might have forced early changes to the emerging nuclear proliferation regime. Although Soviet leadership may have been uncomfortable with a nuclear India, it was not in a position to dictate Indian nuclear policy. India's relations with the West were already at their nadir due to the nuclear sanctions that followed the test. What else was there to lose? We believe that India's decision not to go down the nuclear path after the 1974 test is rooted in the country's preference for strategic restraint over risk taking. The circumstances of the 1998 tests, discussed later, bolster this view of Indian reticence in military matters.

Strategic Assertion Fizzles Out

Turning over the coin of India's strategic restraint, we see the chastening reality of failure when the country has attempted strategic assertion. The 1962 war had resulted from Nehru's naïve and careless policy of forward military deployment without the requisite military preparation. Nehru's belated attempt at strategic assertion against the Chinese juggernaut ended badly. The one success was the 1971 war, with the attendant horrors of Pakistan Army atrocities against Bengalis; and even then India did not press the advantage.

It was not until the mid-1980s, however, that India pursued a series of ambitious strategic projects, all of which were failures. In 1984 India preempted Pakistani efforts to occupy the Siachen Glacier, a strategic position at an altitude of 25,000 feet in the disputed and nondemarcated region of upper Kashmir. An initial Indian success has since proved to be a steady drain on Indian military resources. The game between the two countries to capture heights along the India-Pakistan Line of Control (LOC), as the de facto border is called in Kashmir, culminated in the threat of nuclear escalation in the 1999 Kargil War. Cross-LOC harassment continues today. At least since the 1990s, India has tried to demilitarize Siachen in an agreement with Pakistan, but Islamabad will not allow India a tactical withdrawal unless it pays a price.

After Rajiv Gandhi became prime minister following the assassination of his mother, Indira, by Sikh separatists, he pushed India's strategic objectives and posture further than any Indian leader before or after him. Rajiv Gandhi restarted the nuclear program in response to reports that Pakistan's nuclear program was picking up speed. Working with General Krishnaswami Sundarji, the Indian Army chief at the time, and Arun Singh, his minister of state for defense, Rajiv ordered a dramatic modernization of the armed forces, leveraging India's rapid economic growth—the first time in the post–independence period that the Indian economy expanded faster than population growth. India bought MiG-29s, T-90s, and submarines from the Soviet Union. Moscow even leased India a Charlie class nuclear submarine. The Indian Air Force also bought the Mirage 2000 fighter from France; the Indian Navy bought diesel submarines from Germany; and the Indian Army bought howitzers from Sweden. A corruption scandal centered on the Swedish guns from the Bofors Company contributed to Rajiv Gandhi's defeat in the 1989 general elections.

Buoyed by new military capability, Rajiv made two dramatic attempts at strategic assertion. The first came in 1986 when he approved General Sundarji's plans to conduct a large-scale military exercise on the border with Pakistan. Called Brasstacks, the military maneuvers were later reported to have been open-ended and could have turned into an invasion of Pakistan. Military advice to the Indian prime minister is not publicly available, but General Sundarji wrote after his retirement that Brasstacks was India's last opportunity to decapitate Pakistan's nuclear program and force a Kashmir settlement. In the event, Pakistan threatened to use nuclear weapons and India backed down. A similar scene played out in 1990, when India was compelled once more to accept nuclear parity as the new reality. India's conventional superiority, including its modernization program, served little purpose. Indeed, the wars India would fight thereafter were against insurgencies and demanded troops and superior organization rather than advanced weaponry and technology.

Rajiv's second act of strategic assertion came in 1987 when he sent the Indian Army to police a peacekeeping deal he had forced on the Sri Lankan government and the Tamil Tigers. Both sides rejected the agreement, and the Indian Army was caught between an insurgency on one side and an unhelpful host government on the other. India's only campaign of peace enforcement was a chastening experience. The Indian Army lost more men in that war than in any other in the history of independent India, and the conflict came to be seen as India's Vietnam.

Since then, the problem of how to fight an insurgency has beset India. Once India and Pakistan accepted the basic reality of nuclear deterrence, Islamabad quickly escalated subconventional conflict, causing what nuclear theorists call the stability-instability paradox. Pakistan openly supported an indigenous rebellion in Kashmir and spawned a twenty-year insurgency in the disputed territory that has diverted and bled the Indian Army to the point that the institution, by its own admission, lost sight of its main mission of fighting the Pakistan Army after the Kargil War. The restraint of choice became restraint without choice. No Indian leader could risk the chance of a Pakistani attack on any Indian city.

Crossing the Nuclear Threshold, Finally

India finally broke out of its nuclear restraint in 1998, not due to the pressure of mounting threat but to the international politics of nuclear nonproliferation. Following its cold war victory, the United States spent significant energy in the early and mid-1990s in revamping the international nuclear nonproliferation regime in an effort to cash in on the peace dividend. The Clinton administration sought to extend the Nuclear Non-Proliferation Treaty indefinitely, conclude a Comprehensive Test Ban Treaty, and push along a Fissile Material Cutoff Treaty. These changes in the international nuclear treaty threatened to close off India's nuclear options, which New Delhi had preserved despite international sanctions since the 1974 test. Seeing that the nuclear option was closing down, India tried to test in 1995, but American satellites picked up the test preparations, and Washington was able to pressure New Delhi into backing off. In 1998, however, a new conservative government, buoyed by consensus in India for overt nuclear capacity and set against American nonproliferation fundamentalism, ordered stealthy nuclear test preparations to avoid satellite surveillance. The tests conducted in May 1998 led to widespread criticism outside India but received great support within the country.

The strategic community in India and abroad saw the tests as an indication that New Delhi had finally abandoned strategic restraint in favor of a more active international agenda. Certainly, the revival of the Indian economy a few years later provided the Indian government with greater resources to undertake a massive rearmament program. India's military procurement wish list today confirms that this has indeed happened. Yet, it is important to note that the decision to test in 1998 was reactionary and defensive, driven by the ambition of Washington's nonproliferation agenda rather than a new strategic posture in India. Further, New Delhi fully expected Pakistan to test its own weapons in response to the Indian tests. The Pakistani tests a month later negated lasting strategic advantage. The tests also alerted China to India's growing military potential, though the Chinese reaction to the increased threat from Indian nuclear weapons—as opposed to the heightened threat from the resulting strategic realignment between India and the United States—is not clear.

The tests altered India's strategic landscape, but in unexpected ways that had little to do with breaking out of strategic restraint. Following the tests, the United States placed wide-ranging sanctions on India, but also sought to engage India in an effort to put the nuclear genie back in the bottle. U.S. Under Secretary of State Strobe Talbott initiated talks with Indian Foreign Minister Jaswant Singh in what became the most sustained engagement of India by the United States in history. The Talbott-Singh talks, designed to persuade India to roll back its nuclear weapons program, instead legitimized India's nuclear weapons. The rise of Islamic extremism in Pakistan helped India's case as the region's only stable democracy. During the Kargil War a year after the tests, the United States backed India over Pakistan, the first time in history that Washington came out in unequivocal support of New Delhi. The United States' break from its past support of Pakistan (or neutrality, as in 1965) opened the door to strategic realignment between India and the United States. This realignment, sometimes hesitant and at other times breathtaking, could not have been expected in New Delhi when the Indian government decided to test. In this view the nuclear tests and the unintended strategic realignment with the United States do not suggest that India is abandoning its strategic restraint. Restraint continues to be evident in India's cautious approach to developing its nuclear arsenal since the 1998 tests. The readiness of the Indian nuclear arsenal supports the country's No First Use Policy and is compatible with the civil-military relations of a cautious democracy. Reports in India and abroad suggest that India may lag behind Pakistan in nuclear readiness, including the number of weapons, the delivery systems, and the command and control mechanisms.

Strategic Restraint Today

India's contemporary external security relations suggest continued strategic restraint. Following the Somdurong Cho crisis with China in 1986, India sought to engage China, an effort that culminated in Prime Minister Rajiv Gandhi's visit to Beijing in 1988. The rapprochement eased tensions on the India-China border. Military investment on the border decreased, and the Indian Army routinely diverted its China-oriented mountain divisions to counterinsurgency. Since the 1990s, New Delhi has also emphasized political and economic relations, and China has become India's fastest growing trade partner. The 1998 nuclear tests did not alter this dynamic. Even though Indian Defence Minister George Fernandes sought to justify the 1998 tests by pointing to the Chinese threat, twelve years later no Indian missile threatens China. The hardliners in India's strategic community, alarmed by the China threat, have been largely marginalized, even by the conservative Bharatiya

Janata Party (BJP), which should have been their natural home.[11] The mainstream belief in India has been that the threat from China is not direct, but lies in Beijing's special relationship with Islamabad. It is this link that India has sought to break through rapprochement. China has returned the favor for over a decade. Beijing equivocated between India and Pakistan during the Kargil War in 1999 and has since kept away from the Kashmir problem. After some verbal jousting with China in 2009, the government agreed to an army proposal to raise four new mountain divisions oriented toward the border with China, and the IAF is also reopening forward air bases in the north and east. However, there is no consensus in India that New Delhi should seek military advantage over Beijing. Certainly, India has been unwilling to match Chinese investments in defense modernization.[12]

India has so far tried to deflect the anti-Chinese implications of its growing relationship with the United States; at the same time it has continued to allow the Dalai Lama, the Tibetan leader, to remain in exile in India. The political debate in India over the nuclear deal with the United States, especially as it relates to China, is about preserving the ability to dramatically expand India's nuclear weapons inventory. The parties on the Left, which until recently held the domestic balance of power, opposed the deal not because they seek strategic parity with China but because their leaders do not trust the United States. Some have also expressed fears that close ties with the United States might precipitate Chinese hostility. Only the Far Right is keen to take on China—but many of the same people are equally excited that India may be able to match the United States in some way. India and China continue to negotiate the border dispute with neither ready to compromise or to abandon the talks. At the same time, they are forging ahead on trade and investment. Teresita Schaffer has called the triangular relationship between India, China, and the United States a "virtuous circle," where effort by two sides to come closer is matched by the third.

Public opinion polls in India as well as the actions of most Indian governments indicate that the tendency to restraint runs deep and remains the default option for most Indians. Polls evince an ambiguity about threats and offer no strong guidance to policy or strategy. The Chicago Council on Global Affairs made the most sophisticated attempt to measure Indian views toward foreign and strategic policy in 2007.[13] Terrorism, Islamic fundamentalism, and India-Pakistan tensions all rank higher on India's list of threats than China's development as a military power; although AIDS, avian flu, and other epidemics ranked second only to terrorism (which in the Indian context, is often equated with Pakistan). Most strikingly, Indians rank the promotion of economic and other "quality of life" concerns very highly, more so than their Chinese counterparts, who are less concerned about regional security issues. Of the five issues that the largest share of Indians regard as critical threats to their country's vital interests, four relate directly to regional security.[14] *India Today*, India's leading newsmagazine, declared its own war on terrorism, as it put forth an impassioned case for reforming India's security apparatus after the Mumbai attack.[15]

To the extent that India deviates from strategic restraint, the conventional military balance with Pakistan should be central to that change. Pakistan has never believed in India's posture of strategic restraint. India's global aspirations complicate the communication of that position. Pakistanis see India's rise as an erosion of their own leverage. The ongoing rivalry shapes the nature of demands the Indian armed forces make to their government. The Kargil War in 1999 caught the Indian Army unawares. The 2001–02 Operation Parakram, designed to bring coercive pressure on Pakistan, failed in part due to the lack of military options. In 2008 the government did not even ask the army to mobilize against Pakistan. Since then the Indian Army— and the other services—have sought ways in which to engage in brinksmanship with Pakistan without precipitating nuclear escalation. The army's wish list of new weapons seems to rest on the notion that a sudden but limited attack against Pakistan will not precipitate a nuclear riposte. Consequently, Pakistani efforts to maintain a regional balance of power embroil India in ways that preclude effective military modernization and undermine efforts to achieve great-power status, but the continuing rivalry in the face of mammoth national asymmetry underscores, rather than detracts from, the case for Indian strategic restraint.

We disagree with many analyses of India's military balance with Pakistan. These tend to project imagined, rather than demonstrated, motives and capabilities on India; and only a handful take into account the terrain, political conditions, and nuclear capability of these two countries on the one hand, and the restraint exercised by Indian politicians on the other. A 2009 analysis by BBC defense correspondent Jonathan Marcus is a typical, and much cited study, which concludes that India has an overwhelming advantage. Marcus takes at face value the assertions of India's military rise and the centrality of military power to this rise. He evades the question of India-China military rivalry and attributes to Pakistan a passive strategy rooted in deterrence.[16] Anthony Cordesman, an American analyst writing during the 2001–02 India-Pakistan crisis, offers a more nuanced assessment of the India-Pakistan balance, noting that India's conventional superiority is meaningless as it does not have the capacity to push into Pakistan without risking a nuclear confrontation, that Pakistan has successfully engaged in a "war of nuclear rhetoric and symbolic missile tests" to deter India, and that much of India's armor is in storage and not modern. Both military establishments are rated as competent by the standard of "developing" countries, both have failed to demonstrate the ability to effectively integrate advanced conventional technology into their operations, and both have less than optimal battle management, joint warfare, and combined arms skills.[17]

COUNTERVAILING STRATEGIC RESTRAINT

The conventional explanation for India's slow military development has emphasized the country's poverty. The nationalist critique of the British military policy in India highlighted the undue burden imposed by the imperial state on the people. The post-independence Indian government believed that development, rather than defense, would bring security to the new country. In 1948 the Blackett report recommended pegging defense spending at no more than 2 percent of GDP. The budget decline of the 1950s was largely responsible for the lack of preparedness of the Indian armed forces against China in 1962. The expansion of the 1960s took the budget up to 4.5 percent of GDP, but it fell due to economic stagnation in the late 1960s and through the 1970s. The first period of rapid economic growth of the Indian economy in the 1980s underwrote that decade's military modernization, when defense spending as a percentage of GDP reached its highest-ever level of over 5 percent. The financial crisis of 1991 pushed back budgets, but it put pressure on GDP as well, keeping the percentage high.[18]

Growing Affluence

The explosive growth of the last few years has resulted in an unprecedented increase in defense spending. In 2000 India's defense budget was $11.8 billion. The figure had risen to $30 billion in 2009.[19] The single largest year-on-year increase of 34 percent came in that year, but military budgets have been rising steadily since 2007. The trend in Indian defense spending is likely to continue, though not at the staggering rates achieved in 2007–09. The dramatic nature of the increases has heightened expectations that India's armed forces will acquire significantly increased capacity that could alter the country's strategic posture.

As a percentage of GDP, Indian military spending is now at 3 percent, which is higher than it has been through the last decade, but lower than it was in the last period of modernization in the 1980s. Indeed, Indian defense spending as a percentage of GDP fell to 2 percent in 2007, when the economy expanded rapidly but defense spending did not.[20] The level of defense

Table 1-1. *Percentage Breakdown of Defense Spending by Service,*
Fiscal Years 2006–07 to 2009–10

Service	2006-2007	2007-2008	2008-2009	2009-2010
Army	46.29	49.96	51.53	53.72
Navy	18.95	17.33	15.11	14.54
Air Force	28.39	25.74	25.54	24.30
Research and Development	6.27	6.66	6.05	5.99

Source: Ministry of Defense, Annual Report, 2009–10, p. 19 (http://mod.nic.in/reports/welcome.html).

spending as a percentage of GDP is widely seen as a way to control for economic capacity when comparing defense budgets, but this is a false exercise. The assumption is that military spending should be a function of the size of the economy, a notion inconsistent with the realism of threat-driven military posture. While a bigger economy may mean more to defend, it is not necessarily so. Still, long-term co-occurrence of affluence and military strength is a central proposition in international relations theory.

As Table 1-1 shows, the Indian Army received 54 percent of the total defense budget in 2009. The Indian Air Force received 24 percent, and the Indian Navy, 15 percent. Defense research and development received 6 percent. The army's allocations since 2007 reverse a decade-long trend, where it had been losing budgetary ground to the IAF and the Indian Navy. In particular, the Indian Navy's budget had risen to 18 percent of the total expenditure. The IAF, the country's premier instrument of power projection, is also on a downward trend though its relative decline is slower. Part of the explanation for the reversal of the army's budgetary fortunes lies in the massive Sixth Pay Commission increases. Because the army is disproportionately larger in manpower, it draws the bulk of new resources. However, the strong return of the Indian Army at a time when the air force and the navy have been making large deals indicates the degree to which India remains a land power tied to its historical strategic conditions. It also suggests future difficulties that India must face in rebalancing its forces.

The capital budget for major equipment and infrastructure was $2.7 billion in 2000 and is now $10 billion. In 2009 capital expenditure was about $12 billion, or 40 percent of the budget, while the rest was allocated to the running costs of the armed forces. Revenue spending includes salaries, the single biggest item in the defense budget. Critics of India's military spending say that too much of the budget is consumed by salaries and too little is left for buying new weapon systems and building infrastructure that would

Table 1-2. *Comparative Defense Expenditures, 1998–2008*
Totals in millions of U.S. constant 2005 dollars

Year	India		China		Pakistan	
	Millions U.S.$	% of GDP	Millions U.S.$	% of GDP	Millions U.S.$	% of GDP
1988	11,440	3.6	n.a.	n.a.	2,896	6.2
1989	12,219	3.5	12,276	2.6	2,894	6.0
1990	12,036	3.2	13,147	2.6	3,054	5.8
1991	11,238	3.0	13,691	2.4	3,270	5.8
1992	10,740	2.8	16,534	2.5	3,472	6.1
1993	12,131	2.9	15,331	2.0	3,467	5.7
1994	12,185	2.8	14,607	1.7	3,379	5.3
1995	12,550	2.7	14,987	1.7	3,435	5.3
1996	12,778	2.6	16,606	1.7	3,430	5.1
1997	14,144	2.7	16,799	1.6	3,285	4.9
1998	14,757	2.8	19,263	1.7	3,281	4.8
1999	17,150	3.1	21,626	1.8	3,311	3.8
2000	17,697	3.1	23,767	1.8	3,320	3.7
2001	18,313	3.0	28,515	2.0	3,553	3.8
2002	18,256	2.9	33,436	2.1	3,818	3.9
2003	18,664	2.8	36,405	2.1	4,077	3.7
2004	21,660	2.9	40,631	2.0	4,248	3.6
2005	22,891	2.8	44,911	2.0	4,412	3.5
2006	23,029	2.6	52,199	2.0	4,463	3.3
2007	23,535	2.5	57,861	2.0	4,468	3.1
2008	24,716	n.a.	63,643	n.a.	4,217	

Source: Information from the Stockholm International Peace Research Institute (SIPRI) (www.sipri.org/databases/milex). Data not available is indicated as n.a.

improve fighting capacity. Pay increases distributed by the government's Sixth Pay Commission account for more than half the 34 percent increase in total spending in 2009. The 60–40 revenue-capital spending split is an improvement from the 70–30 division that had been in place for much of the last decade; the ratios were far worse in the 1990s. In the early years of the decade, capital spending had ground to a near halt because of the fiscal crisis and the country's efforts to adjust its strategic vision.

As figure 1-1 shows, Indian military spending is higher than in South Korea and is close to Saudi Arabia's, but remains less than half of China's reported figure of $70 billion in 2009. As a percentage of GDP, Chinese and

Figure 1-1. *Comparative Arms Imports, 1980–2009*

SIPRI trend indicator values in U.S. constant 1990 dollars

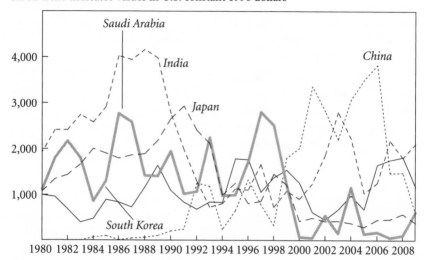

Source: Information from the Stockholm International Peace Research Institute (SIPRI), Arms Transfer Database (www.sipri.org/databases/armstransfers).

Indian spending on defense is similar, but China's total spending far exceeds India's, and the military gap between New Delhi and Beijing is growing rather than shrinking. Pakistan spends more on defense as a percentage of GDP than India, and is able to hold India to a strategic standoff. In absolute terms, Pakistani defense spending has always been less than India's, though historically Islamabad has tried to maintain military parity on its eastern border. In the past Pakistan spent approximately 6 percent of its GDP on defense, though there has been a sharp downturn since 1997. Pakistani military spending in 2007 was about 3 percent of GDP but a fifth of all government expenditure.

The numbers in India and Pakistan suggest a growing divergence in the respective ability of each country to spend on the military. Hardline Indian nationalists have suggested that India adopt the Reagan cold war strategy of spending the enemy into the ground. India could use this strategy against Pakistan; however, recent crises have shown that New Delhi should not assume that the budget gap is necessarily a military one.

India has long been one of the biggest weapons importers in the world. According to Stockholm International Peace Research Institute (SIPRI) data in figure 1-1, India accounts for 8 percent of all known arms imports between

2003 and 2007; it is sandwiched on the list between China (12 percent) and UAE (7 percent). India's arms market is in an unprecedented boom. The IAF is set to become the biggest buyer with 126 Multi-Role Combat Aircraft (MRCA). It has already ordered six Lockheed Martin C-130J medium-range transport aircraft and is considering purchase of a large transport aircraft, the Boeing C-17. The service is also looking at air tankers and airborne early warning platforms while examining upgrades for its Jaguar and Mirage fighters. The Indian Navy has ordered six P-81 maritime reconnaissance aircraft. The Russian retrofit of the aircraft carrier *Admiral Gorshkov* has been ongoing, albeit with recurring problems with pricing and specifications. The navy is also considering two indigenous aircraft carriers and scores of new surface ships and submarines. The Indian Army wants new tanks; light, towed, and self-propelled artillery; armored personnel carriers; tactical air defense; and transport and attack helicopters. All three services seek to upgrade their missiles and munitions, unmanned aerial vehicles (UAVs), electronic warfare capability, battle-space management systems, and communications. Table 1-3 provides a comprehensive but not exhaustive wish list of weapons the Indian armed forces want.

Access to Advanced Technology

Since the 1971 Indo-Soviet Treaty of Peace, Friendship and Cooperation, the Soviet Union had been India's primary military supplier. New Delhi bought some Western weapons, but over 80 percent of Indian weapons platforms were of Soviet origin. The Soviet terms of trade were excellent. The low prices, staggered payment, and rupee denomination allowed India to buy advanced conventional weapons without triggering a balance of payments crisis, which was always imminent because of the country's weak economy. The Soviets were willing not only to sell the weapons, but also to license production and transfer some technology. India assembled MiG fighters, T-72 tanks, armored carriers, and other equipment. The former Soviet Union stopped at the transfer of nuclear technology during the cold war, but Moscow leased a nuclear submarine to the Indian Navy in the 1980s and sold India heavy water for fast-breeder reactors, which produce plutonium that could be used in bombs.

The end of the cold war altered the political justification for Indo-Soviet military trade. After a period of disarray—when Indian officials were going from factory to factory in Russia, the Ukraine, and other former Soviet and Soviet bloc states, trying to buy military spare parts—the special terms were cancelled. Prices went up, though not to Western standards. Russian quality was commensurate with the West's, but India's security threats did not

Table 1-3. *India's Wish List: Some Major Weapons Systems on the Anvil*

System	Units	Vendors or possible vendors	Estimated or contracted cost (U.S.$)
Fighter aircraft	126	Boeing, Lockheed Martin (U.S.), Dassault (France), Eurofighter (U.S.), Saab (Sweden), MiG (Russia)	12 billion
Very large transport aircraft	10	Boeing C17 (U.S.)	6 billion
Medium-range transport aircraft	6 + option to buy 6 more	On order, Lockheed Martin C-130J (U.S.)	1 billion; 1 billion more if option taken
Tanker aircraft	6	Airbus 330 (EU), Boeing, IL-78	1 billion
Naval airborne early warning systems	6	Northrup Grumman Hawkeye E-2D (U.S.)	2 billion
Long maritime reconnaissance systems	8	On order, Boeing P-8 (U.S.)	4 billion
Attack helicopters	22	Augusta (Italy), Apache Longbow (U.S.)	1 billion
Medium-lift helicopters	390	Hindustan Aeronautics Limited (HAL) (India)	n.a.
Light combat helicopters (Army and Air Force)	179	HAL (India)	n.a.
Light observation helicopters	325	Eurocopter (EU), Kamov (Russia)	750 million
Naval helicopters	17	U.S. Navy with Sikorsky and Lockheed Martin as U.S. foreign military sales	n.a.
Aircraft carriers	3	Under contract (Russia) to retrofit and supply *Admiral Gorshkov;* two being built in India	2.7 billion
Submarines	6	Scorpene (France), Kilo (Russia)	4 billion
Nuclear submarines	4	Being designed in India	n.a.
Destroyers, frigates	15	Built at Mazgaon in India and other docks	n.a.
Main battle tanks	124	124 Arjuns (India), unspecified number T-90s (Russia)	n.a.
Light tanks (wheeled or tracked)	200	General Dynamics Stryker (U.S.)	1 billion

(continued)

Table 1-3 *(continued)*

System	Units	Vendors or possible vendors	Estimated or contracted cost (U.S.$)
Howitzers (light, towed, and self-propelled)	450–480	Light howitzer contract to BAE Systems. SWS Defense (Sweden) and Soltam Systems (Israel); Singapore Technologies and BAE in the running for towed and self-propelled guns	2.5 billion
Unmanned aerial vehicles (UAVs), various specifications	n.a.	Israel Aerospace Industries, Honeywell (U.S.), Indian companies	Many disparate programs
Quick reaction surface-to-air-missiles (QRSAMs)	56 launchers and 1,485 missiles	Rafael (Israel), MBDA (EU), Raytheon (U.S.), Rheinmetall (Germany), KPB Tula (Russia)	1.2 billion
Surface-to-air missile programs (Air Force)	n.a.	Under contract (Israel) to buy Barak 8	1.1 billion
Theater air defense (Army)	n.a.	Lockheed Martin PAC-3 (U.S.), S-300, S-400 (Russia), Elements of Arrow (Israel)	n.a.
Tactical communications (Army)	n.a.	Thales, Alcatel (France), EADS (EU), Siemens (Germany), Elbit (Israel), Singapore Technologies, Ericsson (Sweden), General Dynamics (U.S.), many Indian private companies	1 billion
Battlespace management systems (Army)	n.a.	n.a.	2.5 billion
Networkcentric pilot projects (Navy, Army, and Air Force separately)	n.a.	n.a.	1 billion
Target towing, transportation, communication, and aerial photography aircraft	9	Elta (Israel), Embraer (Brazil), Gulfstream, Cessna, Raytheon (U.S.), Dornier (Germany), Bombardier (Canada), Dassault (France)	0.5 billion
Close-quarter carbines	n.a.	n.a.	1.1 billion
Anti-tank missiles	n.a.	Lockheed Martin/Raytheon Javelin (U.S.)	n.a.

Source: Collated from press reporting with assistance from Dhruva Jaishankar. Special thanks to Manohar Thyagaraj of U.S.-India Business Alliance and Woolf Gross of Northrup Grumman for verifying and adding to the list.

n.a. = Not available or applicable.

demand cutting-edge conventional weapons. India awarded Russia its two largest post–cold war military contracts: the Sukhoi-30 fighter-bomber and the purchase and retrofit for the aircraft carrier, *Admiral Gorshkov*. Increasingly, however, India and Russia found themselves in contract disputes. In January 2008, the *Times of India* reported that India had refused to take delivery of a refurbished Kilo-class submarine, suspecting "material deficiencies."[21] Previously, India had strongly protested Russian efforts to add $1.2 billion to the contracted price of $1.5 billion for the *Gorshkov*. Both governments have been trying to minimize differences by emphasizing commercial gains, but special Indo-Russian military trade is clearly fading.

Since 1991 Israel has been slowly selling more to India to the point where New Delhi is now Tel Aviv's biggest military customer. India not only reversed its political opposition to the Jewish state, but also came to see strategic convergence of the two democracies, bookending the swath of political instability that lies in between.[22] India recognized that Israel possessed counterterrorism technologies that it urgently needed. Further, Tel Aviv became a conduit for technology that had been developed through Israel's special relationship with the United States. There has been considerable discussion, for example, over the airborne early warning and missile defense systems; these deals are slowly materializing as Indian efforts to build these systems have not borne fruit.[23]

Israelis—and Russians—have won contracts by offering the DRDO joint development of elements of the project they bid on. The military trade has given India access to new military electronic equipment and technology. Most important, Israel has influenced New Delhi's decision on the feasibility of the border fence in Kashmir, which is believed to have reduced cross-border terrorism. Israel is also a key supplier of unmanned aerial vehicles, which have altered Indian reconnaissance practice. A DRDO joint venture with a Russian missile design firm produced the Brahmos cruise missile, which is ready for induction. In the absence of a public history of the Brahmos, lessons are hard to draw. We do not know the degree to which the joint venture was actually a cover for the Russians to do the job rather than true joint development. The same is true of the *Arihant,* India's "indigenous" nuclear-powered submarine, also likely of Russian origin. History favors a pessimistic view. Despite manufacturing MiG fighters and T-72 tanks under license from the former Soviet Union, India failed to parlay the experience into designing and building the light combat aircraft and the Arjun tank. India is also beginning to buy from the United States, and American companies are pitching their platforms to the Indian Ministry of Defence and the Indian armed forces. Two of the final five contenders for the huge MRCA purchase are American. India has already bought an amphibious assault ship, the former USS *Trenton*, and six specially equipped C-130 transport aircraft, fitted out for special forces use. These two systems give India a modest power-projection capability. We examine America's likely role in Indian military modernization further in chapter 8, but it should be noted here that officials in the Indian government recognize the importance of building constituencies inside the United States that will support improved relations. A case in point is the Federation of Indian Chambers of Commerce, which seeks to link the Department of Science and Technology with a center for innovation at the University of Texas-Austin, in the hope of commercializing DRDO's research.[24] These and other commercial ties provide ballast to the relationship. Buying from the United States represents a change in attitude and process. Indians have long seen the United States as a fickle supplier. In doing business with the United States, then, India is signaling a fundamental change in the level of trust. Moreover, doing business with U.S. companies will require that the Indian system change its approach from one of massive consensus building to a more decision-oriented one, which will expose individual officials to charges of failure and possibly corruption. Officials will have to be shielded from personal attacks if they are expected to make decisions.

In India, the new relationship with the United States and Israel is cause for optimism among those who advocate modernization of the armed forces. They see technology as fundamentally altering the way the Indian military system works. The use of UAVs, for example, is expected to flatten the military command structure by making tactical intelligence available to higher command echelons. Technology access can ultimately reorganize the indigenous research and development system to function more effectively, but only if there is organizational adaptation. The openness that should follow technology transfers—after all, the Indian system will have greater incentive to protect intellectual property—may have the most resounding impact by inviting Indian private sector participation in research and development.

In the eyes of Indian modernizers, India's military trade with Israel was a successful experiment in using alliances to develop indigenous capacity. They would like to see that pattern replicated with the United States. Given the reverse asymmetry, the dynamics of the exchange are likely to be different with the United States; however, as the Israeli case and the nuclear deal show, the payoffs could be substantial. Whether and to what extent the alliance will actually meet India's very specific demands for technology—rather than ready weapons platforms—many observers believe, depends on how close a relationship India develops with Washington. Because India hopes to preserve its strategic independence even as it embraces American technology, competing interests will be a matter of some friction between India and the United States. One side seeks strategic cooperation and profit while the other pursues access to technology.

While Indians understand the deeply political nature of pricing in the military trade, the Western system involves a second layer of pricing complication: once the government allows the sale, private firms set the price. The Indian establishment, in light of its political choices and socialist thinking, has been fundamentally uncomfortable with this idea. Dealing with the Soviet Union was easy. Besides attractive pricing, there was a single-point decision process. Once the political leaders decided on a sale and some general pricing norms, all the other terms were mere details to be firmed up by the bureaucrats. If pricing was a problem, negotiations reverted to the leaders. There were significant problems in adhering to contracts, but the spirit of exchange remained strong, especially at the political level. Until recent deregulation, European arms makers were also in a similar position. The negotiations were conducted by trusted high-level bureaucrats and then vetted by the political leaders. Government approval and pricing were decided at the same time. In contrast, negotiating with the American firms requires separate negotiations with the firms and with the U.S. government. Government approval does not guarantee favorable pricing and vice versa.

Breaking from Restraint?

As Indian armed forces undertake an unprecedented modernization effort, the foundation is set for a great-power military; however, the enterprise awaits strategic intent. Ending India's historical restraint will require more than new resources and technology. In pure resources terms, it is important to remember that while India's recent economic growth may be dramatic, the absolute numbers are still very low. India's technology and industrial base remains relatively modest, especially when one factors in the desire to be autonomous in defense production. According to the World Bank, India's nominal per capita GDP is about $1,000, which ranks it at number 130 out of a possible 170 countries measured. The purchasing power parity figure is higher, but India ranks worse—in the 140s and 160s—depending on who is measuring. To expect the country to devote sufficient resources to cutting-edge military innovation would be erroneous. At best, we are talking about relative shifts in resources that are devoted to science and technology, and we should expect modest outcomes.

Further, the Indian armed forces have been spending steadily more on the purchase of equipment and weapons over the last few years, but the allocations in recent years have exceeded the ability of the services to spend the money. For the first time in history, the Indian armed forces have had more money than they can spend, but this may not be good news since the Indian procurement system is broken. The government has not created legitimate and transparent procedures for buying new weapons so that the deals can survive public scrutiny. Prime Minister Rajiv Gandhi lost the 1989 elections because of allegations of corruption related to a number of weapons deals. Rather than overhaul the system, the government slowed down procurement so that the armed forces were unable to spend their allocations and returned budget funds to the treasury.

With the exception of the nuclear weapons, the history of Indian defense research and development has been an unhappy one. DRDO is the best-funded research institution in India, but it has not produced a single weapons system that could alter the country's strategic condition. In fact India probably lags behind Pakistan, which has received substantial assistance from North Korea and China, in developing missiles. While for twenty years DRDO has tried and failed to produce a "light combat aircraft" (the LCA), Hindustan Aeronautics, a state-run aviation firm more open to outside influence than DRDO, has designed and manufactured a relatively successful light helicopter. The Indian Space Research Organisation (ISRO), the space agency, is more open and more successful than DRDO. Only the Atomic Energy Commission is more closed and more successful than DRDO. Successful military research and development will require a change in both the philosophy of the Indian state and its attitudes toward private industry. If the Indian Air Force buys no more than a few LCAs, for example, we expect its unit cost to compare with the numbers for U.S.–made fighters. For a country that has a per capita GDP that is approximately one-fiftieth of the United States, this level of spending must be prohibitive. The Indian government has given the greatest attention to military research and innovation: New Delhi has spent more money on military R&D than any other category. While it seeks external assistance for these projects, it is fierce in protecting the strategic independence that makes these innovations useful. Despite DRDO's failures, the government has not only persisted in its goals, but also eschewed the overhaul of the responsible agencies.

India's strategic purpose in purchasing the weapons is unclear. The marquee items on the wish list of the armed forces—the aircraft carrier, the fighter aircraft, and the tanks—suggest power projection rather than restraint. Some military power is fungible, but there are limits. How does a new aircraft carrier coincide with India's defense concerns? The quest to buy 126 multirole fighter aircraft will bolster India's air defense and possibly serve the cause of minimum nuclear deterrence, but it is hard to find systematic public analysis of the trade-offs between aircraft and missiles. No country chooses one exclusively over the other, but understanding the trade-off is important to balance investment. This is especially pertinent as Indian Air Force chiefs, like their counterparts all over the world, have emphasized the strategic role of air power. The IAF is notably uninterested in missiles (so far the purview of the army), but the IAF's preference is for aircraft. John Lewis and Xue Litai argue that China very deliberately focused on developing missile forces at the expense of conventional air power.[25]

A similar study of the trade-offs in India probably exists in the world of classified documents. However, given that the purchase is slated to be the biggest peacetime foreign military sale in the world in decades, the lack of public debate on the issue is surprising. Instead, there is consensus in India that these new fighters—in those large numbers—are necessary. The agreement may reflect Indian inability to develop usable missiles, but that begs the question of why this must be so. The delay in the fighter purchase results from fear that corruption charges will bring down the government. All of this and the fact that the IAF has fewer usable fighter aircraft signals that the disjunction between reality and expectation is widening.

Most important, perhaps, strategic restraint has served India well. India has never fought a country more powerful than itself—the war with China was brief and one-sided. Israel, Vietnam, and even Pakistan have all had to innovate because they were taking on larger powers; India's status is that of a large, satisfied, status quo power for which innovation is very difficult if not risky. Why then should it change?

The realist position is that as India's strategic interests grow and its neighborhood becomes increasingly dangerous, the country must step up its defense preparedness. The implication of this argument is that India's leadership must take firm control of the modernization program, altering institutional structures and imposing coordination among state agencies. India's growing strategic community has clamored for this kind of change. However, those advocating strong military rearmament—prominently, Indian scholars such as Brahma Chellaney and Bharat Karnad and a clutch of retired generals, admirals, and air force officers—have become marginalized rather than mainstreamed over time. Advocates of an offensive military posture find it hard to gain traction even within the BJP, the natural political home for robust military policy.

In contrast, the Left believes that massive rearmament is a waste of money, unnecessarily provocative toward China, and an unpalatable association with a fickle United States. The implication of this argument is that India's leadership should step forward and curb the armed forces and their efforts to buy ever-increasing numbers of fancy weapons. Proponents of this argument prefer to avoid military competition with China (especially on behalf of the United States) and seek a more nonmilitary accommodation of Pakistan. The position of the ruling Congress Party, and especially Prime Minister Manmohan Singh, falls in this category, even though this government has allowed dramatic increases in the defense budget. Given that the Congress Party has ruled the country longer than any other political group, it is not surprising that this has been the position of most Indian governments since independence. It is also interesting that the BJP chose to remain within the general parameters of strategic restraint during its time in power.

We believe that this state of arming without aiming will continue into the future. While the behavior of individual political leaders may be suboptimal in defense matters, a kind of collective wisdom has been at play over the years and across political boundaries. The collective wisdom sets down the building blocks of enhanced military power, but not the institutional mechanisms associated with strategic assertiveness. Without strong institutional reform that pushes the development of joint doctrines, integrates the services with political decisionmaking in higher defense planning, and issues clear statements of strategic national goals, increased resources cannot enhance Indian capacity sufficiently to alter the military balance with its main rivals. A more assertive strategic and military posture will be costly, but also bring freedom of action.

CHAPTER TWO

STRUGGLING
WITH REFORM

India's policy of strategic restraint determines the pace, direction, and scope of reform in the country's national security system, which serves as the transmission that converts the country's new affluence and technology into fighting capacity. Indian military capacity depends on a shift of emphasis in the system from research and development to procurement and from pay and recruitment to use-of-force decisions, that is, the broadest conception of civil-military relations.

The Indian government has been more successful in expanding the military, creating new commands, agencies, and positions, and streamlining procurement; it has not been able to change spending priorities, ensure coordination across agencies, alter deep-seated attitudes toward private participation, and deliver transparency in decisionmaking. India's civil-military relations are characterized by political supremacy over the armed forces at a cost to effective military planning. In the words of the Kargil Review Committee, the most important effort at reform since the country's independence, "The framework Lord Ismay formulated and Lord Mountbatten recommended was accepted by a national leadership unfamiliar with the intricacies of national security management. There has been very little change over the past fifty-two years despite the 1962 debacle, the 1965 stalemate and the 1971 victory, the growing nuclear threat, end of the cold war, continuance of proxy war in Kashmir for over a decade and the revolution in military affairs."[1]

We discuss Indian reforms in two separate categories: first, in the military-acquisition process, which includes India's defense research and development and the problem of corruption, which have slowed down military procurement in India over the last two decades. And, second, in higher-defense policy, which includes decisions about a new chief of defense staff position, rebalancing the armed forces in favor of air and naval power, and integrating the service headquarters into the government. Somewhat beyond the purview of this book is how India addresses the relationship between its society and the military—notably the army, which traces its structure to the army created by Lord Clive in the eighteenth century. This is especially evident in the role that caste, class, and ethnicity play in the making of the ground forces.[2] We touch upon these in discussing the army (chapter 3) and in our summary of Indian military modernization (chapter 7).

MILITARY ACQUISITION IN INDIA

Procuring modern weapons is inherently difficult. Weapons are increasingly complex, multipurpose, and costly. Most modern weapons have life cycles that span decades, and the choice of weapon determines the way in which an armed force will respond during a particular period. When cutting-edge technology is used in the manufacture of weapons, the cost, the utility, and the very shape are of a new weapon are uncertain. Choosing the correct weapon system requires not only predicting future threats, but also having a consensus view on how to counter these threats. The choice of a new weapon system must make strategic sense—should the choice be missiles or aircraft—but evaluation of different models of the same type of weapon, let alone understanding the trade-offs between different categories of weapons, is not easy. Matching field test performance and pricing packages is difficult because of how vendors distinguish their products from each other. Also, modernization usually occurs in peacetime without the benefit of testing equipment in an actual war.

Furthermore, the structure of the weapons market is unlike most others. The value of the market may be large, but unit volumes and the number of buyers and sellers are limited. In most countries, the national government is the only buyer and can set prices to its own advantage or proscribe sales. When weapons manufacturers wish to sell to other parties—mainly other governments—they require the approval of their own governments. Given the asymmetrical power of the government in the market, private investment in the manufacture of weapons occurs under very constrained conditions that ultimately subsidize the development process. State-funded laboratories conduct the bulk of research and development in most countries. The government commits to cost-plus weapons and sole-supply contracts to firms

willing to invest in production lines. Pricing becomes even more complicated when technology transfers are included in the international trade of
arms. The seller must price the exchange to compensate the loss of profit
from future sales, but keep the price at a level that does not jeopardize the
current sale. Consequently, the pricing mechanism in the conventional arms
market, except in low-end personal weapons, is political; that is, alliance
relationships determine the price that is paid for weapons. Practically all
countries that produce modern weapons can relate some form of horror
story about the $300 toilet seat.

The Indian government has been on the wrong side of all these problems
and has suffered from a lack of a robust indigenous defense industry. India
produces its own trucks and jeeps, manufacturers its own rifles and guns,
and ammunition for all but the most sophisticated part of its arsenal. During
the Kargil crisis, which saw the extensive use of artillery, there was a frantic
search for such high-end precision ammunition as well as for high-altitude
clothing and even coffins. Under license from the Soviet Union, India has
assembled tanks and aircraft. However, the domestic industry, which, until
recently, was almost entirely state-owned, has failed to contribute meaningfully to the rearmament of the country—except in nuclear weapons.[3] The
billions of dollars of investment in weapons research and development has
not produced anything significant enough to become a game-changer in
India's security landscape. The biggest contribution of indigenous research
to Indian security, nuclear weapons, was not produced by the designated
military research entity, but by the nuclear establishment.[4]

The Procurement Process

Military-procurement decisions in India revolve around five interrelated
questions. First, where will the resources come from? India's rapid economic
growth has alleviated this long-running problem somewhat. Second, which
weapons should India acquire, and how many should it get? What should
the balance be between the services, within them, and in different functions?
For example, what should the balance be between coastal defense, interdiction, and sea control? Or the balance between air defense, ground support,
and strategic bombing for the air force? Third, should the country make or
buy weapons (a question raised by the endemic failure of defense research
in India)? Fourth, if hardware and military technology must be imported,
should the decision be shaped by economic, technical, ideological, or strategic alignments? Fifth, the enormous amount of money at stake raises the
specter of corruption: can India devise a clean procurement system that gives

political, military, and bureaucratic leaders the confidence to make judgment calls in the selection of weapons? The ghost of the Bofors howitzer has haunted Indian defense procurement since the mid-1980s.

Indian Ministry of Defence officials lament the country's inability to come up with a legitimate defense-acquisition process, and argue that this obstructs both defense modernization and the rationale for calibrating the total amount of defense spending. A further complication is the existence of a separate defense finance bureaucracy, a part of the Ministry of Finance, which acts as an additional check on military spending.

After one of the services determines a functional need, the next step is consultations with the state-owned defense research and production establishment. The Defence Research and Development Organisation, the umbrella agency better known by its acronym, DRDO, is a privileged entity that exercises the right of first refusal on equipment demands raised by the services. The head of the DRDO serves as the scientific adviser to the minister of defense, a position in which he has veto power over what India can import. In a number of cases, the DRDO makes the unrealistic case for indigenous production, holding up procurement until it is proved incapable of making the supply. The dual role of supplier and evaluator has resulted in reduced accountability for the dramatic record of its failure.

DRDO

DRDO has not delivered a single major weapon system to the armed forces in five decades of existence, though it has had small successes in projects such as systems integration and anti-submarine warfare sonar.[5] In the 1980s it tried to develop a Light Combat Aircraft (LCA), which we discuss further in chapter 4. The LCA was well beyond the reach of current Indian technology, and American companies approached by DRDO with offers of collaboration were skeptical of its capabilities. DRDO went ahead without any major external partner, announcing a deployment date of 2003; however, by 2010 it had not produced an aircraft that the Indian Air Force wanted to buy. Instead, India now seeks to purchase 126 multirole fighters for $10 billion in one of the biggest single weapons deals in the developing world. A second prized DRDO project was the Arjun tank, which was meant to supplement Soviet-supplied T-72s and T-90s. One study quotes the Indian Army's point person for the Arjun tank project, Brigadier D. K. Babbar, as saying, "The Arjun tank has no future. It still cannot fire straight. The T-90, a far superior tank, can kill the Arjun. We would not cross any border with these tanks." Army chief General J. J. Singh was more diplomatic, "We will see where we can use it to get optimum use."[6]

Initially, the vaunted guided missile program was thought to be successful. But ten years after the nuclear tests, India has been able to deploy only the Prithvi, whose 150-kilometer range and liquid fuel make it of little practical use. The 1,500-kilometer Agni does not appear to have been produced in large enough numbers for induction into the services. Compared to the success of the space program, which provided the missile program with the basic technology, the failure of the DRDO is visible. The missile program has now shifted emphasis from longer-range nuclear-delivery vehicles to air defense, and Indian strategists are deeply worried about losing the missile race to Pakistan, let alone catching up with China. Yet DRDO has the power to kill any procurement proposal from the armed forces. The organization has adopted a classic foot-in-the-door strategy: winning initial support by promising products on the cheap but later citing sunk costs to demand more money. The DRDO argues that the armed forces continuously increase the specifications of weapons systems, so that terms set by the services are impossible to achieve. Agency officials publicly criticize the armed forces for their preference for foreign purchases; some privately suggest that political and military leaders are motivated by the prospect of corrupt gains in defense deals. State monopoly engenders increased opacity that makes specific decisions hard to judge. There is no credible public evaluation even of the AEC's success in nuclear weapons. The weapons program is secret and embedded in the civilian nuclear program. The secrecy is understandable, but the absence of an informed audit delays serious evaluation of cost-effectiveness.

The reasons for DRDO's failure are multifaceted. One review concluded that poor planning, over-optimistic timelines, and a lack of coordination with the armed forces led to cost and time overruns of major defense projects.[7] However, the most important reason is the agency's lack of political leadership. DRDO officials engaged in exaggerated and wildly over-optimistic statements of their own capabilities, and civilian politicians with little knowledge about strategic or military affairs, let alone the intricacies of military technology and hardware, allowed DRDO a free hand for decades. The civilian bureaucrats who advise the politicians are rarely experts themselves, and defense research is conducted virtually without any accountability. On the one hand, political leaders have not forced the military to properly define specifications, and have insisted thereafter that they accept indigenous systems if the initial requirements are met. On the other hand, the DRDO can set the hardware-modernization agenda through its power to veto or delay acquisition from overseas in favor of indigenous research and development. There is in fact a duel between military and scientific professionalism as played out by the armed forces and the DRDO. While the military is interested in getting the best possible weapons irrespective of the producer, the scientific establishment places greater value on the development of indigenous technological capacity even if it does not produce the weapons the military wants.

Traditionally, the quality of Indian weapons has been so poor that pilots favor imported planes over indigenously produced ones. The army, too, has long had problems with indigenously assembled tanks, even those under license from the Soviet Union.[8] The reasons for substandard products are well understood: often the adaptation to Indian circumstances is incomplete or ineffective, especially where DRDO was involved; the state defense-production enterprises are plagued by union interference and do not have to meet an international test of excellence; and the integration of subsystems from many countries is always difficult to achieve. As technology becomes more complicated, costs have risen while quality remains problematic.

In a country where import substitution has been the mantra for decades, the forced import of weapons was politically embarrassing. The Indian government overcame the resistance to importing weapons at huge cost by its generous funding of indigenous research and development, despite a continuous string of failures. But the inability—and unwillingness—of the political leadership to coordinate the demands of the armed forces with the supply from the military research agencies has meant that military modernizations in India have been disorganized and of limited strategic value.

A high-level committee chaired by Vijay Kelkar, a former secretary of the Ministry of Finance, was established in 2004. Its mandate was broad, and it urged a number of steps that would professionalize the defense-acquisition process and bring private enterprise into the defense-production system. It recommended that the ordnance factories be "corporatized," that joint public-private ventures be encouraged, and that select private firms be treated as if they were public sector corporations. Kelkar's committee also recommended that the government develop a fifteen-year defense-acquisition plan and share it with private industry, revoke the ban on defense exports of certain kinds of equipment and to certain states, and create an organization to promote defense exports.

Since the Kelkar report, American organizations, public and private, have experimented in ways to transfer American technology to India and to exploit commercially, technology the Indian defense establishment can produce. One of the most ambitious enterprises is a four-way arrangement between a major U.S. defense firm (Lockheed Martin), University of Texas at Austin, the Federation of Indian Chambers of Commerce and Industry (FICCI), and the Department of Science and Technology. Theoretically, FICCI will assist India in marketing its technologies to Indian and foreign firms, and Lockheed Martin will support an "India Innovation Growth Program" at the University of Texas at Austin in an effort to expand global export opportunities for new Indian technologies. Another major Indian industry organization, the Confederation of Indian Industries, operates a program to increase the private sector's role in defense production.[9]

In 2006 the Ministry of Defence published the Defence Procurement Procedure and the Defence Procurement Manual designed to streamline the process and make it more transparent.[10] Since then the ministry has amended both documents to reflect developing realities. Certain problems remain that the ministry finds difficult to resolve. While the documents provide detailed direction on the process, potential vendors are unable to estimate the size and components of the Indian arms market and thus shy away from making investments. The Indian weapons wish list is widely known, but there is no way of knowing which items will clear first. Without priorities, market estimation is impossible. The market remains arbitrarily determined from year to year, and estimates differ based on which officials lead the services and the departments. Second, there is no clear understanding of how the offset process works. The default in the system is "the more offset the better," but such a stand comes at a cost because vendors do not bid or bid seriously unless they know the true cost of participation. Fundamentally, the government has not been able to solve the problem of corruption.

More recently the problem of the DRDO was at last directly addressed. A 2008 report by a committee headed by P. Rama Rao, a former civilian secretary of the Department of Science and Technology, recommended that the DRDO turn over a number of its laboratories to other government agencies and confine itself to eight or ten critical areas, where it had demonstrated competence. Press reports indicate that the committee's twenty-five recommendations had avoided close scrutiny of the failure of major projects such as the Arjun tank and the Light Combat Aircraft.[11] One year later a high-level committee, headed by the defense secretary, was appointed to oversee the changes. A number of the recommendations were accepted, including shedding eleven of DRDO's fifty-one laboratories, notably those in DRDO's life science stream, which had little to do with military hardware; the remaining forty laboratories were clustered into different streams of defense technology (naval, aero, ground combat, weapons, and electronic warfare).[12] This may be the beginning of the first serious attempt to trim DRDO to a manageable size and portfolio, holding the door open to private-sector participation in defense R&D.

A Nascent Military-Industrial Complex

India's policy of defense autarky, in place from the beginning, makes foreign collaboration very difficult, and discomfort about selling weapons to unsavory or conflict-ridden states limits the market for the few exportable items that India does manufacture. India's domestic industrial base remains weak; there are few opportunities for technology spin-off, although the private sector is eager to enter into the defense R&D and production business. One of the largest associations of Indian companies commissioned a study of opportunities in the Indian defense sector by an international consulting firm, KPMG, which found some Indian firms well-positioned to seek defense contracts.[13] Tata Motors was developing a light military vehicle based on a civilian off-road model; it also purchased Land Rover, which was trying to sell its *Defender,* the British Army's main light vehicle, to the Indian Army. Foreign joint ventures in the defense sector are rapidly forming. In 2009 BAE Systems Europe joined with Indian vehicle manufacturer Mahindra and Mahindra to bid for armored vehicles. In the same year Boeing won a contract to supply eight long-range maritime patrol aircraft in a $2.1 billion deal. In May 2009 the European group EADS signed an agreement with Larsen and Toubro to establish a joint venture that might bid for an estimated $500 million in defense contracts, especially in the electronic sector, over the next six years. This deal was rejected by the government initially, but the partners returned in February 2010 with a new equity structure to satisfy requirements of indigenous ownership in defense contracting firms.[14]

The post-1991 economic liberalization in India brought heightened awareness of the possibilities of technology. While science has always been an instrument of national deliverance, telephone connections were difficult to get. Across India, a new constituency for technology emerged as Indians successfully adapted to the demands of international competition, most dramatically in the software industry. The officers of India's armed forces come from the same middle class that supplies this self-aware new talent to the technology sector. The drive for technological upgrading in the military, therefore, is a part of the larger national movement toward technological advancement. However, for this initiative to manifest in the defense sector, India's military-industrial complex will need to be deregulated, an unlikely prospect given the concurrent fears of corruption.

Inability to Tackle Corruption

In 2006 the somewhat arcane subject of military modernization entered Indian popular culture via a film about corruption in the defense industry.

The hit Bollywood film *Rang de Basanti* ("Colors of Spring") is an exploration of corruption in defense deals following the death of an Indian Air Force pilot. The pilot's fiancée and friends expose the defense minister, assassinate him, and take over a radio station to broadcast the truth. The film struck a deep chord with the Indian middle class, for whom corruption has been a dominant issue for decades.

The arms-acquisition process in India has been haunted for years by the specter of corruption, especially in its imports (*Rang de Basanti* deals with the import of substandard spare parts for the MiG-21). In the early years of independence, a "jeep scandal" ensnared Krishna Menon, the Indian high commissioner in London. Menon escaped personal culpability, but the scandal created a rift in the cabinet—those who disliked Menon for personal or ideological reasons used the scandal to discredit him. Nehru, however, stood by his old friend. It is noteworthy that the acquisitions in the 1960s did not lead to cries of corruption—perhaps because the imminent threats of war overshadowed the waste and corruption that was present.

The most damaging cases of corruption occurred during the 1980s following the second major effort to modernize the military. Prime Minister Rajiv Gandhi led the effort and was assisted by a close friend, Arun Singh and the army chief, K. Sundarji. Almost every major weapons deal concluded by Rajiv's government was scrutinized. The most dramatic was the purchase of the Swedish-built Bofors howitzers. Disagreements over the source and degree of corruption led V. P. Singh, a powerful North Indian politician, to quit Rajiv's cabinet and launch an opposition campaign that called for government reform. The Bofors scandal ultimately cost Rajiv Gandhi the 1989 elections, a defeat from which the Congress Party did not recover until the 2004 elections. It is still unclear whether Bofors had paid money to the Gandhi family or the Congress Party, but there is widespread perception that fraud did occur. The last few years have been marked by defense corruption scandals. The most serious was the exposé by *Tehelka* magazine, which indicted important Bharatiya Janata Party (BJP) politicians and some military officers, and revealed a land scam that involved senior army officers.[15]

The possibility of corruption makes continued investment in unproductive but indigenous research and development politically safer. Since the Indian private sector is only beginning to enter the military-production business, buying usually means dealing with foreign sellers. Advocates for domestic R&D justify support for the DRDO by arguing against the "enriching" of foreigners and in favor of technological development at home. There was particular discomfort about Western private companies, which were characterized by the Indian Left as mercenary and unscrupulous. Ironically, the laws that bind American firms to honest business practices are tougher than those that govern companies from other major weapons-producing states. Russians have also benefited more than other suppliers because they have a reputation of being less corrupt. State-owned weapons makers from the Soviet Union (and now Russia) were reputed to function in an above-board fashion.

The reality, of course, was murkier. Defense deals with the Russians were equally corrupt. In the 1970s and 1980s there were kickbacks and purchases from politically favored Indian companies, which also made contributions to party coffers, and sweetheart deals with pro-government, pro-Congress trade unions. The Israelis have also been implicated in several instances, and in June 2009, the Indian government decided to suspend several companies implicated in a case involving bribery of a former head of the Indian Ordnance Factory Board. The allegations were so serious that the government suspended the companies involved without waiting for a trial or conviction; one Israeli firm, Israeli Military Industries (IMI), and one Singapore company, Singapore Technologies, had their contracts terminated. IMI had recently signed a deal to build five factories in India to produce ordnance and ammunition, and the Indian special forces and Army were especially dependent on Israeli equipment.[16] Other Israeli firms (Israeli Aerospace Industries and Rafael) are alleged to be involved in corruption scandals, but their contracts were not suspended because they were critical to the defense-modernization process.[17] The Singapore firm was going to provide a major upgrade for Indian artillery; after its initial contract was rescinded, the contract process began anew.

These scandals, and others, happen because the indigenous research, development, and production establishment has failed to produce any weapons system of substance despite sustained and significant support. If commissions in weapons contracts raised the price of a working system to the Indian taxpayer, inability to deliver on research and development meant that the taxpayer received no returns on the investment. The decision to make or buy, therefore, cannot be separated from the potential for corruption that plagues every weapons purchase. There is considerable exasperation in India, and while no one argues that corruption in weapons acquisition is a good thing, many defense experts point out that it may be a small and inevitable price to pay if India wants to acquire the right kinds of weapons in a timely fashion. As the head of one of India's leading private firms, now engaged in defense production, noted at a recent DefExpo defense show, "It is time to understand that the gun is innocent." Anand Mahindra was referring to the vaunted Bofors gun, which his firm plans to manufacture in India.[18] The very name "Bofors" has become a byword for corruption in high places and has prevented two generations of political leaders from addressing the military's needs in a timely and effective fashion. One experienced observer of the Indian scene, a former *Financial Times* correspondent in Delhi, reflecting on Mahindra's plea for a fresh look at the defense-acquisition process, calls the Indian armed forces "probably the worst-equipped of any large country in the world."[19]

HIGHER DEFENSE POLICYMAKING

Civil-military relations are always a balancing act between too little and too much control over the armed forces: India falls into the second category. While India compares favorably with some of its neighbors regarding the recessed role of the military, this may have eaten into the quality of strategic decisionmaking. Reforming the Indian defense and security policymaking process has long been a subject of interest to foreign and Indian observers. When George Tanham investigated India's strategic culture in the early 1990s, a significant element in his report concerned the dysfunctional relationship between the civil and military sectors. India's own defense modernizers have been criticizing the existing pattern for three decades. More recently, complaints about the Indian security establishment's inability to respond promptly to new threats of terrorism or to offer viable instruments of coercive diplomacy are really questions that emanate from India's civil-military relations. The country is lauded for preserving democracy from military takeovers, which have occurred in Pakistan and Bangladesh, but, with rare exceptions, the country has also been unwilling or unable to use force to alter its strategic condition.

Whereas the British integrated military advice at the highest level of the Governor-General's Council, independent India has limited military access to key decisionmaking bodies. This situation has evolved in two ways. First, the military's position was downgraded when a civilian defense minister became the highest official in the military department, later the Ministry of Defence. Military proposals now had to be scrutinized in the decisionmaking council by someone who was clearly not a part of the military itself. Eventually the Ministry of Defence expanded in size and influence so that the uniformed services were made subservient to the bureaucracy acting on behalf of the defence minister. The second institutional change was to abolish the post of the military commander in chief, fragmenting the military institution into its constituent services. In theory, if not in reality, the hugely larger army, which had supplied the commander in chief, became equalized with the other smaller services.

Since then, further changes have not addressed the first echelon of civil-military interaction. After the 1962 defeat, the Indian Army created the Eastern Command specifically to manage the Northeast region. Since then, the Northern Command, the most important regional organization in the army, has practically broken off from the 16 Corps headquarters in Srinagar as the Kashmir Command. In 2001 India's first interservice command was inaugurated at the Andaman Islands in the Bay of Bengal. Later a Strategic Command was established for the nuclear program, although operational control remains with the two services (army and air force) that actually operate delivery systems, along with the scientists who are responsible for the warheads. However, the impact of these changes will remain marginal unless the position of chief of defense staff is created.

Demands for such a position have come up repeatedly; the recommendation was included in two commissions headed by former defense minister Arun Singh, the first in the 1980s and the second following the Kargil War. The BJP government asserted that it would consider creating such a position, but did not follow through with the change. Proposals for chief of defense staff to coordinate between the services have been resisted by civilians who fear the creation of a powerful military figure, who could overthrow civilian supremacy. The move is also resisted by the air force and navy, which fear losing the "equality" they share with the much bigger army. Instead, after the 1998 nuclear tests, India created the new position of national security adviser to coordinate foreign policy and defense issues, strengthening the civilian rather than the military side of the institutional structure.

Civilian control in India rests upon an unwritten but strong agreement between the politicians, who are virtually ignorant about military affairs, and the higher civilian bureaucracy, whose expertise is only marginally better but who have an institutional memory and coherence that is an overmatch for even the army. Thus civilian control does not rest upon political leaders exercising their right to know defense questions better, but upon a calculation that the armed services must be kept in their place for bureaucratic reasons.

The civil-military relationship is susceptible to narrow political calculations, especially regarding kickbacks and corruption in the defense-acquisition process. From the politicians' perspective, the huge empire of defense-production facilities, the cantonments, and other high-value but low-profile expenditures on defense are perfect opportunities. This was made evident in the scandals surrounding one defense minister, George Fernandes, but other ministers have also used their position to political advantage. The military is aware of this, but the services have rarely gone public. The tell-all memoir of a sacked Indian Navy admiral serves as an obviously self-serving defense of his record, but it also contains considerable detail about relations between the services, the politicians, and the Ministry of Defence—which comes in for especially strong condemnation.[20]

The policy and budget processes function inefficiently. While there are mechanisms through which the military can offer its suggestions and state its preferences; for budgets and policy, it is entirely at the mercy of the civilian bureaucracy, both in the Ministries of Defence and Finance. Service chiefs may try to reflect service priorities, but they are in competition with other services for funds, and there is no mechanism by which the defense budget is linked to estimates of strategic threats.

Finally, officer promotion at higher levels is determined by seniority. This ensures contentment in the officer corps, but it also means that the promotion of an exceptionally talented officer is dictated by chance. Out-of-turn merit-based promotions are rare. Seniority is favored because of the bargain between the officer corps and the political community: promotable officers know exactly what lies ahead in their career, while politicians deal with a compliant officer corps, albeit one without imagination or creativity. These are skills that are not highly valued by the politicians or the civilian bureaucrats who are at the center of the process: more than in most services, compliance is valued more than originality.

Post-Kargil Reforms

The Kargil War of May-July 1999 precipitated India's most intense and enduring spell of reform in the higher management of Indian defense matters. We examine the impact of Kargil on army thinking in the next chapter, and discuss here the broader observations generated by an official inquiry under the leadership of K. Subrahmanyam, India's most influential strategic thinker. In a rare instance of transparency, the Kargil Review Committee Report was not only tabled in the Indian Parliament but also published and became a best-selling book.[21]

Kargil had concluded with a political victory for India, but the crisis and mini-war had shocked the country and the political leadership, which had gambled on a new peace offensive with Pakistan. Pakistan's incursion across the Line of Control was repelled without an escalation of conflict to a general war, but the conflict was seen as a result of failure in the institutional struc-ture of the military and a flawed civil-military relationship. The conservative BJP government also played up the theme of betrayal, superbly manipulating media coverage to demonstrate Pakistani perfidy.

The committee made three types of recommendations: first, on national security management and decisionmaking; second, on strengthening capac-ity, especially in intelligence, military technology, and counterterrorism; and third, on developing a more open defense policy that included more input from think tanks, the press, and the public.

The committee concluded that the army's response had been rapid, robust, and acceptable. Specifically, the committee's findings disputed the view that the Indian Army had been slow in reacting, had sustained avoid-able casualties, and had not provided its soldiers with adequate extreme winter clothing and appropriate weapons.[22] Rather, the committee empha-sized systemic failures in the identification of the threat and recommended improvement across a range of Indian military capacities. The Indian Army has been in the process of ordering more 155 mm guns, which had finally won India the war. The use of air power was approved three weeks after the intruders were initially discovered. Once the IAF lost aircraft, however, it had to wait until the installation of the LITENING pods to re-enter the war. Air-land coordination was poor initially, but improved through the course of the war. It is noteworthy that the Indian Army moved robustly toward raising its close air-support assets following Kargil. India won the battle, but then victory should never have been in question. The conflict occurred inside Indian-administered territory, and the intruders had little ongoing international support during the conflict, not even from Pakistan. India enjoyed overwhelming superiority in the theater. The Kargil War launched a renewed demand from the military and the strategic community for larger budgets and modernization; these demands would start to be addressed as India's economic condition improved.

In 2000 the government, headed by the more realist BJP, formed a Group of Ministers (GoM) committee to examine the national security system as a whole and to oversee the implementation of the Kargil Review Committee recommendations. Part of the GoM report has been published, but some of it remains classified.

The GoM included the prime minister, and the home affairs, finance, defense, and external affairs ministers, and it included the national security adviser at the time, Brajesh Mishra.[23] The Kargil analysis cited incoherence and mistakes before and during the operation; the GoM report is briefer but more wide-ranging. The GoM report is based on the work of four task forces in all: the task forces on intelligence, border security, and internal security and a task force on the restructuring of management of defence headed by Arun Singh. Although the studies that lay behind the GoM report are not public, their recommendations have been widely discussed, as participants in that process, frustrated at being ignored by the government, have talked publicly. In frustration, Indian commentators have written about "Boforsphobia," the military-babu complex, an astigmatic civil-military relationship, and an army that is unprepared for battle—issues that have become the very titles of a number of recent critiques.[24]

The GoM met twenty-seven times; its conclusions went well beyond the recommendations of the Kargil study. It noted that most of the structures and processes for the management of national security were under stress— they were for the most part over fifty years old. The report stressed that new developments, notably the nuclearization of India's neighborhood, greater domestic turmoil, globalization, new technologies, American preeminence in the post–cold war world, and the emergence of nonstate actors demanded a new approach to national security matters and the use of the military. In a tour d'horizon, it described a perilous environment that presented problems from Pakistan, China, internal security, drugs, illegal immigration, caste, communalism, and left-wing extremism—a catch-all phrase used to describe various separatists, terrorists, Naxalites, and rebel bands, other than those linked to radical Islam. It did not prioritize these threats—at least not in the declassified version.

The analysis in the report was often scathing. There was no synchronization within and between the three departments of the Ministry of Defence. The system lacked a unified and cohesive method of advising the government on military matters. Interservice doctrinal planning, policy, and operational rivalries stymied "jointness" and integrated planning. Overall linkage between planning and budgeting was weak. The Ministry of Defence lacked an efficient procurement process. There was no overall national security doctrine, little prospect for long-term funding, and a dysfunctional relationship between research and development, defense production, and the services that are the consumers of weapons. Further, the report pointed out that sufficient attention had not been paid to the relationship between the armed forces and India's fast-changing society, changes that could affect recruitment policy, weapons development, and the relationship between the private sector and defense production.

Of the GoM's proposals, the simplest and the most startling was to bring the headquarters of the three services officially into the Indian government—they had hitherto been referred to as "Attached" or "Subordinate" offices. Awareness that the tradition in the services and in the government was excessively hierarchical in nature, and that fiscal responsibility and decisionmaking had to be dramatically decentralized, the Indian government altered the Rules of Business to bring about the change.

Second, the GoM called for the creation of a Chief of Defence Staff (CDS) to provide single-point military advice to the minister of defence. The CDS was to be a four star (full general or admiral rank) officer drawn from one of the three services on a rotating basis; he would not revert to his service after his tour was completed. While a miniature Integrated Defence Staff (IDS) was created, there is no chief at present. The IDS that does exist provides some coordination, and has as close to a "jointness" frame of mind as any other body in the Indian government, but it has little impact on how India formulates and implements its military policies. Jointness is noticeable by its absence: of the seventeen commands of the Indian armed forces, with the exception of the Andaman and Nicobar Command and the Joint Strategic Forces, none are in the same location.[25] The report also called for the creation of a Defence Intelligence Agency (DIA) to coordinate the activities of the separate service intelligence functions, and reforms in defense procurement and production, including a new approach to defense contracting and easing of restraints upon defense exports, long-term defense planning, and a radical change in defense research and development.

Anit Mukherjee, a former Indian Army officer who has studied defense reforms, says recommendations that created new agencies, new commands, and new positions were quickly adopted.[26] The position of the national security adviser, established after the 1998 tests, was strengthened; the incumbent in that position has become the primary executive assistant to the prime minister on defense matters. The government set up a new Defence Intelligence Agency, a National Technical Research Organisation, and a task force on border management. The DIA has been established, but has little authority compared with civilian intelligence agencies, which still provide strategic and even tactical intelligence. However, it has taken under its wing other new organizations such as the Defence Image and Processing Centre and the Defence Information Warfare Agency. DIA's role is to coordinate intelligence among the services and provide it to higher defense management, that is, the Ministry of Defence.

A new satellite imagery capacity was added and unmanned aerial vehicles were inducted for intelligence gathering. Further, the services have made a strong outreach effort by establishing their own think tanks and encouraging retired officers to propagate the views of the services in the media. Lastly, the Ministry of Defence publishes a procurement manual that is available to the public that seeks to rationalize the byzantine system of military purchasing, which has always been subject to criticism and corruption. There exist, for example, a Defence Procurement Council, a Defence Procurement Board, and a Defence R&D Board. Changes in procurement procedures are regularly announced, confusing prospective sellers as well as the military and civilian officials who must follow ever-changing guidelines.[27]

On a number of significant issues, however, change has proved to be more difficult. Tentative steps have been taken toward greater jointness, including the creation of a Joint Command in the Andaman Islands (2001), an Integrated Defence Staff (2001), and a Strategic Forces Command (2003). Three years after its creation, the IDS had only a handful of staff officers, but it has grown steadily and has divisions that deal with planning, intelligence, and joint operations. It has also financed a new think tank to work on multiservice and interservice issues.[28] The Strategic Forces Command, which has been headed by a general-rank officer sequentially from each of the three services, does not control India's nuclear assets, which are under the jurisdiction of the air force, the army (missiles), and civilian nuclear scientists. These steps provide a façade of coordination, and are intended to preserve a strong civilian voice throughout the process. Still, divide and rule persists, and it is unrealistic to expect a CDS or a joint staff to persuade the services to form a singular planning process, not to mention an actual joint command mechanism.

Individual service headquarters are still organized separately from the government. In effect, two parallel bureaucracies run defense policymaking: at the service headquarters, military officers draw up plans and policies, which must once again start at the bottom of the ladder in the Ministry of Defence. The ministry maintains its own files, which may not be available to military officers involved in the planning process even though civilian bureaucrats engaged in deliberations generally do not have the military background necessary to make informed decisions. Given this largely dysfunctional arrangement, the possibility of change seems remote.

As for the weapons-acquisition process, a number of Indian companies have been designated as *Raksha Udyog Ratna* ("state industrial treasure") and are now qualified to submit bids for defense contracts. This recommendation to allow such bidding was made forty years earlier by the American consulting firm Arthur D. Little. Finally, the GoM report recommended the establishment of a National Defence University, which would support academic research on security and defense matters, provide a liaison to the academic community, and pay more attention to the civil-military interface at all levels, beginning with the districts where soldiers and civilians seemed to inhabit different worlds. This has yet to happen. The GoM report went into some detail about the lack of interaction between civilian and military authorities, and even enjoined the armed forces to learn about the "obligations and constraints on the civilian side."

Intriguingly, the GoM recommended the report be self-implementing, that is, that the respective ministries establish a separate cell to monitor implementation, with a quarterly review by the cabinet secretary. Informed sources say that this process was started in the Ministry of Defence, but later fell into disuse. There is no available evidence of whether monitoring was applied to the intelligence sector. Historically, fiscal control has been the dominant form of control over defense and military programs; in the absence of serious parliamentary oversight, the Indian government needs to establish a monitoring program to ensure that important reforms are in fact implemented.

Intelligence Reform

From a planning perspective, intelligence reform is a crucial element of changing India's military capacity. India divides its intelligence services between domestic and foreign intelligence. The Research and Analysis Wing (RAW) conducts strategic or political intelligence in the external domain, the Intelligence Bureau (IB) on domestic security matters. Military intelligence is in the hands of the specific services.[29] The Ministry of External Affairs (MEA) lacks an analytical and intelligence capability; the Ministries of Home Affairs and Finance should have an intelligence element, but do not.

In keeping with the requirements of colonial policing, intelligence gathering in India was historically the domain of police officers interested in maintaining political control. The IB, the oldest intelligence agency in India, has been as much a tool of politics and political control as it has been an instrument of national security. Among other missteps, the IB reportedly armed the Sikh insurgency in the early 1980s in an effort to shore up political support for the Congress Party in the state of Punjab. Perhaps the IB's biggest political-military error was made by Director B. N. Mullick during the run-up to the 1962 war. Mullick told Nehru that the Chinese government would accept India's forward policy without military engagement. Although in the beginning this was the case, as winter approached and Indian posts became hard to resupply, the Chinese military began to engage Indian soldiers at the posts. Many soldiers were left to fend for themselves. Eventually this culminated in war and defeat.

The intelligence failure led to the establishment of RAW in the late 1960s. The bulk of its cadre was drawn from the police and the military. Gradually,

RAW has built up its own staff, but it is not professionalized. Formal education requirements are little more than language training. No effort was made to separate collection and analysis to prevent conflicts of interest. Most important, the external intelligence system works at a political level, with little regard or knowledge of military matters. On the other hand, the military intelligence function resides within the services and has little authority to operate beyond the tactical horizon.

The lack of coordination has contributed to the three largest intelligence failures in recent history: the 1962 war with China; the 1988–90 intervention in Sri Lanka, where RAW misjudged its protégé, the Tamil Tigers; and more recently, a series of intelligence failures— highlighted by the Kargil Committee—that led to the limited incursion by Pakistan into the higher Himalayas. As in 1962, the failure occurred at two levels. First, Indian intelligence failed to convincingly report to the political leadership on the Pakistan Army's true intentions even as Prime Minister Nawaz Sharif embarked on rapprochement with India. As in 1962, intelligence analysts failed to argue convincingly about a political judgment, which is difficult to achieve under any circumstances. The bigger intelligence failure was the inability of the Indian system to detect the incursions. Again the failure was more operational or even tactical rather than strategic, but it was repeated in 2008 with the failure to detect and then adequately respond to the Mumbai terror attack launched from Pakistan.

While there have been numerous failures of military intelligence, it is hard to expect service intelligence to function entirely on its own without direct support from RAW and the IB. A Joint Intelligence Committee (JIC), an institution copied from the British, came under the cabinet secretary after the 1962 war. In 2007 the JIC was given an independent chairman. Historically it served as a forum for unwanted officers who were banished from active policymaking. It now reports to the national security adviser, who also supervises the National Security Council Staff (via a deputy). A system of deputations from the military to the intelligence agencies is in place, but, more often than not, such postings rule out promotion for officers within the military. As a result, officers seconded to an intelligence agency prefer to join the cadre of that agency, thereby acquiring the imperatives of the intelligence agency. On the other side of the coin, there is perhaps a greater problem— intelligence agencies seldom take inputs from military intelligence seriously. The intelligence flow is predominantly one way. The military expresses a demand, and the intelligence agencies supply it. More important, the intelligence chiefs brief the prime minister on a daily and weekly basis. By their very nature, these briefings are more political and strategic than military.

Military intelligence has no forum to present information to the highest authority except when crises are imminent, and by then the damage is done.

Although they purport to supply strategic intelligence, the intelligence agencies are highly operations-oriented. Unlike Western intelligence systems there is no wall between collection and analysis, on the one hand, and covert action, on the other. Indeed, the agencies think that such divisions foster lack of expertise and prefer a more integrated approach. The model, however, best serves operational—though not military operational—goals. Indeed, the successes in Indian intelligence have largely been in covert action. The Indian Peace Keeping Force (IPKF) debacle might be blamed on intelligence failure, but the role of the intelligence agencies in supporting the Tamil insurgency movement in Sri Lanka was highly effective. The agencies played a stellar role in arming and organizing the Mukti Bahini in East Pakistan in the run-up to the 1971 war. Recent—and unconfirmed—reports that Indian intelligence agencies had perfected a system of reprisals for terrorist bombings in India by Pakistan's Inter-Services Intelligence (ISI) suggest a high degree of sophistication in covert action, albeit in a limited geographic area.

The same agencies, however, failed to predict the trajectory of politics in Bangladesh after India helped to liberate the country. In Sri Lanka, they failed to provide good intelligence on the Tamil Tigers even though Indian agencies had supported the emergence of the organization. In Kashmir, Indian intelligence agencies have been able only belatedly, after almost two decades of civil war, to separate indigenous Kashmiri groups that are fighting for independence from the Pakistan-backed insurgents who want Kashmir to become a part of Pakistan. The intelligence agencies failed in Punjab as well—first with the rise of Bhindranwale, then with the transformation of the Golden Temple into a militant fortress, and later, in failing to see clearly the impact of the Longowal Accord. The problem then is this: although the intelligence agencies are supposed to perform a strategic role, they do so in a limited way, mainly through covert action. The agencies perform poorly with actual intelligence gathering and analysis—that is, the prediction of political judgment, correct estimation of enemy intention and capacity. Given that the system itself is fractured, and military intelligence too limited in scope, the most dramatic cases of failure could not have been avoided.

In the case of the intelligence services, as in the case of the armed services and the Ministry of Defence, secrecy and past penetrations inhibit reform; this in turn limits intelligence sharing, making it hard to deliver intelligence to consumers. There is a half-hearted emulation of U.S. and U.K. services (RAW was established with CIA assistance), but RAW fails to support policymakers and the armed services. Instead of further concentration, a diversification of analysis is long overdue, with MEA acquiring its own strategic intelligence along the lines of the Department of State's Intelligence and Research Division. The same is true for the finance and home affairs ministries.

Reforming the Army-Society Relationship

Finally, there is one area in need of reform that has received very little attention, partly because it is enmeshed with domestic politics and partly because the armed forces—notably the army—and the political community have agreed not to talk about it: this is the peculiar structure of the present-day Indian Army, which was laid down by Lord Clive in the mid-eighteenth century. The air force and the navy have "modern," merit-based, and entirely secular systems of recruitment and promotion, but the army still bears the marks of its historical origins.

Clive borrowed the "sepoy system" from the French. It stood the test of time; there were few mutinies and the sepoys (now *jawan*) performed admirably. The sepoys were locally recruited, but could serve anywhere in India and abroad; they were commanded by an officer corps that was recruited and promoted on the basis of merit.[30] The Indian Army was further honed in the aftermath of the 1857 Mutiny and withstood massive expansion when it was transformed into an expeditionary force in the course of the two world wars. The Indian Army became the largest volunteer army in history, reaching over two-and-a-half million men, and was certainly one of the most professional of large armies. It now draws its officer corps from a middle class, and its soldiers theoretically from the peasantry, but the rapid change in India demands the re-examination of this structure. Such re-examination will not come from civilians; they keep their part of the postcolonial bargain by leaving such matters as recruitment, organization, and structure in the hands of the army itself. It will not come from the army, which is embroiled in insurgencies (discussed in chapter 6), pressed to defend a long border with Pakistan and China, and now even more in demand for joint exercises with an increasingly large number of friendly foreign armies. The only point of accord between the armed services and the political community is the centrality of pay: too much as far as civilians are concerned, too little according to the chiefs, who for the first time in history, spoke out unanimously in opposition to the 2009 increases proposed by the Sixth Pay Commission (a central government entity that sets civilian and military pay levels every ten years). Their joint opposition forced the government to retreat.

While they agree on pay, none of the services has addressed such questions as officer shortage (in the army), relations between the officer corps and the increasingly educated *jawans*, the greater entry of women into the services, and representation in the other ranks of Muslims and various castes and regions. These issues are left unexamined, not least because no data are publicly available. A recent seminar on military sociology correctly concluded that not only were these and other important questions not being asked anywhere, no useful answers were being proposed to them.[31] Although we cannot deal with all of these questions, a few merit comment.

The Indian Army reportedly suffers from an acute shortage of junior officers, some 13,000 or as much as 30 percent of total billets. The billets remain unfilled because the military leadership does not want to risk current force cohesion by expanding the social pool of officer candidates. A natural expansion of the officer corps might have been possible by encouraging enlisted soldiers to seek commissions, but it would jeopardize social harmony in the officer corps. The objections are not unlike the protests Kitchener faced when he inducted Indians to be officers in the Raj's Army. The impact of officer shortage on military effectiveness is recognized, but the institution seems unable to change things. The army's failure in this regard is critical because the ranks of the junior leadership account for the greater part of its military effectiveness. The high casualty rate of junior officers shows that they lead from the front. The shortages, therefore, can be expected to have a magnified impact on performance.

The situation is exacerbated because the army has been unwilling and, perhaps, unable to devolve leadership down the chain to junior commissioned officers and noncommissioned soldiers. At the same time, the army itself has grown older as most soldiers stay for the full twenty years of service in order to become eligible for pension. It would make sense to promote from within or push command responsibility down the chain, but neither has happened. Although no law prohibits enlisted men from seeking commission, the practice is discouraged. A middle-class officer corps has trouble socially accepting the few enlisted men who become officers.[32] What has improved, however, is that more sons of *jawans* now aspire to be officers, but the officer corps still retains its conservative views about "the right type" necessary for military leadership. The attitude reflects the caste, class, and ethnic consciousness of Indian society at large—and while the military is no place for social experiments—the army loses out on a full-strength officer corps because it is unable to make changes to its recruitment, training, and promotion practices.[33]

The effects of the shortage are debated. On the one hand, the army has had such a shortage for decades, suggesting that the shortage is manufactured; the army frames its problems as an exaggerated need for greater numbers. On the other hand, there are statements by qualified military experts,

Indians and others, and evidence from incidents that suggest that in fact the shortage of younger officers may limit operational abilities. Typically, under-strength units are filled out when they enter counterinsurgency duties or are posted to a militarily active border, but this further stresses manpower; and multiple assignments to such postings are apparently one of the reasons for low recruitment.

Could the officer shortage be filled in other ways, assuming that the threats persist? There could be increased promotion from the other ranks (almost unheard of in India); there could be more female recruitment to the army (also rare); there could be other entry points that are untapped—a replication of the Officer Training Academy (there is only one, in Chennai) and entry via the national Cadet Corps, India's equivalent to the American ROTC.

There could also be a rethinking of the junior commissioned officer—that class of officers, which stands between the soldier and the officer. This institution goes back over two hundred years and was an important cul-tural bridge. But many JCOs are older; some were found unfit for combat at higher altitudes. Does the JCO still serve the role of cultural link? What about opportunities for the JCO to move up to commissioned ranks? Does the JCO still command the same respect he did in the days of the British? The rapid spread of education in recent years means that older JCOs tend to be less educated than younger *jawans,* many of whom are matriculates, even in the Gurkha regiments. Some informed observers believe that the JCOs are actually a barrier to modernization: they are not as adept at modern technol-ogy, their language skills may not be as good, and there is no need for them to serve as cultural links as the officers are closer to the *jawans* in terms of social origins. They do not exist in the air force and navy—why does the army need them?[34]

In the context of India's ponderous bureaucracy and status-quo legacy, the recent burst of reform is impressive, but the Indian government contin-ues to fall further behind the rapidly modernizing private sector in reform, innovation, and fresh approaches to difficult problems. The government is still searching for a better way to coordinate military research and develop-ment with the demands of the services. Indeed, it has not been willing to subject the military research agencies to public audit despite repeated failures over decades. Instead, with the ascendant economy, the government is in the process of approving a raft of new weapons purchases from foreign suppli-ers. Furthermore, there appears to be no effort to balance the purchase of new weapons either between the services or across functional requirements. The Indian Air Force's hesitation in committing to a close air support role for the Indian Army operations has led the ground forces to seek their own air assets, a point on which interservice conflict continues. Lastly, despite the growing threat of insurgency and terrorism within India, police modernization received a small part of monies devoted to military modernization until the 2008 Mumbai attacks.

Like most other states, India finds it easier to add and expand than to reorganize and innovate. Modernization efforts have been largely linear. Troop numbers have increased, new weapons have been added, and new commands have been created; but these efforts have not been accompanied by a re-examination of organizational fundamentals.

CHAPTER THREE

Army
Modernization

The extent to which the Indian armed forces modernize will depend greatly on the ability of the Indian Army to accept a reduced position in the service triumvirate. The army eclipses the other services in size, budget, and military operations. Though it has been losing ground to the Indian Navy and the Indian Air Force on capital spending, the army still accounts for 50 percent of Indian defense budgets. In the last decade, the Indian Army has tried to improve across a range of capabilities that define modernization for most professional armies: mobility and precision ordnance, electronic warfare, communications, and personal equipment used by soldiers especially in the context of counterinsurgency. Further, increased military-to-military interaction with foreign powers is changing the Indian Army's modus operandi, for example: following the U.S. Army's release of the new counterinsurgency manual in 2006, the Indian Army published a remarkably similar document. The strategic impact of these changes is harder to see. How does the army justify the purchase of hundreds of new tanks and other legacy systems that are less relevant to the country's strategic context today?

We begin by looking at past military change in India in an effort to draw out contributing factors. We then examine back-to-back crises between India and Pakistan following the nuclearization of the subcontinent. The lessons of the crises led to the development of the new army doctrine of Cold Start, which seems to be driving the modernization agenda of the service, but is, in fact, a parochial army effort without the benefit of strong political direction.

RECOVERY AND CONSOLIDATION

The first major change in Indian defense was strategic. After independence the Indian government decided that the military was a poor instrument of policy. Accordingly, New Delhi pushed aside military matters in order to focus on development and diplomacy. India's defeat by China in 1962 led to independent India's first systematic military rearmament.[1] Defense spending almost doubled, reaching a peak of 4.5 percent of GNP in 1963–64, but decreasing again to 3.3 percent after the 1965 war with Pakistan. Despite the increases, Indian defense spending remained lower than the military expenditures of its neighbors and to global standards.[2] The army expanded rapidly, going from ten to twenty-five divisions within a few years. It acquired a range of new weapons, including better tanks, artillery pieces, and personal weapons. The army raised eight specialized mountain divisions; many of these were later moved out of the Himalayan region. The equipment had been paid for by the United States, and their purpose was to defend the border, and so deter future Chinese invasions.

The army's command structure was reorganized. The Western Command (created in 1948) grew out of the Delhi and East Punjab Command, which was created to restore order during Partition and had directed the ill-fated Punjab Boundary Force. The First Kashmir War (1947–49) was the impetus for the creation of a Northern Command. The experience of the 1962 war necessitated the relocation of the seat of the Eastern Command from Lucknow to Calcutta. The reorganization moved commanders closer to theaters, but did not significantly alter the decisionmaking system.

The expansion after the 1962 war prepared India for the wars of 1965 and 1971. In 1965 the Indian and the Pakistani Armies fought each other to a standstill, without resolution of any of the major strategic issues. In 1971, however, the Indian Army conducted a blitzkrieg in the eastern theater, liberating Bengalis from West Pakistan's domination and helping create the new state of Bangladesh. India did not press the advantage in the west, where the state of the conflict remained unchanged from the previous war. In light of the military defeat, India and Pakistan signed the Simla Agreement in 1972 committing themselves to the peaceful resolution of the Kashmir dispute. Thereafter, both India and Pakistan would become beset by domestic unrest. In 1979–80 Pakistan became the frontline U.S. ally in the covert war to expel the Soviet Union from Afghanistan.

Round Two in Indian Modernization

Meanwhile, the army's first major task of the 1980s was a counterinsurgency campaign against Sikh separatists that led to Operation Bluestar, a military assault on the Golden Temple in Amritsar in 1984 that alienated the Sikh community as a whole and led to a mutiny by large numbers of Sikhs in the army itself. The event was a factor in the assassination of Prime Minister Indira Gandhi by her Sikh bodyguards. At about the same time, India engaged in a localized conflict with Pakistan over control of the Siachen Glacier, a 20,000-feet Himalayan perch that offered some tactical advantage to the side that controlled it. India was able to reach greater heights before Pakistan and has managed to hold on since then at considerable cost in men and matériel. Except for these limited demands, the Indian Army was left in a state of benign neglect until encouraged by a new generation of political and military leaders and by the buoyancy in the Indian economy. The army and the other services launched a second round of modernization in the mid-1980s.

Under General Krishnaswamy Sundarji, one of the most ambitious service chiefs in Indian history, the army promised to abdicate strategic restraint. Given the changing nature of warfare and Pakistan's imminent nuclearization, Sundarji argued for mechanized armor forces, which could strike preemptively to end Islamabad's nuclear ambitions. The strategy of rearmament and assertion was backed by Prime Minister Rajiv Gandhi and his close friend, Arun Singh, who effectively ran the Ministry of Defence as a minister of state. Accordingly, the army bought new tanks, armored fighting vehicles, modern artillery, ground-attack missiles, air defense systems, and the country's first attack helicopters.[3] The most prominent item was the Bofors howitzer, which ultimately cost Rajiv the 1989 elections after a senior member of his government accused him of corruption.

Much like Kitchener eighty years before, Sundarji reorganized the army into strike and holding formations. While in the past Indian infantry had moved on foot and vehicle transport, Sundarji put them in Soviet infantry fighting vehicles called BMPs, joining infantry and armor on a sufficiently large scale for the first time in India. Like Kitchener, Sundarji realized he could not transform the entire army. Pouring resources into select formations, Sundarji created mobile strike corps of armor and mechanized infantry capable of deep penetration into Pakistan. These were called Reorganized Plains Infantry Divisions (RAPIDS), and were complemented by a comparable change in light infantry intended for defensive use in the mountains (called RAMIDS).[4]

Technological modernization and reorganization contributed to and benefited from doctrines notable for their offensive spirit. Unlike the 1960s when change emerged from defeat, the Sundarji modernization included new doctrines framed by the anticipation of a crisis generated by Pakistan's nuclear program. He decided to use Brasstacks, a military exercise he had inherited as army chief, to test the army's growing capacity vis-à-vis Pakistan.

Brasstacks was an updated variant on massive maneuver warfare like the German Schlieffen Plan, the armor swings across the North African desert in World War II, and the Israeli assaults that broke the Egyptian Army in 1967.[5] Maneuver on this scale required wholly new military organization. For Brasstacks, the Indian Army put together the biggest land army maneuver by any country since World War II.[6] As 400,000 troops in strike formations gathered in the Rajasthan Desert on India's western border across from the Pakistani province of Sindh, together with logistics trains and reserve call-up, the Pakistan leadership feared another Indian effort to break up their country.

We do not fully understand the motivation of the political leadership in allowing Brasstacks to proceed, but at least one participant in the deliberations in New Delhi has called the military and political objectives "open ended." Several of the Indian participants in what became known as the Brasstacks crisis subsequently reminisced that if India had ever had a chance to permanently remove the Pakistani threat without fear of nuclear retaliation, Brasstacks was that chance.[7] The exercise may have been intended to provoke a Pakistani response and thereby legitimate a larger Indian assault across the international border. There was also the option of moving across the Line of Control and seizing parts of Pakistan-controlled Kashmir, as well as of attacking Pakistan's nuclear facilities, which were by many accounts on the verge of producing fissile material. These would have been bold acts of strategic assertion, and the army was on board with a strategy it had helped to design.

The exercise caused a military crisis between India and Pakistan. Pakistan had moved its own northern reserve forces so as to face the Indian state of Punjab, then in a situation of armed rebellion. A. Q. Khan, the head of Pakistan's nuclear program, gave an interview to an Indian journalist declaring his country's ability and intention to use nuclear weapons if attacked. It is unclear what effect the threat had on India's leadership, but New Delhi suspended Exercise Brasstacks, and Indian Prime Minister Rajiv Gandhi and Pakistani President Zia ul-Haq met at a cricket match to signal de-escalation.

After the Brasstacks crisis had been defused, the logic of Sundarji's transformation disintegrated. Pakistan accelerated its own nuclear program and crossed the nuclear threshold, making large-scale conventional war in the subcontinent unthinkable. The risk of doctrine-led rearmament lies in the fact that the assumptions of the doctrine—that India would fight a conventional war—were invalid. Certainly, Sundarji's belief in the possibility of preemption, including the willingness of the Indian political leadership to order it, was misplaced. Frustrated with the indecisiveness of the political leadership, Sundarji wrote a thinly disguised book of fiction during his retirement, where he described India's political leaders as being blind to the consequences of Pakistan's nuclearization: He averred that it eradicated all of India's strategic advantages, notably its size, its greater wealth, and its strategy of painfully and slowly acquiring technological self-sufficiency.[8]

The Indian Army, reorganized by Sundarji to conduct blitzkrieg, turned instead toward counterinsurgency, at one point simultaneously fighting three irregular campaigns. The Indian Army, already embroiled in Punjab and Assam, took on the added task of peacekeeping in Sri Lanka. The Sri Lankan campaign failed; and a bloodied Indian Army eventually withdrew in 1990. To this day, the army of independent India has lost more men in Sri Lanka than in any other foreign conflict. By then the opportunity of preemption had passed. During a military crisis in 1990, Pakistan let it be known that it had and was willing to use nuclear weapons if India attacked. New Delhi backed down again. Thereafter, the Indian Army became enmeshed in another counterinsurgency campaign, this time in Kashmir and in a conflict that would stretch the institution unlike other earlier efforts. It is a measure of the army's tenacity that it was able to change yet again. Indeed, the Indian Army has repeatedly had to switch roles, but this has taken time and proved costly.

From the perspective of modernization, however, implications are pessimistic. Army doctrine may propel change, but the overall strategic restraint preferred by leaders across the political spectrum suggests that the direction of the change may itself be inconstant. The third round of modernization emerged from General Sundarji's preemptive thinking on Pakistan, but the political leadership did not exploit the opportunity to act, and Islamabad's announcement of its definitive nuclear capability in 1989–90 invalidated the very concept of preemption. Since then the Indian Army has moved toward a posture of deterrence, but was impeded in the 1990s by reduced defense budgets and the lack of political attention to military matters.

KARGIL AND ITS AFTERMATH

Once conventional war became impossible, Pakistan openly supported the Kashmir insurgency; thus for the next decade the Indian Army, for its part, was diverted to counterinsurgency. The Pakistani intrusion into Kargil in 1999 caught the army unawares not only from the intelligence point of view, but also in its readiness to fight a conventional war. By its own assessment, the army was caught in a "defensive mindset" as it had been overly focused on counterinsurgency in Kashmir.[9] The jolt that Kargil delivered produced new thinking about army modernization.[10]

The 1999 Kargil War built a new constituency for rebalancing army functions and reforming the larger defense structure. The Kargil Review Committee, which had been set up by the government to report in detail on the onset and conduct of the war, called for a much larger shift of the counterinsurgency burden to entities such as the central paramilitary police called the Border Security Force and the Central Reserve Police Force.[11] Indeed, the committee cautioned against the reduction of army numbers to release resources for modernization. It argued that while the army had to maintain and support winter posts along the Line of Control as an immediate measure, it could not be expected to physically defend every inch of Indian territory. Instead the committee called for a less restricted military posture to punish violations at the Line of Control. This entailed an expansion of military capacities across a range of functions from intelligence gathering to rapid mobilization as well as the rejection of international efforts at even-handedness between India and Pakistan after the initial aggression had already occurred.

On army capacity specifically, the committee recommended improving coordination between government agencies, expanding air and electronic surveillance, and technological enhancement, especially in the personal weapons and equipment of the troops. The recommendations of the review committee strengthened the case for capital spending after nearly a decade. Indian military spending surpassed 3 percent of GDP for the first time in the decade; an upswing had already started in 1998—the year of the nuclear test— and the Indian economy was beginning to generate truly rapid growth for the first time. Efforts to move away from counterinsurgency duties, however, proved difficult despite marked increases in paramilitary police forces.

A crisis in 2001–02 further accentuated the lessons of Kargil. On December 3, 2001, terrorists attacked the Indian Parliament. The Indian government claimed that the attackers were Pakistani; employing the same principle of defense enunciated by the Bush administration in the war on terror, it mounted a full-scale military mobilization on the Pakistan border. There is consensus that India was on the verge of attacking Pakistan between December 13, 2001, and January 2, 2002. This maneuver had been practiced the year before.[12] The army's name for the mobilization was "Operation Parakram"—the nomenclature is important as it was not called an "exercise" like Brasstacks. The political leadership ultimately decided against a war, and the crisis de-escalated into a stalemate.

Many arms analysts interpreted India's effort at compellence (the use or threat of use of force to compel an adversary to act or cease to act) as deficient on a number of counts. The time it had taken to muster forces had cost the army the element of surprise. The enormous size of the forces had created difficulty in deployment and maneuver. Pakistan had been afforded time to craft a political response. By the time the strike force had reached its forward concentration, President Pervez Musharraf had delivered a speech to mollify international opinion on Pakistan's role in fomenting terrorism in India. The formations in place on the border before mobilization lacked offensive punch, and while they were deployed on the border, they had limited mobility and firepower, and were ready only for border defense tasks such as stopping infiltration.[13] Pakistan, it seems, had found a way to undercut India's conventional superiority, push its own agenda, and force India into a position of restraint.

The Rediscovery of Limited War

To find a solution, Indian Army planners turned to the early era of superpower nuclear competition, and, in particular, to the military posture of American and Soviet forces in Central Europe, which were held in defensive formations but could rapidly transition to offensive operations in a crisis. The ability to move quickly from defense to offense enhanced their deterrent value since the other side remained apprehensive that an offensive operation could be launched with no warning. Future wars between India and Pakistan, given the nuclear weapons and the international environment, would be short and sharp.[14] India needed a credible dissuasive capability against Pakistani aggression.[15]

General S. Padmanabhan, the chief of staff during the crisis, initiated rethinking on doctrine and strategy. The army began to think smaller and faster, put military units on the Line of Control on continuous high alert, and assumed a more offensive posture. To ensure deterrence, retaliation had to become automatic, bypassing the hesitation and timidity of the politicians and bureaucrats.[16] The Indian Army's doctrine became colloquially known as "Cold Start," an idea that the next war with Pakistan would start suddenly, require the army to undertake quick offensive action, and return to a holding role just as quickly in order to preclude nuclear escalation.[17] Credible capacity to do this would deter Pakistan's low-level provocations such as violations of the Line of Control, support for the Kashmiri insurgency, and terrorist attacks against India.

The Indian debate over limited war replicated the exposition of limited war doctrine by American and European theorists during the 1950s; Robert Osgood has defined limited war as one "fought for ends far short of the complete subordination of one state's will to another's, using means that involve far less than the total military resources of the belligerents and leave the civilian life and the armed forces of the belligerents largely intact."[18] Just as limited war theory (with its roots in Chinese military thought and Karl von Clausewitz) was relevant in a nuclearized European front, it was also relevant in the nuclearized India-Pakistan context: it was possible for states to fight a limited conventional war under the nuclear umbrella. [19]

Cold Start was officially promulgated at an army commanders' conference on April 28, 2004, by Padmanabhan's successor, General N. C. Vij. The doctrine stressed smaller, mobile, and integrated units, with close air support, moving quickly enough to avoid nuclear weapons. In a discussion with the press, Vij noted that the era of long wars was over, and that "our future wars, if any, will be for a short period and intense."[20] The era of ponderous mobilization was finished. Sundarji's war plan had required over a week to mobilize formations located in Central India, a considerable distance from the border. This mobilization not only allowed Pakistan to prepare its own response, it also gave the international community time to intervene, and after Brasstacks every major exercise along the border carried with it the potential for a new crisis. Further, the delays and large forces involved in mobilization encouraged a strategically restrained civilian leadership to hesitate and wait rather than striking early and decisively. The army needed the capability to strike instantly across the border, exacting a price for Pakistani provocation without starting a general war. Just as Pakistan had hitherto hoped for a firebreak between subconventional and conventional war in Kargil, India now began to expand the space between limited and general war.

Cold Start envisaged the movement of up to eight Integrated Battle Groups (IBG), each consisting of armor, mechanized infantry, and artillery, with integrated close air support. They were to be based on the border; their location would allow one or more of them to attack instantly—from a standing start. Instead of the traditional holding or blocking formations, tasked to resist a Pakistani attack, all forces on the border would be capable of offensive action, as well as standing up to a Pakistani probe. Once the IBGs were in Pakistan, the army's main armor reserve forces could start moving. They could either reinforce one or more IBGs, or strike across the frontier in an area that was weakly defended by Pakistan. Conceivably, they could also deploy in such a way as to block a Pakistani force headed toward India. All of this was presumably to be done in such a way as to avoid a Pakistani nuclear response to India's initial armed entry.

Cold Start is an alternative to the "all or nothing" posture of the massive, but slow-moving strike forces based far from the border. By preparing to launch a quick attack along one or more of eight axes, Cold Start theoretically presents Pakistan with very difficult defensive choices. India might strike jihadi training camps in Kashmir or the Punjab or Pakistani military installations, infrastructure, or even smaller towns as part of a strategy of punishment in response to a terrorist attack. India could cross the border (or the LOC) in pursuit of militants fleeing from India, using larger forces to support special operations forces.

Beginning in March 2004, Cold Start was extensively tested. The assessment of senior army commanders was that Cold Start had been validated even though the scenario had involved actions (attacks into Pakistan) that crossed stated Pakistani red lines.[21] These exercises were not conducted with the participation of civilian policymakers; no one appears to have tested the willingness of political leaders to issue orders to send the Indian Army across the border in force, nor, at least in their unclassified form, did anyone explore likely Pakistani responses.

Within the army, the creation of a South Western Command represents a step forward; there is evidence that offensive units are now forward deployed, and that the supporting infrastructure for the Integrated Battle Groups is being built. Interservice and civil-military tensions remain significant barriers to the doctrine's implementation. As one observer has written, "In framing this doctrine as an integrated doctrine, and in calling for integrated battle groups with a presumptive unified command, the army appears to be pushing for its view of joint warfare. This view has faced stiff resistance in the past from the air force, and is very likely to get bogged down in a familiar, unproductive turf battle."[22] The execution of Cold Start requires improvements in the quality of weapons and army leadership. All of this suggests a picture of a military organization that is several years away from full implementation of its new war-fighting strategy.

Weaponry for Cold Start

The Cold Start Doctrine is predicated on—and drives—the army's efforts to transform itself from a ponderous giant to a nimble and deadly force. The doctrine seeks to provide the political leadership with viable options against Pakistan; however, a strategy of compellence seems so high-risk that the political leadership is unlikely to embrace it. There is little reason to expect the Indian government to abandon strategic restraint for a more assertive policy, but the army's plans continue regardless. Arguably, this is as it should be: the military prepares while the political leadership exercises caution on the question of use of force. However, the disconnect between strategy and doctrine also means that today's modernization decisions may have little bearing on developing useful options for the government in managing the Pakistan problem.

The army's main modernization goal is greater mobility in case of another conflict with Pakistan. A request for proposals for 400 helicopters, mainly for transport, was issued in 2008 for a total of $2 billion. The leading contenders for the helicopter order appear to be Western companies such as Bell, Sikorsky, and Augusta Westland. The army already has 330 T-90 tanks from Russia on order, in addition to the several hundred it plans to produce indigenously, all destined for the Pakistan front.[23] In January 2009 it submitted bids for 155 mm self-propelled howitzers valued at $2 billion, for which companies from Sweden, Israel, and South Africa were in the running.[24]

A more muted modernization program, the Future Infantry Soldier as a System (F-INSAS), considers the needs of the individual soldier from side arms and night vision goggles to body armor and uniform. While this effort may have the greatest impact on counterinsurgency, the army's primary war-fighting activity, the program's fragmentary requirements mean that a demand and supply coalition is harder to develop despite a surge of interest after the December 2008 Mumbai attacks. The Indian Army's War College in Mhow is F-INSAS's primary advocate; there does not appear to be a momentum among suppliers (as in the case of the fighter aircraft) to push this through, so most counterinsurgency purchases may be made from foreign sources. Further, the potential demand—of upgrading almost a million soldiers—is so large that even India's expanding budget is not sufficient.

The army is improving command and control systems in order to create fast-moving pieces. Tata Consultancy Services, one of the world's largest software customization firms, won the contract for creating a new army digital network. According to reports, the new digital communication network has reached battalion headquarters, but needs to be connected to surveillance assets such as satellites and unmanned aerial vehicles as well as to other services. The air defense network, the most important interservice tactical coordination problem, leads this effort. The Indian Air Force has lately come to recognize that the army's plans lack emphasis on logistics. One reason for the neglect is that the army does not see itself in long-range extended missions that require higher-order logistics support, but the slowest part of the system determines battlefield movement despite new mobility platforms.

One new development shows promise for both reform and modernization. As successive Indian governments moved closer to the United States from the 1990s onwards, it has become easier for army strategists (and for their counterparts in other services) to emulate American doctrine without being accused, as they would have been fifteen years earlier, of being pro-American.[25] The development of new thinking on the subject was pushed along by the American example of Desert Storm and Desert Shield. The army's schools and research centers studied and investigated the "Revolution in Military Affairs." The process began with the so-called Kickleighter proposals for U.S.-Indian naval cooperation at the end of the Clinton administration. Slow but steady growth of service-to-service cooperation led to further emulation of American practices but also made that emulation politically acceptable within the Indian context.

Tripwire and Civilian Control

The central component of Cold Start was a short lead-time between decision and action—a matter of minutes and hours, rather than days or weeks. Its proponents argued this would "compel the political leadership to give political approval *ab initio* and thereby free the Armed Forces to generate their full combat potential from the outset."[26]

The military, mainly through its surrogates of retired officers, has driven the Cold Start debate. Cold Start has allowed army commanders and hawkish civilians to advocate circumvention of civilian reluctance to use force.[27] Their attitude stems from a combination of irritation with Indian civilians (especially the timid but oppressive bureaucrats) and anger at Pakistan's ability to taunt India by putting it on the defensive as in Kargil or its support for terrorists and extremists, which precipitated the 2001–02 crises. Conversations with numerous serving and retired officers indicate that for some senior officers Cold Start was as much directed against Indian civilian leaders as it was against the actions of the Pakistan Army.

Political commentary on Cold Start is conspicuous in its meagerness. One critic of Cold Start has written that "the army appears to be unwittingly narrowing the window of opportunity available to diplomats and crisis managers," yet there was nothing unwitting about the army's preference for Cold Start.[28] In the view of one of India's most senior and experienced politicians, familiar with the problem and interviewed for this book in February 2008, India cannot take the risk of attacking Pakistan; it does not know where Pakistani assets are located. He added that while Indians tend to assume Pakistani reasonableness in a crisis, they don't understand the problem of Pakistan's irrationality; they assume that Pakistan will be normal.

Even one supporter of Cold Start, retired brigadier, Gurmeet Kanwal, notes that the strategy requires a high degree of generalship, achieving India's military aims quickly without crossing Pakistan's nuclear threshold, and before the international community calls for a cease-fire.[29] In this scenario the choice between peace and war or escalation and retreat would be in the hands of the Indian Army, something that the politicians and the civilian bureaucracy will be reluctant to grant. In fact, their reluctance will be stronger as Cold Start allows, at least in theory, the decision to esca-late—to turn a defensive formation into an offensive one—to be made by local military commanders. This would require generalship of a very high order, one that fully understands the international, political, and strategic implications of barely predictable consequences. Since the army controls India's nuclear-armed missile force, it is especially important for the politi-cal leadership to keep escalation decisions in its own hands. While Indian army generals are not regarded as especially innovative, let alone disobedi-ent, there may be a situation where the entire escalatory process is in the hands of a single service and a single officer and a more adventurous general (such as Sundarji) is in charge.

On a broader level, the army has, for the first time in its history, begun to speak out publicly and critically on important foreign policy topics. Not only have top brass opposed as "fatal" any settlement with Pakistan on the Siachen Glacier, anonymous army "spokesmen" have opposed any demili-tarization of Jammu and Kashmir. The army expressed its public opposition to any such agreement with Pakistan only four days before the departure of the minister for external affairs, noting that disarmament along the Line of Control was not possible as it could not afford any such measure, given its history of four invasions—one from China and three from Pakistan.[30]

THE ARMY'S PATH AHEAD

There is no question that the Indian Army is searching for change—its jour-nals and seminars dwell on transformation and related subjects. Army officers once studied the various technologies and organizational innovations lumped together under the rubric "Revolution in Military Affairs." Now the talk is of "hybrid" war, the need to transform the army from a conventional force to one capable of "contesting multi-directional and multi-spectrum threats."[31]

Transformation of the army will come from resolving the five-front problem. The army is tasked with a mind-boggling range of duties. The first is countering proxy wars, probably sponsored by Pakistan at present, but conceivably by China in the future. For this kind of war, special training in counterinsurgency is important. Second, the army must be prepared to fight domestic insurgency, backing up the police and paramilitary forces, but intervening directly where necessary. Third, the army has to be prepared for a conventional Chinese probe across the Himalayas. Fourth, the army wants to adopt a strategy that enables it to move against Pakistan at will, mobilizing its own troops so quickly that Pakistan does not have a chance to anticipate the move. Finally, the army is responsible for a good portion of

India's nuclear deterrent, in the form of land-based nuclear-tipped missiles. Thus this one service is wholly or partially responsible for the full spectrum of warfare, from insurgency to atomic war.

The politicians, who must drive strategic policy, do not understand the necessity of deterrence, the fundamental task toward which the Indian Army appears to be moving. The political position was inadvertently captured in a comment by Defense Minister George Fernandes in 2000 when he described Indian defense policy as nonaggressive, nonprovocative, and based on the philosophy of "defensive defense."[32] Deterrence is the threat to respond to an action, either by successfully resisting that action (deterrence by defense) or by punishing the other side (deterrence by punishment or retaliation), if it does act.[33] However, compellence (as noted earlier, the use or threat of use of force to compel another to act or to cease to act) is not well understood. India tried compellence in the most recent crisis with Pakistan, and is now reshaping its ground forces to pursue a compellence strategy, while deterring Pakistan and defending against a Pakistani attack.

Regardless of the technological advancement, the army must accept that Cold Start assumes that escalation thresholds (red lines) will be known, and unwelcome escalation can be prevented or managed. The doctrine assumes that Pakistan will not know the axis of attack and will accept a limited Indian incursion, if it is convinced that incursion will be limited. Given past intelligence failures, this may require operational secrecy that inhibits close coordination between separate army units, between the army and the air force, and between the military and civilians.

Cold Start also represents a pure maneuver strategy. As Edward Luttwak observes, maneuver doctrines offer a higher level of both risk and reward than does a war of attrition.[34] The vulnerability of maneuver strategies, Luttwak notes, is their dependence upon the precise application of force against identified points of weakness.[35] Cold Start's emphasis on maneuver demands radical change within the army itself. Maneuver strategies need highly trained people, junior officers, and enlisted senior personnel, who can take the initiative and assume responsibilities beyond their pay grade. Officers and NCOs need to be problem-solvers rather than stolid plodders. The strategy also requires a different approach to information management across the ranks of hierarchy.

Presumably, this new ability and the demonstrated will to act should deter future Pakistani attempts at cross-border terrorism. Close consultation with the Indian Air Force, and perhaps with the Indian Navy, a combined service approach to warfare, and a streamlined decisionmaking process are also necessary. The army demands "jointness" for ground operations in India, but resists the appointment of a true chairman of the Joint Chiefs. Future joint commands in India proper are likely to be headed by army generals, although those set up outside of mainland India could be led by one of the other services, as is the Andaman Islands Command. India is some distance away from a Goldwater-Nichols transformation; the present Joint Staff is a token operation; the army would resist jointness except to the degree that it can compel air force cooperation

Pakistan's Response

With a few exceptions, the Pakistan Army has taken Cold Start and the idea of a preemptive Indian attack very seriously.[36] Politically, the strategy has been useful to Pakistan as its diplomats and generals can contend on the international stage that India is in fact an aggressive country, which is planning a first strike against Pakistan. When an Indian Army chief, Deepak Kapoor, gave a casual speech referring to the army's ability to fight on two fronts and prevail in a limited war against Pakistan and China, a wide range of Pakistani officials and strategists responded furiously, citing this as proof of India's aggressive intent.[37] While Kapoor's statement triggered a Pakistani response, Indian journalist Shekhar Gupta notes that no one in India takes such statements by Indian generals seriously—the power rests with the politicians.[38] If nothing else, Cold Start has been a boon for the Pakistani establishment; however, its extreme response may also indicate pervasive paranoia.

Pakistan can plan its military responses accordingly. Cold Start compels it to consider its own preemptive strike. As one Pakistani analyst writes, "Given the Indian Army's ability to spring a major surprise, the Pakistan Army must not completely rule out preemption by attempting to destroy the India Army's IBGs before India can bring them to bear on Pakistani defences."[39]

Further, Pakistan's intelligence-gathering requirements have increased exponentially. Because of Cold Start Pakistan must maintain round-the-clock, all-weather surveillance and reconnaissance of all eight IBGs to avoid surprise (through whatever technical and human intelligence it can gather). Such sensitive military action puts a premium on sound intelligence and rapid decisionmaking in Pakistan and India, and, in a sense, Indian security depends on the least responsible or reliable link in the Pakistani chain of command. Ironically, the more that Pakistan is demonized by Indian strategists and politicians, the greater is the likelihood of Indian self-deterrence. Similarly, it is in Pakistan's interest to occasionally appear to be unreasonable and unpredictable, and thus accentuate Indian uncertainty about its response to an Indian attack.

A limited cross-border occupation of Pakistani territory may not lead to a Pakistani nuclear response, but it may provoke a conventional one, and Pakistan will select the place of crossing that will put maximum pressure on Indian politicians. The 1987 Brasstacks crisis is an example: the Pakistani Army moved so as to threaten the Punjab, which was then in the midst of an uprising by Sikh dissidents. The IBGs will have to account for the location and possible movement of Pakistan's two major armor formations, Army Reserve North and Army Reserve South.[40] They are powerful enough to disrupt India's decisionmaking and action cycle, forcing it to consider escalation by activating more IBGs or bringing the strike formations forward.

Fourth, Pakistan could cross the nuclear threshold. While the head of Pakistan's Strategic Plans Division, Lieutenant-General (retired) Khalid Kidwai, has publicly articulated a series of red lines, other Pakistanis have issued statements that increase ambiguity. Indian officers have complained that Pakistan has issued too many red lines, but a strategy of calculated ambiguity makes perfect sense.[41] Figuring out the Pakistani nuclear threshold will involve dangerous brinksmanship, but Pakistani strategists prefer the security of ambiguity, forcing a timid Indian political establishment to choose whether or not to attack.

Finally, the strategy is also relevant in another contingency: Pakistan in disarray. This is what concerns Pakistan most. In a Pakistan gravely wounded by internal disorder, a preemptive cross-border assault by one of the Integrated Battle Groups could embarrass Pakistan's government, demonstrate its incompetence, and thus support Pakistani dissidents and separatists. This scenario played out in 1971 when India launched covert operations in East Pakistan before the invasion in what K. Subrahmanyam called the "opportunity of the century."

No Cold Start after Mumbai

The Cold Start Doctrine did not prevent the 2008 commando attacks on Mumbai. It may be unrealistic to expect the doctrine to deter such attacks, but this was precisely the case made for the doctrine. Whoever in Pakistan launched the Mumbai assault—or whoever could have stopped it—was undeterred by Indian claims that there would be a price to pay for such action. Indeed, if the attacks were designed to trigger a new crisis between the two countries, Indian restraint was highly appropriate, as the attacks were launched by a group beyond the government's control.

As a doctrine, Cold Start is suitable for destroying terrorist training camps in Pakistan, but obviously carries the risk of nuclear escalation. Undoubtedly, the army had some contingency plans to cross the border and strike at a Pakistani facility or valued target. However, it seems the Indian government did not ask the army to mount a retaliatory campaign.

Without action, the strategy reminds us of the South Asian game of *Kabbaddi*, a kind of touch wrestling, characterized by a great deal of posturing but little violence—in other words, a strategy perfectly suited to India's tendency toward strategic restraint.

The China Front

India and China share a 2,500-kilometer land border. China humiliated the Indian Army in 1962 and is one of Pakistan's closest allies today. There are expectations in the country and in the United States that in Asia, India will emerge as a military balance to China. However, China has not been a central feature in the Pakistan-centric army debate over military modernization.

After 1962 the shattered Fourth Division was reconstituted as a Mountain Division (stripped of its armor, heavy artillery, and large vehicles). Three new divisions were raised for service in the Northeast, and by 1965, according to the military expert Ravi Rikhye, eleven divisions were deployed there—primarily for duty against China—along with a number of independent brigades in Ladakh and other northern sectors.[42] Over time these China-oriented units have been retasked against Pakistan, both in East Pakistan and in the West, and to counterinsurgency in the 1980s against the Sikh insurgency in the Punjab. In 1989 further redeployments were undertaken to cope with the insurgency in Kashmir. The Eighth Mountain Division, the primary force for defense against China, was reallocated to Northern Command for counterinsurgency. In the 1990s as India and Pakistan engaged in talks designed to demilitarize the border between them, some Eastern Command divisions were reclassified as army reserves.

Today, the Indian Army has thirty-seven divisions, of which seven are committed to the China border, three against Pakistan in Jammu and Kashmir, and three on the Punjab-Rajasthan border. Two more divisions are being raised and two others will be in the offing by 2012.[43] The increase in numbers is the first expansion of military manpower for external defense for almost three decades. In 1982 Prime Minister Indira Gandhi ordered a systematic improvement in Indian military capacity against the Chinese, but with Rajiv Gandhi's opening to China in 1988, these measures were scaled back and finally discontinued in the 1990s. Thereafter, the threat from China was to be managed through diplomacy. The increase in numbers is seen in army circles as a credit for a recent chief, General Deepak Kapoor, but comes at a time when the government has clearly preferred not to militarily antagonize China, which is less restrained in its comments on army doctrine and strategy than, say, Pakistan.[44]

The increase in manpower reverses the troop-for-technology trade-off that enabled modernization. However, with India's defense budgets growing at a faster rate than the services can spend, the money will help pay for the size expansion of the army. This further delays the difficult decisions about retrenchment that the army must take to become the smaller, faster, and deadlier force required for deterrence and, in particular, for its Cold Start doctrine. The irony is that India remains politically committed to a policy of accommodation with China, based upon a greatly expanding trade with Beijing. Indeed, the army has been engaged in visible confidence building with the Chinese that has included high-altitude soccer matches.

Rethinking the Army's Role

The notion that the Indian Army may once again play a larger role in stabilizing the insecure parts of Asia, as it did under the Raj, was forwarded by a leading Indian civilian strategist, C. Raja Mohan, and not a general. In the summary of an important study of India's military future, one of the army's most imaginative (retired) theoreticians writes that in the next few decades few provocations could cause India to launch a major cross-border operation on land, and those launched are likely to be restricted in scope and nature.[45] Instead, national strategy will compel India to expand its sphere of influence "with the ultimate objective of shaping the regional environment" mainly through the development of maritime power.[46]

Overall, it is not surprising that democratic India has sought military reform in the wake of military failures. The changes that occurred have mainly expanded force size, added new weapons, and created new agencies, commands, and positions; but they have not tackled the difficult tasks of retrenchment, coordination, and strategic balance. There is no established political lobby arguing for change and reform, and no significant civilian expertise in military matters, and the few ex-officers who ventured into politics have not excelled—with the exception of Jaswant Singh, still an important figure in the conservative-nationalist Bharatiya Janata Party.

The 1965 stalemate and 1971 victory froze the civil-military balance. As long as the military appeared to succeed, the system was allowed to proceed without regard for future challenges. Consequently, efforts to change either the Indian Army's antique social structure or the civil-military balance have generally failed. One exception occurred when Indira Gandhi appointed an army chief out of the order of promotion—that civil-military structure persists to this day. Besides its problematic relationship with politicians, the army must figure out how to be three or four armies at once. Should it focus more on insurgency, which the prime minister has publicly stated is India's greatest threat, and deepen its counterinsurgency capabilities, displacing some of the less reliable paramilitary forces? Or, as some prefer, prepare for a classic armor battle with Pakistan, albeit one conducted in the shadow of nuclear weapons? Or, should it pursue a risky strategy of deterrence by punishment, applicable both to Pakistan and China (two nuclear weapons states)? Finally, should the Indian Army prepare for an extraregional role, perhaps engaging in more UN Chapter 7 (peacemaking) activities, or should it stay with its traditional peacekeeping?

In our view the army should not pursue provocative strategies such as Cold Start; the strategy, which cannot be operationalized without generating a serious crisis, may be easy to defeat, and thus hard to initiate. Nor should the army settle for minimally invasive peacekeeping operations; it could be effectively deployed in Chapter 7 operations in the right set of political circumstances. The army does have to confront the domestic terrorist threat, where it is far more capable than the paramilitaries; this may mean a formal division of the army into two services. As for the use of coercive threats against Pakistan, the army must offer positive rhetoric instead of only criticisms, a political strategy that may transform Pakistan into a normal state. In order to do this, army leaders must rise above the rhetorical excess of recent years and stop the demonization of Pakistan. Blaming Pakistan for all of India's ills is not a strategy; it is an example of what Hans Morgenthau called a "policy of making faces." The Indian Army must also play its part to deter Pakistan or induce it to cease its support for terrorism and insurgency in India. Cold Start and other similar maneuvers generate risks that few (if any) Indian politicians are willing to run. The Indian Army must plan for war with the politicians that it has, not the politicians it would like; however, the ultimate responsibility for developing a strategy that uses the army in the successful management of the Pakistan problem rests with the politicians, not the army.

CHAPTER FOUR

AIR AND NAVAL MODERNIZATION

While the modernization of the Indian Army sets the pace of military change in India as a whole, rebalancing the armed forces in favor of air and naval power will be the proof of real transformation. The sheer potential is breathtaking. Indian air and naval capacity will determine the quality of its China deterrent more than its ground forces, which must be defensively organized due to the terrain. India could potentially upend the artificial balance of power Pakistan has been able to maintain and return to prominence in the Indian Ocean region, reviving a past going back to the British Raj and beyond. Effective air and naval capacity could liberate India from being—and being held hostage as—a land power. In short, India would be able to break out of the tradition of strategic restraint.

However, expectations of an air and naval transformation depend on the country's strategic direction. The new Indian government initially received a recommendation for a navy of sixty-nine ships, but shifted away from air- and naval-power-projection capabilities to army-led defense with the rise of the Pakistani and Chinese threats and the political preference for caution in military posture. Today the Indian Navy has approximately thirty-eight principal combatants.[1] India's restraint has served it well; it has precluded air and naval rearmament. The expectation now that increased spending on air- and naval-rearmament will precede strategic assertion might be putting the cart before the horse. Further, the Indian Navy and Indian Air Force have neither evolved in tandem between themselves nor with the Indian Army.

The Rise of Air and Sea Power

Two events, one just before independence, the other immediately after it, shaped the future of the navy and the air force for many years. In February 1946, a mutiny broke out on Royal Indian Navy ships based in Bombay. It spread to Karachi and Calcutta. Over fifty ships and many shore establishments were involved. It was led by Indian sailors inspired by the trials of three Indian Army officers who had defected to the Japanese side, and fought the British. Any plans for an expanded navy had to be put on hold until it could ensure that its sailors were loyal.

Then, in October 1947, after raiders from Pakistan entered the princely state of Jammu and Kashmir, the Maharaja signed an instrument of accession to the Indian Union and the IAF established an air bridge to Srinagar using three Dakotas, a move that saved the city. In this first war for Kashmir, the Dakotas flew up to a hundred sorties a day, and IAF fighter aircraft engaged in fire suppression around the Srinagar airfield. The air force also airlifted troops to Chusul (15,000 feet) and Leh, an astonishing feat given the unpressurized planes and the improvised landing strip. Even today, landings and take-offs from the 11,000-feet high Leh airfield are a thrilling experience.

Thus the IAF was thrust into the vital role of preserving the Indian Union, while the navy was being rebuilt. The IAF was short of equipment and had no bombers, but Indian technicians rehabilitated forty-two scrapped B-24 American bombers. Some continued flying in transport and maritime reconnaissance roles until 1968. In 1953 the air force acquired night-time intercept capacity with the first-generation jet, the British Vampire, and in 1956 the service got its first helicopters.

Despite the acquisition of a few modern squadrons, offensive air power was neglected in defense planning; air defense was the IAF's main role for most of its modern history. There were memories of Japanese attacks on a few Indian cities; in 1962 there was also the fear that China might attack Indian cities in the east, when Nehru sent a frantic request to President John F. Kennedy for American air cover. This request was a closely held secret for many years; Nehru and the Indian government never discussed it publicly. Later the request was dismissed as having been made under extreme pressure. If it had been accepted, it might have put India on the same footing as Pakistan, a dependant ally of the United States.

In retrospect, the inability of the government and the military leadership to coordinate air and ground power in the war with China was one reason the army was easily defeated—no IAF planes had been sent up. After the war, American and Commonwealth Air Forces flew an air defense exercise in India's northeast. However, at that time India was not politically ready for a closer relationship with the United States, which may have meant American or British intervention in the Kashmir dispute. Instead, New Delhi, which had begun to purchase from the Soviet Union just before the 1962 war, expanded its Soviet military purchases by buying MiG-21 interceptor fighters.

The war with China shook India; improving the armed forces became a top priority. As part of the post-1962 buildup, the Indian government stipulated that the Indian Air Force and the Indian Navy grow to sixty-four combat squadrons and fifty-four principal combatants, respectively. Neither service reached those numbers. At their largest in the late 1980s, the IAF was forty-five squadrons, and the Indian Navy had forty-four principal combatants.[2] By the mid-1990s, the impact of the Soviet implosion was in full view and the numbers of working squadrons and principal combatants were down to forty-two and thirty-eight, respectively.[3]

The expansion had scarcely begun when the IAF had to go to war in 1965. P. V. S. Jagan Mohan and Samir Chopra, who have written a history of the 1965 air war, report that 40 percent of Indian air assets were in the northeast, positioned to meet a Chinese attack. Thus Pakistan had both numerical and technological advantage in the west.[4] Initial Pakistani attacks hit a number of Indian airfields. However, the IAF was not able to turn the war in its favor with better aircraft utilization, reconnaissance, and air combat skills. The headlines featured the supersonic duel between MiG-21s and the American-supplied Sabre; the gallant Gnat pilots used their superior skills to thwart the Pakistani fleet of supersonic American-built fighters.[5] It is important that during the war some British Hunters and Soviet Sukhois were used to attack Pakistani airbases and other targets. Since the focus was on the ground war, where air power had no impact, the IAF's offensive strikes have not been widely recognized, but they were the first-use instance by India of offensive air power.

Ironically, air power did not capture the popular imagination or the attention of the strategists in 1971 as it did in 1965, perhaps because India was able to assert air superiority quickly. In the 1971 war the IAF was competent: Pakistan had little air capability in the east, and what did exist was quickly subdued. The IAF successfully executed an air-drop of Indian para commandos, who played a role in bringing the war in the eastern theater to a quick end. In the west, the IAF launched attacks on Pakistani civilian facilities, notably the country's energy infrastructure: refineries, gas and oil storage tanks, and power stations. These were both limited and strategically irrelevant since there were no plans to launch a major attack on West Pakistan, nor to defeat

Pakistan comprehensively, but complemented the navy's attack on Karachi port. The IAF did prevent attacks on Indian cities with air defense interception, but P. C. Lal, the wartime air chief, later wrote bitterly that the Indian Army had essentially ignored air power in the war.

Naval Incrementalism

In the first three decades of independent India, the Indian Navy took a very different path to modernization than the IAF. Partition hurt the navy more than the army or the IAF; it had to purge its ratings of politically unreliable sailors, but its officers were perhaps the best educated of the services and certainly saw more of the world than officers from the army or air force. Further, they had the advantage of starting from scratch. There was little in the way of historical baggage.

In 1947 the Indian Navy had no capital ships, no shipyards under its control (Garden Reach and Mazagaon Docks were privately owned until the Indian government took them over years later), and Indian resources allowed acquisition of only a few castoffs. A naval plan paper produced in 1948 proclaimed a ten-year strategy for developing a sixty-nine-ship navy, "structured around a balanced fleet of two light aircraft carriers, three cruisers and twelve destroyers. There was no plan to induct submarines."[6] Where the development of ground and air power were reactive, the Indian Navy benefited from clearer political vision. K. M. Panikkar, a respected scholar and administrator who served as India's ambassador to nationalist and communist China, wrote a Mahan-esque tract on the importance of Indian maritime power that still serves as a blueprint for naval modernization.[7] Unlike the other two services, the navy adopted a different developmental model emphasizing in-house shipbuilding capability. The initial enthusiasm for naval growth dwindled, however, as the realities of military rearmament became clearer and the army's needs became urgent. India was also in the fortunate position of being able to free ride on the U.S. and British naval presence in the region. In 1950 the government released a recast Naval Development Plan calling for a smaller navy (forty-seven ships) by 1960.

In the mid-1950s India entered into an agreement with the United Kingdom for new ships, culminating in the purchase of the ex-HMS *Hermes*, a small aircraft carrier renamed the INS *Vikrant*. In the 1960s the navy added the third operational dimension when it purchased Soviet ocean-going submarines. But the most important investment the navy made was in developing its in-house capacity for ship design and construction. Twenty-five years after independence, the navy commissioned the indigenously built INS *Nilgiri*, a modification of the British *Leander* class.

Given the ground-war threats, the army, supported by the air force, received most of the attention. The navy's share of the defense budget accordingly went from 11.7 percent in 1960–61 to a mere 3 percent before and after the 1962 conflict with China. It crept up to 8.2 percent in 1970–71, and to 10.57 percent in 1978–79. By the 1970s the elderly World War II ship inventory approached block obsolescence, but naval expansion took place very slowly, and was affected by the general downturn in defense spending of the mid-1980s. The deferral of modernization dealt the greatest blow to the two technology-intensive services, the navy and the air force.

Where the army and the air force focused on war-fighting and technological improvement, respectively, the navy focused on ships. This was very much in keeping with the political vision adopted by Nehru and the British physicist P. M. S. Blackett, emphasizing indigenous infrastructure development. In a later piece, Panikkar proclaims that "on borrowed science defence cannot flourish." He points to Japan's failure to develop modern planes and ships during World War II when it had been cut off from the world.[8] What the navy added to the policy was to keep the development effort within the service rather than hand it over to the Defence Research and Development Organization. In contrast, the army and air force, which turned to the DRDO with their requirements, have not seen any major weapons platform emerge.

In contrast, the 1971 war brought the Indian Navy to the fore. In one of the most celebrated operations in recent maritime history, the Indian Navy towed missile boats to the Pakistani coast, attacked the country's main port at Karachi, and blockaded the harbor for the duration of the conflict. There was an implicit threat of a long blockade, although both India and Pakistan could no more fight a long war in 1971 than they could in 1965 because both were dependent on resupply from outside powers. The Indian Navy lost a destroyer, but a Pakistani submarine was sunk off the Indian east coast naval port of Vishakahapatnam. Toward the end of the war the United States ordered the USS *Enterprise* battle group into the Bay of Bengal in a show of gunboat diplomacy. The putative *Enterprise* intervention defined a new low in U.S.-India relations.

It also gave the navy an immediate security-related objective. Where in the past the service had focused on shipbuilding, now it turned its attention toward naval doctrine. The *Enterprise* episode, redolent of European interventions three hundred years earlier, caused a radical turn in the navy toward a sea-denial strategy.[9] For years thereafter, Indian naval strategists characterized the United States as seeking to establish a foothold in the Indian Ocean in order to contain India. The "Enterprise Syndrome," as some have called it, led leading strategists such as K. Subrahmanyam to argue on behalf of attack submarines that could launch long-range missiles and deter future great-power naval intervention, as well as interdict Pakistani shipping.

The *Enterprise* episode also opened the doors to Soviet naval sales. Consequently the Indian Navy's fledgling submarine arm saw the fastest growth over the next two decades, mostly with Soviet help. Anti-submarine frigates were also purchased from the Soviets to bolster the British-designed frigates purchased earlier. The Soviets sold long-range naval patrol vessels. India allowed the Soviets access, on a temporary basis, to some of its ports—other ports were reserved for British-origin ships, and the navy tried to keep the two apart, complicating maintenance in port and at sea. From 1971, the date of the *Enterprise* sailing, to the early 1980s, the United States was regarded as a malevolent country by much of the Indian military, especially the navy. The Soviets were considered to be reliable and steadfast, even if their equipment was not up to Western standards. India also bought a second ex-U.K. aircraft carrier in the mid-1980s, configured for short take-off and landing planes.

The IAF Reaches for a Strategic Mission

For most of its history the IAF was an air defense force designed to thwart enemy attacks. This suited India's liberal political establishment, which had memories of the attacks in the 1940s by German, American, and Japanese aircraft on innocent civilians. It was not until India edged toward becoming a nuclear weapons state that the IAF was able to develop the doctrine, and persuade the politicians, that it had to become a truly balanced, modern air force.

Air Commodore Jasjit Singh, a former fighter pilot and a leading Indian air power theorist, writes that the IAF's early development at the "lower-end of tactical air power" tethered the service to very limited goals.[10] Unlike the navy, which benefited from Panikkar's clear vision of Indian maritime influence, the IAF was unmoored without sound civilian leadership.

After the success of the Srinagar air bridge, the IAF did not know what its future would be and was consequently unable to decide on sizing and technology. In the first decade of independence, the IAF remained a transport service. Nehru's British adviser on military science, Blackett, recommended that India restrain its ambitions about military modernization. The enormous cost of acquiring offensive air power was also daunting. An incipient debate existed between the strategic and auxiliary roles of air power, but the IAF was unable to choose. Air Marshall P. C. Lal's unprecedented denunciation of the Indian Army after the 1971 war was not that the IAF had been denied a strategic role, but rather that it had been excluded from planning and decisionmaking during the war. He demanded a combined arms approach, which under the circumstances would have meant significant commitment to close air support for army units. However, the reality was that army planning had excluded the IAF because Pakistan had few air assets there—and deliberately limited in the west where the objective was to keep the conflict from escalating before the east had been won and secured. The IAF's role was to provide tactical reconnaissance and, in one joint operation, air-drop about seven hundred Indian paratroopers. It was not asked, nor did it suggest that it could secure victory.

Doctrinal Development

Several events conspired to propel the IAF toward a more strategic "war-winning" role, beyond a transport and air support service. The first led to the IAF becoming the first service responsible for delivering India's nuclear weapons. The second was the air war in Iraq, where an India-trained air force fled from the United States and its allies, and air power played a critical role in the quick defeat of Saddam's ground army. Finally, the IAF's limited operations during the 1999 Kargil War revealed both the problems of air power in a limited war under nuclear conditions, and also some of the opportunities that an adventurous air strategy might provide.

The test of a single nuclear device in 1974 raised the issue of preparedness for a nuclear war; the air force was the only service, even if by inference, to move in this direction. The first major acquisition following the "peaceful nuclear explosion" showed the air force had been thinking about nuclear delivery. After three decades of focusing on air defense interception, the IAF acquired a modern two-engine strike aircraft: the Anglo-French Jaguar, supplanting the slower and more vulnerable *Canberra*. British Aerospace, the Jaguar's manufacturer, had offered the plane to India as early as 1968, but New Delhi had rejected it for fear of accepting another orphan aircraft, such as the Gnat,[11] which would make India dependent on a single supplier for spare parts. Once the Royal Air Force bought the Jaguar, however, IAF interest revived. The aircraft's two engines provided an additional margin of safety, a requirement for deep incursions into hostile airspace, as well as additional insurance against bird strikes at low altitudes. The Jaguar deal included progressive manufacture in India itself, and even today the Jaguar assembly and repair lines operate in Bangalore, using 1950's technology for this sturdy aircraft. Neither the government nor the IAF publicly mentioned the nuclear delivery role, but the decision to buy the Jaguar came a few years after the 1974 nuclear test, presumably sufficient time to conduct a serious evaluation.

India bought enough Jaguars to raise four squadrons in the mid-1980s, and developed a maritime variant, although it is hard to tell from their configuration which if any of these planes were meant for nuclear use. Other fighter purchases of the 1980s—the Mirage-2000 and the MiG-29—were multirole weapons systems. Buying one aircraft type instead of two—specialized for attack and specialized for air defense—was cheaper, and their multirole qualities obscured their exact role. Those who were concerned— Pakistan and the West's nonproliferation lobby—assumed the worst; the uncertainty about delivery vehicles was part of India's stated policy of nuclear ambiguity.[12]

The success of opaque nuclear deterrence in the 1980s and 1990s depended on limited planning. India's new aircraft gave the country a latent strategic capacity, but the demands of nuclear ambiguity obstructed thinking about air power. In 1993, fifteen years after India acquired the Jaguar, American scholar George Tanham found that the IAF still had not developed a strategic mindset.[13] Tanham widely polled Indian military and civilian opinion in the early days after the cold war to determine whether the Indian Air Force would lead India's military transformation. It was institutionally cohesive, modern in its equipment, steeped in sophisticated air campaign theory, and the only functioning Soviet-supplied air force outside the Soviet Union itself.

Tanham was surprised at the IAF's conspicuous lack of investment in electronic equipment and force multipliers critical to turning fighter aircraft into strategic instruments of military power. He correctly identifies civilian influence as the main detractor of strategic air power, but also cites that the IAF itself accepted its subordinate role. He wrote that "the air force has found it easier to justify and persuade civilians of a need for air defense aircraft and transports than for other types of aircraft. For example, the acquisition of the Mirage 2000 was justified on the basis of its air defense capabilities, and as a counter to Pakistan's F-16s, although it is really a dual-purpose aircraft with important attack capabilities." On electronic equipment, he found, "for its part the air force appears not to have fought hard for such equipment and has opted for more aircraft instead."[14] Tanham concluded that the IAF's top priority was still air defense, followed by strike missions against Pakistan, close air support for the Indian Army, airlift, and strategic reconnaissance.[15] Furthermore, Tanham observed other deficiencies, notably in training and readiness.

When Tanham studied the IAF, it was in sad shape—it had not figured prominently in the Sundarji-Arun Singh concept of a land assault on a (nonnuclear) Pakistan; its role was to be air defense, close air support, and attacking Pakistani targets in aid of ground operations. With the end of the cold war, the IAF was particularly hard hit for spares from the defunct Soviet Union; Indian missions scoured the former Soviet Union for MiG and other spare parts, With difficulty, it was able to build a new supply chain, one that eventually included Israel. After a high of 96 percent in 1971, serviceability was stagnant. Pilots had averaged 180 to 200 flying hours a year in 1988–89 (as they did in 2009), but this dropped to 120 hours in 1992–93. The decrease was reflected in total flying hours, which dipped in the post–cold war years but revived with the onset of prosperity and development of a secure source of spare parts.[16]

Tanham's observations galvanized the Indian debate over strategic air power. Indian air power theorists responded with voluminous writing on how the IAF could indeed change the course of the war. Air Commodore Singh, then director of the government-funded Institute of Defence Studies and Analyses (and later head of the air force–backed Center for Air Power Studies), approvingly cited Lord Trenchard's observation that not only did the air force influence the conduct of war and conflict in all three dimensions—land, sea, and air—the navy and the army could not affect air power and its freedom of action. He and others advocated for the establishment of a Strategic Command with the IAF in charge. The nuclear Strategic Forces Command did come into being in January 2004, with an air force officer as its first commander, but its second commander was an army general, its third, a naval officer; also, the IAF shares operational control over nuclear assets with the army.

The IAF absorbed the lessons of the allied air campaign over Iraq; the outcome was an Air Power Doctrine, the "culmination of the IAF's research into the changed nature of air warfare, its implications for the force, and the challenges of operating nuclear weapons."[17] The doctrine, promulgated in 1997, argued that offensive air operations must be given equal priority with air defense, that the IAF might have to reduce its force levels, but that the reduction would be offset by an increase in technological capability. It emphasized so-called force multipliers, notably technologies such as aerial refueling, electronic warfare, and electronic countermeasures; and it strongly emphasized improvement in command, control, communications, and intelligence structures, and a revamped modernized air defense and communications network. It also claimed the exploitation of space for military purposes for the air force.[18]

The Air Power Doctrine had to take into account the IAF's marginal performance during the Kargil War. For the first time precision-guided munitions were fired in anger by the IAF, but they had little battlefield impact. While some Pakistani outposts were demolished, artillery pounding and a courageous ground assault by the infantry turned the tide. The IAF lost two fighters and a helicopter. Indeed, one lesson of Kargil was that close air support was risky to expensive equipment, and that in the next such conflict, the IAF might do better to skip the ground war and go directly to coercive strikes on high value targets. Retired air force officers are no longer guarded about publicly expounding that "India needs to shift its stance to a more offense-oriented doctrinal thought process, notwithstanding our innate desire for peaceful and harmonious relationships all around."[19] In classical air power justification, Air Marshall A. K. Tiwary criticized defense, especially ground defense, for not winning wars. He argued that a defensive strategy takes too long, costs more than offense, and does not take advantage of India's vast size.

Not surprisingly, the IAF's thinking is most precise when it comes to Pakistan. In the next subcontinental war, the IAF would like to transcend air defense and ground support in favor of offensive air power. It intends to secure air superiority and follow through with limited but well-directed attacks on enemy targets that would demonstrate the futility of Pakistani escalation.[20] With a clear and unambiguous declaration of intent, communication of this intent to the adversary and other powers, and with dedicated high-tech strike squadrons launching surgical strikes, India need not fear retaliation by any enemy.[21] Whether Pakistan is likely to allow the marked asymmetry in air power to continue for long is uncertain. Even if we assumed Indian ability to impose air superiority, there is no guarantee that the IAF will be able to hit the right targets at the right time. Certainly, it is doubtful that the IAF can knock out Pakistani nuclear weapons, the only real surety against Pakistani escalation. IAF officers provide similar analyses of Chinese targeting strategies—with even weaker justification.

Ultimately, the exact strategic role the IAF plays, the timing of such a role, or which material accoutrements of strategic capacity beyond more and newer aircraft are required is unclear. The IAF's justification for strategic air power responds not only to the changing threats India faces, but also to the Indian Army's new war-fighting doctrine, embodied in the Cold Start concept. When the army released its new war doctrine, giving primacy to land forces in joint operations, IAF officers unofficially told the press that the days when the air force could be treated like a high-technology artillery regiment were over.[22] IAF sources told the press that "as air operations have become much more sophisticated [,] it will be unfair to treat us as secondary players under the command of the army as is being suggested in their war doctrine."[23] They bridled at the suggestion that the army could have tasking authority on air assets.

India's politicians, innocent of such matters, regard these disputes with incomprehension, and with some irritation and exasperation by those civilians responsible for acquiring strategic delivery vehicles. Theoretically, the IAF has freedom to deploy its forces as it sees fit, within the larger framework that grants the military considerable tactical authority. However, politicians, to the extent they are aware of the consequences of an aggressive air power strategy, are reluctant to appease the air force. They wish to guard war and peace decisionmaking within their own domain rather than relinquishing it to an air force or army officer who commands the air or missile assets.

The IAF underscores the growing importance of air power by pointing to the experience of U.S.-led coalition operations in Bosnia, Kosovo, and Afghanistan and to the experiences of the Israeli Air Force in the Bekaa Valley in Lebanon. Tiwary writes of contemporary American air power as the "zenith of offense in the fluctuating race between the defense and offense."[24] However, the analysis reflects unsubstantiated optimism. It does not take into account the sobering conclusions of the Gulf War Air Power Survey or analyses of the air campaign over Kosovo, which showed that the coalition air campaign destroyed less than 10 percent of Serbian military assets.[25] At the very least, the Kosovo War presents a complex case of compellence not easily explained by air power alone.

Moreover, it is worth noting that U.S.-led coalition forces have operated in highly asymmetric environments, whereas India faces enemies who possess nuclear weapons. The power parity in the subcontinent implies that strategic air power is of little use—and indeed India's strategic restraint precludes such use of force. The Indian Army's bid to acquire ground attack helicopters, thereby sidelining the IAF, reflects similar thinking.

The five nuclear tests in May 1998, once again raised the question of nuclear delivery. Soon after, India placed orders for the Russian Sukhoi-30 attack planes, which are likely to supplant the aging Jaguars and other high-performance planes in the nuclear-delivery role. In the meantime the IAF has lost its monopoly on the nuclear delivery role to the army's missile force; this is not merely a step in the direction of a putative "triad" of nuclear delivery techniques, but also a way of balancing the services, and ensuring that none has a monopoly on any single critical weapon.

The uncertainty about the enemy, the theater, and the nature of future war contrasts with the IAF's real strategic capacity in airlift and aerial reconnaissance. Airlift is an IAF tradition, which goes back to World War II, when Northeast India and Calcutta were critical links in operations over the "hump" to China. Airfields, built mostly by American engineers, blanketed India's Northeast, and Bangalore became a major hub for aircraft repair and maintenance. Today, India has one of the world's largest proved airlift capabilities. In 1988–90 India carried out two military airlifts with strategic implications.

In 1988 it flew a para battalion to the island state of the Maldives to assist a government under military attack. The IAF executed one of history's largest airlifts on the eve of Desert Storm in 1990–91, evacuating 170,000 Indian citizens from Kuwait to India. This involved IAF transport planes and state-owned civilian aircraft and was an extremely popular use of military power, analogous to the navy's role in the tsunami relief operations of 2004. For its joint exercises in Europe and elsewhere, the IAF airlifted its own supplies, accompanying the fighters to the training sites. India is likely to expand its impressive airlift capacity. It has approached the American firm Boeing about purchasing the C-17, a heavy-lift plane with a very long range, giving it the potential to project forces and material throughout the Indian Ocean region. The C-17 would replace some of India's Soviet-era heavy lifters.

How might India's airlift capacity be used in the future? Exercises and training missions are necessary, as is emergency evacuation or humanitarian airlift, but there seems to be little interest in deploying this capacity for only peacemaking operations. As noted, the Indian Army no longer has a force designated for airlift, and the strategic community talks about such an airlift only in theoretical terms. Should it decide to increase its presence there (as advocated by some realist strategists), India could use the airlift to deliver troops and emergency equipment to Afghanistan, but mainstream thinking resists this idea, no matter what the strategic stakes are in Afghanistan.

The IAF's record in reconnaissance is also impressive but fading as far as manned aircraft are concerned. The IAF flew one of the world's most advanced high-altitude planes, the Soviet MiG-25 Foxbat, for decades before retiring them in 2006. The outcome of those flights and their benefits to Indian security are unclear because of the secrecy of operations, but the Foxbat's range included all of Pakistan and much of China. Like America's U-2 and Blackbird spy planes, the Foxbat was made obsolete by military satellites; their loss cost the IAF an important strategic role.

In years past UAVs were purchased separately by all three Indian services from an American firm and used as target drones and for reconnaissance. The IAF is one of the recipients of unmanned aerial technology purchased from Israel; it operates two different Israeli technologies. Recently a DRDO program has sought to develop a UAV, but crashes have marred the program, forcing the IAF and Indian Army to continue reliance on imported UAVs and other MiG jets for short- and medium-range reconnaissance.

The IAF does not manage India's military satellites, but IAF officers have argued for an aerospace command that will presumably bring space-based military assets under its control. This seems very unlikely, given that expertise in space is concentrated in the civilian Indian Space Research Organisation, which may one day be competitive with America's NASA.[26] The air force says that adversaries in the next war will target India's space program, and only the IAF can provide extended protection.[27] Since India does not make long-range reconnaissance aircraft and the technological suites that they now carry, the only alternative is to buy abroad. The IAF has shown interest in Boeing's P-8, which competes with Northrop Grumman's E2C (considered by the Indian Navy), setting up the prospect of interservice rivalry for the short-range reconnaissance and interdiction roles.[28] The failure to detect terrorists who sailed from Karachi to Mumbai lends urgency to this role, and both services are scrambling to produce options.

The IAF's Technology Trap

More than the other two services, the IAF is caught between the enormous expansion of relevant technology and its astronomical cost. Operating at the leading edge of technology is difficult for any air force, and it is certainly expensive given the skyrocketing cost of modern aircraft. This makes the IAF especially sensitive to guns-versus-butter comparisons in India. The cost of a SEPECAT Jaguar was about $8 million a unit in 1979 and the Su-30MKI was approximately $40 million a unit in 2000, while the Multi-Role Combat Aircraft (MRCA) are expected to amount to over $80 million each only a decade later. Each aircraft may perform far better than its predecessors, but ancillary costs and infrastructure over its lifespan have also grown rapidly.

Even as the IAF developed an ambitious air power doctrine, some question whether it is being downgraded through attrition. In 2009 the IAF was reduced to thirty-two squadrons (576 aircraft). By the time the first planes are delivered, theoretically in 2012 but probably much later, the IAF will have shed three more squadrons to an all-time low of twenty-nine. Without a formal decision to reduce the size of the air force, it will decline in numbers because of block obsolescence of its MiG fleet and the aging of other aircraft. The IAF's main hope is that it will be able to preserve its numbers at near-present levels through a government decision to buy large numbers of very advanced aircraft—the MRCA and the Su-30. However, the lengthy and ever-changing procurement process, and the inherent difficulty of operating at the advanced edge of several technologies, means that it may be years before the IAF is equipped with these theoretically supreme aircraft and capable of performing the air defense and offensive air-delivery roles to a standard of effectiveness that matches two potentially hostile air forces, the Pakistan Air Force and the People's Liberation Army Air Force.

From 1960 to the present the IAF has flown aircraft manufactured in many different nations. There has always been a mix of imported aircraft,

aircraft assembled from imported components, aircraft built from a mixture of imported and indigenous components, and a few planes that were built entirely out of Indian parts.[29] The variability in the quality of these aircraft was notorious, and apocryphal stories abound of pilots asking whether a particular plane was imported or built in India, usually preferring the former to the latter.[30] Regardless of quality, this presents the IAF with a logistic nightmare, and inhibits the basing of planes in different parts of the country.

More than the navy, the IAF is in a perpetual struggle to procure both funding and suppliers who can deliver the best available weapons at an affordable cost. "Best available" has usually meant "not as good as Pakistan," but recent acquisition of very high-performance Russian aircraft, notably nearly a hundred Su-30s, gives the IAF a seeming qualitative edge that may or may not translate into air superiority in the next war. Modernization of the air force must balance the requirements of strategic independence, quality technology, the possibility of indigenous production via technology transfer, and the avoidance of dependence on a single supplier. The latter is especially difficult to achieve in the procurement of aircraft, which must be bought in large numbers to be cost-effective.

"Made in India"

Whenever India has attempted to build its own planes, it has stumbled. The history of the attempt to gain autonomy and build a multirole aircraft in India—or any aircraft, for that matter—is one of serial and dismal failure.[31]

Guided by Blackett's framework, and catalyzed by bad experiences with technology denial, India moved early to an indigenous program of design and manufacture of the most advanced military technology (aside from nuclear weapons), as in high-performance jet combat aircraft. The overall strategy was to shift away from purchasing foreign technology to indigenizing the system, component by component; and then producing it in India with suitable Indian-inspired modifications. The net result would be combat aircraft in adequate numbers and at reasonable prices, as well as security from any technology-denial regime that may be imposed in the future. By and large, the strategy has failed.

The three major experiments in this direction, the HF-24 (Marut), the advanced jet trainer, and the Light Combat Aircraft (LCA) are very instructive. They demonstrate the problems that India has had in pleasing its ultimate customer, the Indian Air Force, and the difficulty of jumping from basic to advanced aerospace and engine technologies. However, while the effort has had public and popular support, these systems served (and in the case of the LCA, still serve) symbolic goals, not substantive ones.

The first attempt to build an indigenous combat aircraft was a costly disaster. The HF-24 was designed by a German team hired by India. During World War II, the team had worked for the Focke-Wolf aircraft firm.[32] The HF-24 was a twin-engine, light interceptor or bomber. It never reached its design goals, in large part because India could not fit a proper engine to it. The team tried an underpowered British engine as well as engines from the Soviet Union and the United States, settling on an engine to be supplied by Egypt, which also used German scientists. All were inadequate, and the plane killed a number of test pilots and performed poorly in combat against American-supplied Pakistan fighters. For years the HF-24 was celebrated as having brought India into the jet era; in turn, it necessitated the purchase of a replacement from the Soviet Union, the Sukhoi-7, which also was highly vulnerable in combat. Ultimately, very little infrastructure was built up. Thus when India undertook its next experiment in aircraft self-reliance, the Light Combat Aircraft, the requisite foundation was not in place.

Second, there was a failed attempt to build a basic jet trainer in India, this time with a Soviet-supplied engine that never worked properly. The requirement was an intermediary jet trainer, which would allow pilots to transition from propeller to high-performance jets (the Soviet MiG-21 was a notoriously hard plane to learn to fly). After thirty years of complaining, the IAF was allowed to place orders for the British Hawk jet trainer in 2000. The inability to procure the trainer in time, coupled with the aging fighter fleet, gave the IAF the dubious distinction, since rectified, of having one of the world's worst accident records.[33] The slow and convoluted acquisition process explains the interminable delay over the Hawk, but the overconfidence of Indian designers, the distrust of the United States as a supplier (not, in this case, misplaced), and the urge to indigenize advanced technology were all responsible for the failure of indigenous development of a Light Combat Aircraft.

Although the LCA was conceived in the 1980s, nearly thirty years later it is still over budget and behind schedule. India's attempt to build an aircraft comparable to the best contemporary American and European designs remains something of a joke.[34] When its specifications were shown to American aircraft companies in the late 1980s, they responded that someone had circled all the "hot" technologies of that era (for instance, fly-by-wire, heads-up displays). In the end the American firms backed off, which was just as well as they would have been prohibited from cooperation with the LCA once sanctions were imposed after India's 1998 nuclear tests. The advocates of self-reliance in India were correct in that the United States was not a trustworthy supplier of advanced military technology; however, they were wrong to expect a feeble Indian aerospace industry to produce frontline equipment.[35] Fifteen years late, the LCA is in 2010 moving into the "final development" stage with a contract with a European defense company to integrate its electronics; weapons may still take another three years to gain operational clearance.[36]

The air force was always skeptical of the LCA. For years there has been an ongoing battle between the IAF, which prefers India to buy verified foreign technology, and DRDO and the Indian defense production establishment, which claims it can deliver sanction-proof aircraft with the best or at least "good enough" technology, on time and within budget.[37] The LCA is slated to replace the MiG-21s, but remains a paper plane twenty-five years after DRDO set out to build it to modest international standards.

While IAF officers tend to favor foreign over indigenous technology, they remain acutely aware that foreign purchases compromise India's position; for political reasons, they may be denied critical spare parts, equipment upgrades, and repair facilities. There are several instances when the Indian services, especially the air force, faced technology denial or arms embargos. The first such occasion was the British denial of aircraft engines. In 1951 the British initiated the first of many Western attempts to influence Indian policy by a go-slow delivery of Goblin engines for the new Indian jet fighters.[38] Further, until recently the United States would not sell aircraft or critical technology to India. There was a fear during the cold war that technology might leak to the Soviets (in fact, the United States clandestinely procured Soviet technology through India). There was also concern about fueling an arms race between India and Pakistan, and in the 1990s India was punished for its nuclear program. The United States carefully monitored the transfer of U.S.-origin technology to India from third parties, thus halting the sale of Swedish aircraft (with their American engines) to India.

These aircraft were generally optimized for a single role, but the service adapted single-mission aircraft to its own purposes, so there was a steep learning curve and many accidents. The Soviet-era MiGs were also "hot" aircraft, but unforgiving of young pilots. It was two decades before the IAF was allowed to purchase an intermediary jet trainer, the British Hawk.

The MRCA and Expansion

In 2000 the air force requested urgent replacements of its aging fleet, seeking an MRCA. Eight years later, the Ministry of Defence finally invited six main foreign bidders to enter a competition; this defense contract of Rs. 42,000 crore ($10 billion) is India's largest. India proposes to buy eighteen fighters off-the-shelf (one squadron) and seeks help in manufacturing another 108 domestically. There is an option to purchase another sixty-four fighters under the same terms and conditions. These include a massive direct offset of 50 percent (not the normal 30 percent) directly related to the aircraft or to India's defense manufacturing sector.[39] This option is intended to help the government's own defense production infrastructure and, perhaps, the few private firms that have been specially designated for defense contracting work.

The Ministry of Defence prognosticates that the fighters are likely to be in service for forty years, and vendors will be required to provide lifetime support and performance-based warranties.[40] The six companies to which requests for proposals were issued included two American firms and one each from Russia, Sweden, France, and a European consortium. The selection process that precedes the final contract will take at least four years, and aircraft may not be delivered until at least two years after that.

Doctrinal Development

Trying to analyze the IAF's failure to modernize, George Tanham noted that in the 1980s it was characterized by its fighter pilot mentality, lack of managerial skills, promotions determined strictly by seniority— blocking the way for younger promising officers—and lack of understanding of air power by civilian bureaucrats. Tanham then went on to make the telling point that the IAF itself was partly to blame with its lack of interest in long-range planning; obsession with acquiring greater numbers of aircraft; and inattention to modern electronics, force multipliers, and other less glamorous but vitally important needs. He concluded by predicting that "without change in IAF policy, leadership and accepted roles of the air force, and visibility, . . . the future is more likely to resemble the past."[41] Events belie this prediction, and in matters under its own control, the IAF has moved toward becoming a truly modern air force with a strategic mindset.

The IAF has aggressively pursued a strategy that meets a wide range of threats. It backs its demands by suggesting that a large number of fighters are completing their service lives. The previous chief of the IAF, Air Chief Marshall S. P. Tyagi, wrote to Defense Minister Pranab Mukherjee complaining that IAF numbers were dwindling so fast that Pakistan would soon have more fighters than India unless the MRCA contract were quickly concluded. Well-informed analysts disputed those figures, arguing that upgrades and overhauls could keep existing aircraft going until the Sukhoi-30 production plant was in full flow.[42] The IAF has never reached the squadron level assigned to it after the 1962 war (sixty-four squadrons); at its peak it had forty-five squadrons and currently has thirty-nine, approximately half of which are tasked for air defense. The numbers are expected to decline to thirty-two squadrons with the retirement of older MiG-21s. However, this decrease need not mean a degradation of capability, as a single modern Sukhoi-30, now manufactured in India, can deliver as much ordnance as a squadron of MiG-21 FLs at greater ranges and with greater accuracy.[43]

The IAF has developed an air doctrine that articulates the importance of air power for the defense of India. However, the doctrine is only one step toward fielding a modern air force that is equipped to take on the substantial threats posed by Pakistan and even China. The technology-intensive IAF has been displaced from its long-range reconnaissance role, and the army has moved quickly to assert a more offensive doctrine even as it is mired in counterinsurgency. The IAF can contribute little to either kind of war and is wary of being drawn into counterinsurgency where Indian citizens may be harmed. Instead, it promulgates the classic air power argument that planes can replace both navies and armies, especially when engaged in a game of nerves or an escalation scenario with an opponent. This, however, has little appeal to India's strategic policy community, notably politicians and bureaucrats, who are wary of escalation.

India's Naval Growth: Slow but Steady

In 1978 the Indian Navy announced a twenty-year modernization plan intended to develop true blue water capability. Over the next decade, India acquired conventional submarines, large destroyers, and maritime reconnaissance; and received Soviet assistance to build extensive port and dockyard facilities in Cochin and Vishakapatnam.[44]

In comparison with the Indian Air Force, India's Navy has benefited from modest but unambiguous and long-term political support. The need to rebuild the politically unreliable navy after partition provided time to develop a strategic framework, which was, in fact, available in the writings of the influential K. M. Panikkar. The IAF never had a Panikkar—a respected Indian civilian advocate. Panikkar's framework of naval power, especially reclaiming the Indian Ocean littoral as an Indian area of influence, underlies India's repeated efforts to expand sea control. The Indian Navy has also diverged from the IAF in the pursuit of technology as the means to its goals. Whereas the IAF has been frustrated by the sheer difficulty of acquiring or producing the "latest and greatest" in technology, the navy has been more successful by aiming at lower-end established technologies. This was exactly the approach Blackett advocated in his 1948 report, but the army was too busy fighting to think seriously about weapons development; the IAF, like other air forces, followed the technology-pull view of modernization.

Notably, the navy kept the shipbuilding effort within the service; it used the DRDO only for smaller equipment such as the sonar arrays.

The Indian Navy may have enjoyed high political support and acted more judiciously in the pursuit of new technology, but it did have to make classic naval choices in the first two decades after independence: Should the navy protect the coastline or secure Indian shipping? Was the navy to assume an important role in an offensive against Pakistan? Was it to go after Pakistani shipping, or was its primary role to defeat the Pakistan Navy on the high seas? Then there were the choices that involved a particular mix of ships in the navy's inventory: Was sea denial a higher priority than protection of shipping, and if so, was it best achieved by acquiring more submarines or by a second (or third) carrier? Was the navy to play a role in extending Indian power, and if so, was this by an expansion of its amphibious and troop carrier capabilities or by offshore missiles and air power? Unable to answer these questions with any confidence, the navy pursued the Panikkar vision in incremental fashion, according to the dictates of its meager budget.

The early vision outlined by Nehru and Panikkar was sea control, a reflection of the influence of British naval power. This vision was, however, at odds with the reality of a weak Indian naval capacity that could neither control nor deny the sea to any major power. The 1971 *Enterprise* episode redefined the naval environment for India; the navy moved toward sea denial, which was aimed as much against the Americans as the weak Pakistan Navy. India shifted focus to expansion of the submarine fleet; over the next decade, it acquired submarines from the Soviet Union, culminating in 1988 with the controversial three-year lease of a single Charlie class nuclear submarine.

Once the possibility of another *Enterprise* intervention had faded, the vision of sea control reasserted itself. The Indian Navy acquired its second carrier—the refurbished HMS *Hermes*, which had been the flagship of the British task force in the 1982 Falklands War. There was a greater focus on surface presence with the acquisition of aerial reconnaissance, guided missile cruisers, and fleet replenishment ships. For a variety of legacy reasons, most important among them the network Soviet weapons-makers had built in New Delhi over the years, Moscow remained the primary supplier to the Indian Navy, but the navy continued to build its own ships. In the mid-1980s the navy also contracted to buy and build smaller submarines from the German HDW, but the deal was mired in a corruption scandal along with the Bofors gun imbroglio. The navy procured the initial vessels but further development based on the HDW design stopped after the government cut off contact with the German firm and Indian shipyards were prohibited access to foreign technology.

The Navy Regroups

The end of the cold war cut the navy adrift. To its credit, however, it was the first service to adjust to the geopolitical transformation. First, it rediscovered Panikkar's old dream of maritime influence in the Indian Ocean region. Over the next decade, the Indian Navy and its supporters developed a maritime vision that was essentially decoupled from direct military threats to the country. Second, the navy was the first Indian service to view the United States in a new light. In 1991 the navy convinced the political leadership to allow it to sign the Kickleighter Proposals, the first substantive military-to-military cooperation agreement between India and the United States since the interlude after the 1962 China war. The navy was the first service to develop a regular rotation of mid-level officers to American war colleges, despite the ill-feeling that continued from the *Enterprise* episode. A 1998 navy *Strategic Defence Review* obliquely referred to the need to deter possible U.S. gunboat diplomacy even as it vigorously pursued close ties with the U.S. Navy.[45] However, the Indian Navy has also embraced a new role that puts it in direct competition with the other services; it plans to build a ship, a nuclear-propelled and nuclear weapons–capable submarine, which could instead turn out to be a naval white elephant.

Between 1986 and 1996, the Indian Navy placed no new orders for principal combatants. During the 1990s, it added five previously ordered vessels: three Kilo-class submarines, one corvette, and one tanker.[46] Between 1997 and 2000 the navy placed orders with Russia for two more Kilo submarines and three frigates. In 1994 the navy also opened negotiations for a Russian aircraft carrier, the *Admiral Gorshkov*. However, delivery of the ship has been delayed, and Russia has increased the price for the retrofit. The navy is in something of a quandary over this—it has already made advance payments, which could be appropriated if the sale were cancelled. Moreover, the navy is optimistic that Russia will sell India a nuclear submarine in the future. As the Indian Navy tries to rise up the technology ladder, it too becomes more vulnerable to cost and foreign supply problems. The navy may be in a better place than the IAF, however, because the Indian government has approved indigenous manufacture of two submarines (Project 75), three frigates (Project 17), and three destroyers (Project 15A), as well as the Air Defense Ship (a small aircraft carrier).

A Nuclear "LCA"?

A nuclear submarine project, originally and euphemistically called the Advanced Technological Vehicle, is an extended collaboration between the navy, a private firm (Larsen and Toubro), a nuclear laboratory, and Russia. It was begun in deep secrecy in the 1970s, about the time the Soviet Union built a special dockyard at Vishakapatnam, but it soon became common knowledge. The nuclear laboratories are trying to produce a reactor that will propel the ship. The *Arihant* was launched in July 2009—the tenth anniversary of the Kargil War—through the simple process of allowing water to flood its dry dock (it had no means of propelling itself). No pictures were published of the event, presumably because a very large contingent of Russian technical experts was on hand. The vessel is a scaled-back Charlie class Russian design with four instead of eight silos for missile launch. The *Arihant* will itself be a "technology demonstrator" when it joins the fleet. Two others are planned, although it is not clear what kind of missiles they will carry or how many more vessels of its class will be launched. The forecasted operational date is 2012.

From the perspective of modernizing the Indian Navy, of greater import than the technological import is whether or not the *Arihant* signals Indian intent to have global nuclear delivery capacity or at least capacity to reach major Eastern Chinese ports, or whether it is the last gasp of a long and costly project that will be slowly terminated. The *Arihant* program is justified by Indian naval writers and the navy's own doctrinal pronouncements as the third leg in the triad of land, air, and sea-based deterrents. We will discuss India's nuclear strategy in the next chapter. The *Arihant* raises questions of how much is sufficient for the Indian state: how many nuclear weapons and of what size must it be able to deliver and to which countries in order to have a credible deterrent. It also raises questions of command and control, as the *Arihant* would not have direct communication with the Indian political leadership, and we do not foresee any Indian government yielding this power to the military in the near future. Our guess is that the expected date of commission will be stretched out indefinitely, but the *Arihant* will intensify pressure on the Indian government to make decisions about its nuclear policy. It will also force the Indian Navy to make choices among its priorities. A nuclear submarine, with a complement of missiles, at over $3 billion a copy could consume a large part of the navy's budget, forcing it to abandon plans for a second or third carrier or restricting the size of other surface combatants, as well as indigenously produced submarines. As in the case of the LCA and some tank projects, Indian policymakers, and even the navy, may be content to produce one or two prototypes, and rely on tested and relatively inexpensive air and missile assets for nuclear delivery. Britain seems to be moving in this direction.

In 2010 the Indian Navy is expected to be smaller—at thirty-three principal combatants—than it was in 1990, but it will be organized into two carrier task forces. It would have the ability to assert sea control much farther than in the past. In 2007 the navy also acquired a major amphibious capability in the form of the former USS *Trenton*, renamed the *Jalashwa*, which became the second biggest ship in the Indian Navy. The *Jalashwa* can put over one thousand troops ashore via six helicopters or smaller landing craft and can, if necessary, launch Harrier jump jets, already in service with the Indian Navy.

Maritime Doctrine

In 2004 after the army and the air force had issued similar documents, the navy unilaterally promulgated an Indian Maritime Doctrine. It visualized four naval missions: military, diplomatic, constabulary, and "benign," the last entailing humanitarian relief and rescue. Based on these missions the navy has deduced it needs a maritime force architecture that, in the medium term, would include two operational aircraft carrier groups (presumably with three carriers) capable of exercising "sea control" in the entire Indian Ocean region. This would be supplemented by suitable submarine and aviation assets, amphibious forces, and mine and countermine capabilities.[47] In 2006 a "Roadmap to Transformation" outlining the new maritime strategy was discussed at a Naval Commanders Conference, providing more details about the navy's plans for rescue-and-relief operations and interoperability with the other armed forces and with the forces of other countries.[48]

The doctrine indicated a more expansive view of Indian maritime security, focused more on economic and energy security than on the role of naval power. According to British naval theorist Geoffrey Till, the change reflects the rise of broader maritime issues.[49] Till writes that in the past, navies were "national" or Westphalian, judged in terms of other navies; and their goal was sea control, the maintenance of local, regional, or global *naval* dominance. The great theoretician of sea power was American Alfred Thayer Mahan, who wrote that the ultimate test of navies was whether they prevailed in combat. In recent decades, however, globalization has forced navies to become more alert to security of access and trade: the war against renewed piracy, disaster relief, and protection of offshore mineral rights and facilities such as oil and gas platforms. The relevant doctrine for our contemporary age was promulgated by Sir Julian Corbett, a British naval historian and theoretician who averred that navies could play many roles besides preparing for the climactic battle at sea—a battle that may never come.[50] These roles have historically been the bailiwick of navies in peacetime. This shift in the balance between naval supremacy and a more complex menu of maritime roles and missions dictated by interdependence and globalization plays to the historical strengths of the Indian Navy, and is the reason why man for man and rupee for rupee it is emerging as India's most important service, at least from the perspective of foreign powers.

The navy's essential dilemma is that it is hard for this capital-intensive service to do everything, or even to do a little of everything. The cost of one carrier (approximately $1.5 billion) or one nuclear-powered missile-submarine (about $2.9 billion) is equivalent to about 375 to 725 main battle tanks or 17 to 33 combat aircraft. On the other hand, in the attempt to cover many roles and missions, the navy has built its technical and organizational capabilities to a very high level, which may be better exploited if India gains access to advanced technology (a scenario that raises the question of public versus private sources of technology).

Though naval strategists argue that only the navy can correct the imbalance in India's international security priorities, the service lacks real political influence in New Delhi. There is no parliamentary lobby that pushes for naval construction and enhanced budgets, let alone for a rebalance of the services. Until very recently Indian industry has not been interested in the navy and naval construction. This may change with the opening of the defense sector to select Indian firms—one of them is involved in the construction of the first nuclear submarine.

Since the 1990s the rise of the Indian economy has revealed growing maritime, rather than merely naval, needs—raising the prospect of greater spending on the navy after years of stagnation.[51] The navy has been asked to safeguard the offshore oil and gas fields north of Bombay, and protect India's vast Extended Economic Zone (EEZ) from claims by other states, especially Pakistan. After 1998 the navy has sought a role in India's nuclear weapons program; various schemes were developed to build a sea-based nuclear deterrent force. The American Tomahawk attacks in both Gulf Wars made a deep impression on Indian Navy strategists; India lacked such a capacity—although it was one of the first navies to launch seaborne missiles in its attack on the Karachi fuel and gas depots in 1971. The Indian Air Force and the Indian Navy remain rival claimants for the maritime reconnaissance and missile defense missions, respectively.

Thomas Barnett, an American naval theoretician writing in 2001, summed up four possible future scenarios for the navy. The first was to constitute a minimum deterrent force, relegating the navy to a position of inferiority vis-à-vis the army and air force, and focusing largely upon the naval threat of Pakistan. The second was a sea-denial navy focused mainly on the threat from China, but having more general capacity to exclude outside influence in the region. Both futures would allow continued Russian influence with anti-ship capabilities and protection of territorial waters and offshore facilities—and would not be transformative. The third alternative is a regional stabilization navy, responsible for the preservation of the Indian Ocean as a safe transit for global commerce. Most Indian navy officers see themselves in this status quo scenario. Finally, there could be an international coalition navy, a force capable of acting independently when necessary, but especially skillful at coalition operations with other major services, notably the U.S. Navy.

The Indian Navy operates successfully throughout the larger Indian Ocean region and occasionally beyond. It has done maritime patrolling in the Strait of Malacca alongside the U.S., Australian, and Singapore navies. Its finest hour in recent years was disaster relief efforts for victims of the 2005 tsunami in the Indian islands of Andaman and Nicobar as well as in Aceh, Indonesia, and Sri Lanka. In 2006 the Indian Navy evacuated 530 Indians and others from Lebanon before the Israeli air strikes. The navy also conducts maritime patrolling; after a series of attacks on vessels carrying Indian crews in the waters off the coasts of Somalia and Yemen, it was allowed to base a frigate in these waters. In November 2008, among the first such actions by any major-power navy, INS *Tabar* set alight a Thai commercial vessel believed to be in pirate control off the Somali coast. There is also talk of a UN naval peacekeeping force, which could provide international legitimacy for the Indian ship(s).

The navy is of two minds regarding a strategy toward Pakistan or China. The Indian Maritime Doctrine and its precursor, the *Strategic Defence Review: The Maritime Dimension*, did not suggest how Indian naval power could alter the balance with Pakistan or offset China's growing naval capacity. This reticence is evident in the public comments of navy leaders.[52] As the Chinese used to do when talking about the United States, Indian naval officials speak of the huge gap in terms of budget and ship numbers between India and China, and India's interest in cooperative rather than competitive relations with all navies. Admiral Mehta and others argue that India's advantage will be in advanced technology, not sheer numbers. Indian Maritime Doctrine deals with Pakistan indirectly as one of many littoral threats in the Indian Ocean including possible subversion in the Maldives as well as piracy. According to the doctrine, the navy expects to assert control and even project power into enemy land. To what extent this is feasible with respect to Pakistan is open to question. The advantage that the Indian service has in relation to its Pakistani counterpart is in the weakness of its enemy: the navy in Pakistan has always been in disrepair.

Political restraint may have caused the navy's public reticence about competition with China, but the navy leaks plenty of anti-China stories to the Indian press, especially about Chinese naval works in Burmese and Pakistani ports.

The navy's inability to offer forthright responses to the challenges from China and Pakistan—the nation's primary external security challenges—mars its potential candidacy to be one part of the country's nuclear triad. Navy analysts and their supporters speak and write of a sea-based deterrent, yet the inability to articulate a meaningful wartime role reduces the navy's political capacity to bargain for more resources and ultimately hurts its ability to pursue transformation.

To confront China, India would have to close the budget and numbers gap between the two countries. This would require huge investment and modification of the navy's force structure.[53] If the Indian Navy is to become truly modern, if it is to develop a high level of competence in the many different roles that modern navies are expected to perform, it will need not only greater funding but an expanded infrastructure (at least one new port is being constructed on India's southwest coast). On its own, it cannot begin to make amends with regional rivals, notably Pakistan;[54] but its political masters have encouraged it to develop a closer relationship with the United States, a new development that we discuss in chapter 8.

INSTRUMENTS OF POWER PROJECTION

A military transformation in India depends greatly on how the country expands its air and sea power assets relative to its ground forces. The Indian Air Force and the Indian Navy have gained in their relative share of the defense budget in the last two decades. The Indian Air Force has had the greatest increases of all three services as the country sought to develop the rudiments of a nuclear deterrent. The Indian Navy, the most neglected of the three services after 1962, saw its share of the budget surge from 12 to 18 percent until 2008. But the shifting of priority to air and sea power has tapered off temporarily as the government adjusts to the massive salary hikes ordered in the Sixth Pay Commission. The Indian Army, as the largest service, benefited in proportion to its numbers; it reversed the trend favoring the navy and the air force.

The prospects for change differ between the Indian Navy and the Indian Air Force. Because the navy produces and uses a few large units with long life spans, it has a decades-long strategic and production timeline, and an expansive view of India's maritime interests, which resonates with those Indians who have great-power ambitions. The navy's seamanship is rated as NATO-quality by U.S. navy officers who participated in joint exercises or who sailed alongside Indian Navy vessels in such closed-in seas as the Persian Gulf. The navy attracts some of the best human material for both the officer and enlisted classes. It has learned to master operations across the Indian Ocean region and operates two separate fleets. Although the navy's agenda may have little to do with Pakistan today, it places India in an advantageous maritime position over the next several decades. Additionally, there are demands that the navy become the true strategic force for the country, but such a role will require nuclear submarines armed with intermediate-range ballistic missiles. As the smallest service the navy does not have the political support and wherewithal to become the instrument that alters India's strategic condition.

In contrast, the IAF is struggling to keep up in technology and numbers in a prospective climactic battle with Pakistan or a long drawn-out contest with China. At this point, the IAF is primarily designed as an air defense force with limited offensive capability. Instead of growing, the air force has been losing its numbers and continues to be dependent on foreign sources (or the unproductive DRDO). Comparatively, the IAF is an excellent service; the air force's missions are truly strategic—failure to defend or to deter may result in a catastrophic attack on the Indian homeland. The IAF is split between the demands of the army for air support, its dependence on foreign sources for critical advanced technology (and the inability, so far, of Indian laboratories to produce modern weapons), the requirements of nuclear delivery and air superiority, and the vision of a globe-girdling space power. The IAF competes with the IN for reconnaissance and with the army over the ground support and air defense roles. The IAF and the army have yet to work out an airlift strategy.

In terms of modernization, the IAF is the most vulnerable of all services to technology shortfall. While weapons modernization depends on system integration for maximum results, it is easier for the navy to get by with less sophisticated technology because its ships perform so many different roles. Displaying the flag or disaster relief or fighting pirates does not require sophisticated technology. On the other hand, the difference between a plane optimized for a ground attack versus one with an interceptor role is so great it remains vulnerable to a skilled opponent or to a minor breakthrough in electronics technology. In terms of quality, the Pakistan Air Force was always as good as, if not better than, the IAF. Although this is not measurable except in war, the IAF's nominal superiority in numbers did not, until recently, translate into air superiority. The air balance with China is even harder to imagine; in the case of a war with nuclearized Pakistan or China, one of the main considerations will not be victory in the air, but the use of air power to avoid escalation. Indeed, the calculation between nuclear rivals is how to use air power on the margins; as in Kargil, a clear breakthrough may lead the other side to escalate spatially or militarily.

CHAPTER FIVE

THE RELUCTANT NUCLEAR POWER

India's May 1998 test of five nuclear weapons was a major break with the past; many predicted that India's trajectory henceforth would be of greater assertiveness. This view was reinforced by India's declaration that, unlike the single test in 1974— euphemistically termed a Peaceful Nuclear Explosion—the 1998 tests were aimed toward perfecting usable nuclear weapons. Further, India indicated that specific security threats had driven it across the weapons threshold, particularly China's growing power and hostility to India. However, India formulated a "draft" doctrine to guide its use of the new weapons, and while India's overall rise as a power is attributed in large part to its new nuclear status, New Delhi has moved cautiously and slowly as a nuclear weapons state. Pakistan has been far more assertive in this regard.

India's caution and measured pace have been the hallmark of its nuclear weapons program, which itself was enmeshed from the beginning with an attempt to use the atom for peaceful purposes. India had a strong interest in nuclear energy even before independence.[1] India's early success in nuclear research was due largely to the remarkable Homi J. Bhabha, who saw nuclear energy as a means to accelerate the development process by leapfrogging over outmoded technologies. Bhabha was close to India's first prime minister, Jawaharlal Nehru, who accepted India's comparative advantage in nuclear energy—with its scientific expertise and large thorium deposits—but opposed the atomic bomb. This was not the case for Bhabha, who became the Indian Atomic Energy Commission's (IAEC) first chairman as India embarked on a small but sophisticated program of civilian nuclear research. Bhabha ensured that a part of the program continued to consider the atom's military use. India acquired two nuclear power reactors, one each from Canada and the United States. By 1965 Bhabha and his team had reached a standing where India could seriously consider becoming a nuclear weapons state. India's nuclear program included a reprocessing facility that produced about eight kilograms of plutonium a year, enough for at least one nuclear weapon. Although dependent on foreign sources for reactor technology, heavy water, and enriched uranium; India achieved autonomy in some areas of design and construction.

However, instead of moving quickly to a weapons program, India embarked on a series of wide-ranging debates over "going nuclear," encompassing not only strategy but also politics, morality, and economics.[2] On the one hand, the 1962 military humiliation inflicted by Beijing and the 1964 Chinese test at Lop Nor weighed heavily on the minds of the Indian leadership. Another Chinese invasion of northern and eastern India seemed probable. Homi Bhabha, who was familiar with theories of deterrence, argued that India should seek a security guarantee from the major nuclear weapons states or pursue the bomb. There was some expectation that the United States and the United Kingdom would provide such an umbrella; the Indian government sounded both states out after the 1964 Chinese test (Nehru also pled frantically for the transfer of B-47 bombers, capable of delivering nuclear weapons of that generation). Disgraced after 1962 and preoccupied with conventional rearmament, the armed forces stayed out of the debate. The decision about the nuclear weapons program was entirely the concern of civilians—politicians, bureaucrats, and scientists.

On the other hand, a nuclear weapons program in addition to the massive post-1962 rearmament threatened an already weak economy. Moreover, Nehru had an abiding political and moral aversion to nuclear weapons that he continued to hold after the 1962 defeat. American officials discussed guarantees or a security umbrella for India should there be another attack from China; some in the U.S. government supported an Indian nuclear weapons program. Chester Bowles, the American ambassador, favored a nonpunitive policy for India were it to move in this direction.[3] However, Nehru was restrained in following the nuclear path given his own advocacy of nonalignment—close ties with the United States would result from a nuclear deal— as well as American and British efforts to compel India to negotiate with Pakistan on a Kashmir deal. His nuclear advisers favored a weapons program if nuclear disarmament were not to happen soon. For them, it was either nuclear disarmament or the bomb option.[4] Although the technical infrastructure for a nuclear weapons program remained, it was hidden away.

Once the great powers had engineered a cooperative formula to manage the spread of nuclear weapons, they wanted India to join up. The 1968 Nuclear Non-Proliferation Treaty (NPT) did advance long-stated Indian goals of ending the nuclear arms race and allowing the pursuit of nuclear disarmament as well as offering civilian nuclear technology to signatories that renounced nuclear weapons. In practice, however, both objectives were ephemeral. Signing the NPT would have ended India's nuclear option, opening Indian nuclear facilities to full-scope inspections and safeguards without a parallel guarantee that the great powers and China would dismantle their nuclear arsenals. After much debate, India decided to remain outside the NPT, continuing low-level R&D and fissile material production. The decision to keep the nuclear option open reflected India's deep-seated need to maintain foreign policy autonomy, and also demonstrated its recognition that the weapons program was possibly just as important as the civilian one.

The 1971 victory over Pakistan transformed India's strategic position once again. New Delhi moved closer to the Soviet Union, and Indira Gandhi, prompted probably by domestic problems, approved a single nuclear test in 1974.[5] Although India was confident enough to test a device, it was less confident about actually pursuing a functioning weapon. Thus the test was billed as a "peaceful nuclear explosion"; those involved saw it more realistically. Dr. Raja Ramanna, a key figure in the 1974 test, frequently spoke before his 2004 death of the military objectives of that event, and of Homi Bhabha's interest in a weapon. The United States and other Western nations imposed sanctions and restrictions as stipulated under the NPT and their own nonproliferation laws. Even the Soviet Union backed away temporarily from India. Pakistani Prime Minister Zulfikar Ali Bhutto, having lost the 1971 war, promised his nation would acquire its own nuclear weapon even if the people had to eat grass.

Yet after the 1974 test, the Indian nuclear program was quiescent. Key players retired and faded away after a blaze of nationalist glory. The nation became preoccupied with domestic problems that culminated in Indira Gandhi's defeat in the 1977 general elections.

The neglect of nuclear policy was reversed only in the mid-to-late 1980s when leading Indian strategists concluded that Pakistan was close to or already in possession of the bomb. They were correct. In addition to intelligence from their own sources, Indians had only to read the increasingly frantic public statements by American officials warning Islamabad it should not cross certain "red lines" as it moved toward a nuclear weapons program; Chinese assistance was also a widely known fact. Two individuals, General K.

Sundarji, who headed the army between 1986 and 1988, and defense expert K. Subrahmanyam mounted a strong and successful case for an Indian bomb. Subrahmanyam has been for decades and remains the nuclear "guru" to a generation of Indian scholars and journalists. Sundarji was one of the few officers who had given serious thought to nuclear weapons. Sundarji directed a government study commissioned by Arun Singh (Rajiv Gandhi's Minister of State for Defense) in 1988. This team's threat assessment was persuasive enough to win widespread support.[6] The report set forth a graded series of nuclear and non-nuclear threats to India; these were primarily from China and Pakistan, but also from the United States or some other outside power that might intrude on India's natural sphere of influence. After 1972 the dominant Indian view was that the country was up against an unholy triad of these three states; the nominal ally, the Soviet Union, made a dedicated effort to reinforce this Indian view of encirclement.

Citing the American nuclear theorist Kenneth Waltz, Sundarji and Subrahmanyam asserted that the acquisition of nuclear weapons made states more cautious, and disputed the Western allegation that nuclear weapons in the third world were inherently more dangerous than they were elsewhere. Their view held that the best option against Pakistan was to limit military conflict to the conventional level where India had a clear advantage. India was advised to declare a No First Use doctrine to minimize the possibility of preemption, but to back it up with a small deterrent force capable of destroying high-value targets. China was a more complex challenge because of its size and military power. Certainly, India was not going to match China's conventional or nuclear forces. The answer was to develop a missile capability that could reach a few Chinese urban targets. Indian military R&D shifted significantly to missiles during this period, as well as to a nuclear-powered submarine that could deliver them.

Beyond Pakistan and China, the threats were more indirect. U.S. nonproliferation efforts were interpreted as a contain-India strategy. The United States had asked India to give up nuclear weapons, but it had never held China accountable for supplying nuclear technology to Pakistan. Additionally, the United States had been unwilling to try to halt the Pakistani nuclear program until it was too late. These strategic nuclear calculations were once again accompanied with offsetting efforts to put the nuclear genie back in the bottle, a reflection of India's deep reluctance to pursue a deployed, working nuclear arsenal. In 1988 Prime Minister Rajiv Gandhi proposed an action plan for phased global and regional nuclear disarmament. It was a last ditch diplomatic effort to stop the Pakistani nuclear program. In the action plan, India for the first time proposed regional disarmament alongside global

reduction of nuclear weapons. The great powers paid the proposal no attention, and some Indian critics decried it as too late and naïve. Amidst mounting evidence of a serious Pakistani weapons program, some of it based on
official American warnings to Pakistan not to cross certain lines, Prime Minister Rajiv Gandhi in 1989 authorized the Defence Research and Development Organisation (DRDO) to restart the nuclear program in cooperation
with the Indian Atomic Energy Commission.[7] The objective was to develop
an unassembled nuclear weapon, but also to have all the other elements of
delivery and organization put in place.

Design teams in the Bhabha Atomic Research Centre (BARC), along with
scientists from the DRDO, began working toward a test after Rajiv's order in
1989. This work benefited from a considerable amount of public information about the physics of nuclear weapons. Indian designers had access to
high-performance computers as well as the knowledge that certain configu-
rations were known to work. The Indian team worked on several different
systems: a refinement of the 1974 plutonium bomb, components of a thermonuclear design, and perhaps tactical and battlefield weapons. This work
ultimately produced the 1998 tests that brought India's nuclear capacity out
into the open.

Going Nuclear, Abandoning Ambiguity

While India tried to calibrate its response to the threat of an expanding Pakistani nuclear program, it lost its chief strategic partner, the Soviet Union, as
the balancer to both America and China. With the end of the cold war, the
United States sought to consolidate the peace dividend, aggressively seeking
renewed emphasis on nonproliferation. The Clinton administration sought
the indefinite extension of the NPT and negotiated the Comprehensive Test
Ban Treaty (CTBT) and Fissile Material Cut-off Treaty (FMCT). As a state
opposed to these regimes, India became a prime target of U.S. nonproliferation policy. Senior American officials stated that Washington's goal was to
"cap, reduce, and eliminate" the nuclear programs of states that were not
signatories of the NPT.[8]

After the cold war, three different Indian schools of thought debated
nuclear weapons.[9] The first group consisted of the neoliberals, who were
concerned mainly with economic growth. Dominating Indian policy in the
early 1990s, they launched the economic reforms following the balance of
payments crisis in 1991, and were wary of an assertive foreign and security policy that could jeopardize India's economic recovery. A second group
was the Nehruvians, who were the traditional proponents of India's nuclear

ambiguity, drawing inspiration from "the third way" in foreign policy. As delineated in chapter 1, Nehru believed that equidistance from the super- powers enabled India to preserve its freedom of action while obviating the need for a costly military buildup. This approach was the foundation of India's long history of strategic restraint. Apart from nonalignment, the subordination of military power to diplomacy, the unwillingness (except in 1971) to initiate war, and the hesitation to press the military advantage even after victory all resulted from the fundamental Nehruvian unwillingness to bear the high costs of assertive security. The neoliberals and the Nehruvians had been in a coalition that kept the nuclear option open.

A third group advocated a strong defense, demanding not only testing but also a full nuclear triad. They wanted a modern nuclear arsenal similar to the American, Soviet, Chinese, British, and French systems—one that included land, sea, and air-based delivery systems and the most modern weapons designs, that is, thermonuclear warheads. They believed that India could launch itself into great-power status by presenting the world with a fait accompli, India as a new nuclear weapon state. Unlike the neoliberals and the Nehruvians, these hyperrealists believed in the utility of force in interna- tional relations. Military rearmament would either deter Pakistan or force it into excessive military spending; many Indian strategists believe the Soviet Union collapsed because it could not keep up with lavish American defense spending. As for China, it had to be deterred from encroaching into the regional politics of the subcontinent. Indeed, a revitalized India would force the United States to acquiesce to an Indian sphere of influence, thus allowing India to control the seas of Southeast Asia and the Persian Gulf.

Finally, the scientists were an important factor, participating sparingly in the public debate but leaking information to further their goals. The scien- tists were divided on the utility of a nuclear weapon, but were united in their anger at the West, notably the United States and the United Kingdom for denying them ostensibly harmless technologies for their laboratories, or refusing to cooperate with them on scientific projects because such equip- ment and such cooperation might have "dual use."[10] This was especially irksome to those scientists who cared or knew little about military affairs, and who felt that the West used a spurious pretext to eliminate a potential competitor. Additionally, Indians were driven to show the West that they could do high-quality and original work on their own, in spite of technology- restraint regimes. Many Indian scientists were nevertheless also incensed at restrictions imposed by the same Western countries that worked hand- in-glove with dictatorships and undemocratic regimes around the world, notably Pakistan and China, while they denied democratic India legitimate access to technologies that could alleviate India's poverty (even if some of that technology had potential military applications).

As pressure from the United States built up in the early 1990s, Indian nuclear policy, supported by the neoliberals and the Nehruvians, sought escape through diplomacy. India made a strong case against the indefinite extension of the NPT in 1995, but the United States bypassed the Conference on Disarmament and won indefinite NPT extension in the United Nations General Assembly. Soon after, the United States energetically advanced the CTBT. India had been a cosponsor, but it retreated from arms control advocacy when its own nuclear option was put at risk. The defining moment came on June 20, 1996, when India's ambassador, Arundhati Ghose, negotiating the CTBT at the Conference on Disarmament, publicly stated that signing the treaty would compromise India's security interests. This was perhaps the first time India cited "security" as a reason to withdraw advocacy of arms control agreements. The major nuclear weapons states, which had by then worked out a number of compromises among themselves, did not accommodate India. India was outmaneuvered in the entry-into-force provision of the treaty, which, unlike the NPT, required ratification from forty states for it to apply to all the others. India could not stall, as it had done with the NPT. American nonproliferation policies, in this case backed by China and Europe, were inexorably closing down India's nuclear options. On the military side, the apocryphal lesson from the 1991 Gulf War was never to fight the United States without nuclear weapons. India was not looking at a war with the United States; it wanted to resist American pressure on issues from nuclear proliferation to trade policy, even though American support in the multilateral lending institutions was essential to the Indian economic reform program. Economic and security imperatives clashed with each other.

With the door closing on India, the Nehruvians defected from the "do nothing" coalition that tried to maintain India's nuclear option and joined the coalition that wanted to test in order to keep the option viable. The Congress-led P. V. R. Narasimha Rao government seriously considered conducting tests and sent out teams to prepare the site of the 1974 explosion in the Thar Desert of Rajasthan. When American satellites picked up the activity, Washington tried to dissuade New Delhi. Under pressure, the Rao government backed down, but a new domestic constituency for testing was now in place. The CTBT debate succeeded in accomplishing what thirty years of insecurity and uncertainty had not: it united Indian opinion against a treaty that had originally been proposed by India.[11]

The hyperrealists who all along had supported Indian nuclear testing and weapons development had a natural home in the Bharatiya Janata Party (BJP). They also had the support of those scientists who favored nuclear testing and weaponization. Since the decision was made in utter secrecy, and only a few people knew about the plans for the tests, there was no public debate on the wisdom of finally breaking through the nuclear barrier, although the issue of "going nuclear" had been debated exhaustively over the years.

In the previous ten years, the BJP had risen from the margins of Indian politics to become the second largest national political party. Its rise had been accelerated by a staunchly nationalist platform that, among other things, advocated testing. The growing importance of the issue caused the BJP to adopt it specifically as an election promise. The general elections brought the BJP to power for the first time in March 1998; two months later India conducted five nuclear tests. BJP's alacrity to test took observers by surprise. Even India's defense minister, who was in the government as a representative of a BJP coalition partner, was ignorant about the tests until the final moment. The initial reaction in the United States was a sense of betrayal; apparently, Indian government representatives had assured Washington that tests were unlikely. Moreover, the BJP had mounted an elaborate and effective deception plan; the tests had come as a complete surprise—and shock—to American officials.[12]

BEING NUCLEAR

The tests may have served as an end in themselves, but the government was faced with difficult choices regarding the kind of nuclear program it would pursue and the strategic doctrine it would develop. The BJP-led government was soon to fall, but it commissioned a "Draft Nuclear Doctrine" from the newly created National Security Advisory Board (NSAB).[13] Since the NSAB had only advisory standing, and some members were working journalists, creating a serious conflict of interest, its work was regarded skeptically by many observers. The NSAB was not representative of all views; its members bickered publicly, and a number of the original members were removed when the group was reconstituted in early 2000.

The NSAB produced a catchall document, designed to please many important interests, and still set clear parameters for Indian nuclear weapons development and strategy. It embraced the idea of nuclear deterrence, but called for a minimum deterrent: just enough to deter an unnamed adversary from launching a nuclear attack on India. Perhaps the most important argument in the doctrine was the claim that India need not engage in an arms race with its likely opponents; a small force would suffice. Nevertheless, this minimum deterrent would require a triad of air, ground, and sea-delivered weapons to ensure the survivability of an Indian nuclear force. Further, the Draft Nuclear Doctrine declared that India should adopt a declaratory policy of No First Use against other nuclear states, and No Use against non-nuclear states. It also called for progress on global disarmament.

The Draft Nuclear Doctrine was the focal point for internal and foreign debate over the Indian nuclear program, but it could not settle the major questions concerning the Indian nuclear program. The anti-nuclear community, which was still strong, attacked the Draft for obvious reasons. They were joined by a few hawkish strategists who argued that the document did not go far enough or was inconsistent. Many former serving officers thought the Draft was motivated more by politics than strategy.

The 1999 and 2001–02 crises with Pakistan raised questions about the utility of nuclear weapons.[14] The 1999 crisis offered two lessons: India's nuclear arsenal did not prevent Pakistan from launching a subconventional military probe, and any subsequent Indian response would have to take Pakistan's arsenal into account; thus regional war in South Asia would have to be carefully limited. The 2001–02 crisis confirmed the latter lesson, as India dared not risk a wider war in retaliation for another perceived Pakistan-supported terrorist attack. Both crises also drove home the lesson that the United States and other foreign powers would play a role in regional crises.

The tests ended the option strategy and tenuously set India on the path to nuclear weaponization. "Seemingly" and "tenuously" are necessary qualifications because eleven years later there is no consensus on the meaning of weaponization. There is doubt about the status of the Indian weapons program, and there is considerable confusion about how nuclear weapons will fit into the Indian grand strategy. Some Indian politicians and administrators familiar with the program have also worried about its technical soundness. Despite the claims of its scientists, they see India in no position to move ahead and design, develop, build, and deploy a triad that would give it an air, sea, and land nuclear capability. The seaborne capability is the most technically improbable and politically unappealing because of the command and control problem—nuclear submarines require delegation of launch authority to the military on the spot. The debate is muted because the U.S.-India nuclear deal legitimized the Indian weapons program. This agreement says nothing about India's military program. After the Indian weapons program acquired international legitimacy, interest in nuclear strategy and doctrine quickly dissipated.

TRADING SECURITY FOR INFLUENCE

Indian decisions on nuclear matters will have profound implications for Asian stability and long-term Indian-American relations. These are (1) "sizing" the Indian nuclear program to meet likely threats; (2) development of a nuclear doctrine; (3) crisis management; (4) arsenal maintenance, including the development of a command-and-control structure compatible with India's democratic system and its unique civil-military relationship; and (5) India's policies on the spread of nuclear weapons. Analysis of these five points must be tentative due to the evolving nature of the nuclear program, but some projections are possible.

How Many Are Enough?

For the next five to seven years the number and types of Indian nuclear weapons are fairly predictable, given known capacities to generate fissile material and to reprocess fuel that contains plutonium. Table 5-1 summarizes estimates by a number of independent sources: at the upper end it is possible that India may have two hundred weapons, at the lower end, around sixty. These are likely to be first- and second-generation devices, unless India were to undertake a new round of testing to validate thermonuclear designs that might be mounted several to a missile warhead. However, if it dipped into its unreprocessed used fuel supplies, India could build as many as a thousand nuclear weapons.

Pakistan is already reachable by aircraft-delivered Indian nuclear weapons and has responded with a vigorous program of missile development and testing. India can deliver a few nuclear weapons by air to several western Chinese cities; perhaps by 2015, India's nuclear-tipped missiles and bombers will be able to reach all of Pakistan, major eastern Chinese cities, many American allies, American overseas bases, and perhaps the American homeland.

As India has buried its weapons program in a professedly civilian or peaceful nuclear infrastructure, estimates of India's capabilities are approximate. Still, present physical limitations are evident.

A few nuclear hawks would like a widely deployed arsenal of thermonuclear weapons, enough to boost India to the major league of nuclear weapons states. They envision seaborne delivery systems that would permit India to field a nuclear force in neighboring oceans, and a rail-based system that would ensure mobility and the preservation of a second-strike retaliatory capability.

Table 5-1. *Estimates of Indian Nuclear Weapons*

Source	1998–2002	2004–10	Future estimates
David Albright (2000, 2003)	Low-45 Median-65 High-95	Low-65 Median-85 High-110	n.a.
Bulletin of the Atomic Scientists (2002, 2005)	30–35	45–50	n.a.
Cirincione, Wolfsthal, and Rajkumar (2001)	50–90	n.a.	n.a.
Congressional Research Service (2005)	n.a.	30–35	n.a.
Bharat Karnad (2002)	n.a.	*122 (proposed)*	*408 (proposed)*
Raja Menon (2005)	n.a.	200	*400 (proposed)*
Mian, Nayyar, Rajaraman, and Ramana (2006)	n.a.	100	n.a.
George Perkovich (1999)	25–50	n.a.	n.a.
R. Rajaraman (2008)	n.a.	130	n.a.
R. Ramachandran (1999)	35	n.a.	n.a.
SIPRI (2000)	25–40	n.a.	n.a.
Ashley Tellis (2001)	50	70–76	n.a.

Sources: Ashley Tellis, *India's Emerging Nuclear Posture: Between Recessed Deterrent and Ready Arsenal* (Santa Monica, Calif.: RAND, 2001), pp. 484–93, 692; Joseph Cirincione, Jon B. Wolfsthal, and Miriam Rajkumar, *Deadly Arsenals* (Washington: Carnegie Endowment for International Peace, 2002), pp. 191–206; R. Rajaraman, "Implications of the Indo-U.S. Nuclear Deal for India's Energy and Military Programs," in *Indo-U.S. Nuclear Deal: Seeking Synergy in Bilateralism*, edited by P. R. Chari (New Delhi: Routledge India, 2009), pp. 133–34; Sharon Squassoni, "Indian and Pakistani Nuclear Weapons," CRS Report for Congress, Congressional Research Service, Library of Congress, February 17, 2005; George Perkovich, *India's Nuclear Bomb: The Impact on Global Proliferation* (University of California Press, 1999), pp. 2, 430; Robert S. Norris and Hans M. Kristensen, Nuclear Notebook, "India's Nuclear Forces, 2005," *Bulletin of the Atomic Scientists* (September-October 2005): 73; R. Ramachandran, "Pokhran II: The Scientific Dimensions," in *India's Nuclear Deterrent: Pokhran II and Beyond*, edited by Amitabh Mattoo (New Delhi: Har-Anand, 1999), pp. 35–36; Raja Menon, "Nuclear Stability, Deterrence and Separation of India's Civil and Weapon Facilities," in *Strategic Analysis* 29, no. 4 (October 2005): 604; Zia Mian and others, "Fissile Material in South Asia: The Implications of the US-India Nuclear Deal," *Science & Global Security* 14, nos. 2, 3 (December 2006), pp. 117–43; and Bharat Karnad, *Nuclear Weapons and Indian Security* (New Delhi: Macmillan India, 2002), p. 617.

The dominant Indian position is that India's nuclear forces should be large enough to survive a first strike, thus deterring both Pakistan and China; and that a small but robust (and technically advanced) Indian arsenal would be sufficient. However, since deterrence is first and foremost a guess about psychology and mindsets, the Indian nuclear establishment argues that it must be free to adjust its arsenal to meet the rise and fall in threats.

This argument leads them to uncertain strategic ground. First, there is no sense in increasing one's nuclear forces unless the other side is aware of the increase, hence there is always pressure to maintain a large reserve production capacity to guard against future nuclear threats. Yet this capacity will be seen as a floor rather than a ceiling by potential enemies. This is the stuff of which arms races are born.

Second, "how much is enough?" is hard to answer as calculations of "unacceptable" damage may vary from regime to regime or from time to time. Will a stable, prosperous, and cautious Chinese leadership be deterred by the threat of a few nuclear warheads aimed at some of its major cities, or must India demonstrate the capability to destroy many more urban centers? The same calculation will have to be made in the case of Pakistan, where leadership is likely to be more unpredictable in the future. Will India have to destroy Lahore four or five times to show Pakistani leadership the gravity of its intention, should Pakistan escalate to nuclear use during another India-Pakistan crisis or war, or will a single weapon, or perhaps two, be sufficient?[15]

Third, will India have to plan for a contingency where it will be forced to use nuclear weapons against both Pakistan and China, and perhaps in the future, against Iran or another new nuclear weapons state, or even against the United States or another Western country seen as hostile to core Indian interests?

Finally, will the Indian government's threat assessment be accurate and reliable? India's judgment about nuclear capabilities, let alone intentions, of other states has often been at wide variance from reality. It seriously underestimated Pakistan's capabilities (and intentions) for at least twenty years. It exaggerated the United States' hostility for an equal length of time, and it has paid surprisingly little attention to China's nuclear program. It is also doubtful whether India and Pakistan have sound estimates of the number of nuclear weapons the other possesses or has deployed. Ambiguity may be dangerous in a crisis. Each side may assume that the other cannot escalate or has used all of its nuclear forces or is preparing to strike first because of limited nuclear arsenals. The relationship between two countries with adequate fissile material and inadequate information will be driven in the direction of a classic arms race. The situation is further complicated when China's nuclear arsenal is considered. Pakistan sees China as a deterrent to India; on the other hand, the China factor may motivate India to go to war against the weaker state, Pakistan, sooner rather than later.

If Indian strategists err on the side of caution, the risk of a nuclear arms race is somewhat greater unless the Indian government is more transparent about its nuclear ambitions and enters into discussions with likely nuclear rivals—China and Pakistan—about levels that deter, but do not provoke. It may take the Indian strategic community some time to come to this position; if it does not, an arms race or perhaps an arms walk, may be expected with steadily escalating numbers, more accurate and reliable delivery systems, and increasingly larger warheads—a scenario requiring a fresh round of nuclear testing. India could be one of the nuclear "big boys," a status that some of its strategists crave, but one that will not make India more secure.

Nuclear Doctrine

The core assumptions of the Indian nuclear doctrine after the 1998 tests extended the Sundarji and Subrahmanyam approach that India should seek primarily to deter Pakistan and develop a missile capacity to balance China while using diplomatic channels for other nuclear issues. In essence, India's nuclear doctrine has been one of minimum deterrence, limited deployment, de-mated warhead and delivery systems, and No First Use.[16] India has not chosen the nuclear war-fighting option with a fully deployed triad. This may happen in the future if the Indian economy allows increased defense spending and if Indian nuclear and weapons technologies improve. However, it is difficult to envision even the right-wing BJP taking this path, given the deep-rooted strategic restraint in the country. The dominant view concerning nuclear weapons among the Indian leadership is political. As Jaswant Singh has argued, "There is an inescapable conclusion to be drawn about the nuclear reality: of recognizing both the deterrent factor of such weapons and, paradoxically, their actual non-usability in conflict."[17]

India's nuclear doctrine, evident in 1990 but declared openly after the 1998 tests, established that India would await a nuclear attack before using its own weapons in a retaliatory blow. The philosophy underlay Prime Minister Vajpayee's statements and subsequent declarations by other officials. They rejected a first-strike nuclear attack against Pakistan. India's No First Use Policy, in conjunction with the threat of a devastating retaliatory strike, suggests that it would adopt a counter-city strategy if attacked with nuclear weapons.

The first few years of overt nuclearization did not raise questions of nuclear war fighting. Instead, as India and Pakistan continued to fight proxy wars, experience cross-border terrorism, and engage in skirmishes; it became clear that nuclear weapons could not deter these other forms of conflict. First Pakistan in 1999 and then India in 2001–02 sought to use the nuclear umbrella to compel the other to accede to its demands.[18] It is not clear whether the Indian establishment fully accepts the consequences of nuclearization at lower levels of conflict. The Kargil Review Committee Report, the most comprehensive examination of Indian security, denies that nuclear weapons had any role in the war.[19] The report assembled considerable evidence that Pakistan intended to pressure India in Kashmir before the Pokhran tests, concluding that the tests alone did not prompt Pakistan to use nuclear capability to re-open the Kashmir issue.[20] However, Pakistani officers interviewed both before and after the war saw the Indian tests as legitimizing the follow-up Pakistan tests, thereby restoring parity between the two countries. Many Pakistanis saw the possibility of increasing pressure on India over Kashmir through strategic parity.

Since the last crisis in 2001–02, Indian officials have placed greater store in confidence-building measures (CBM) with Pakistan. These agreements, however, are not regarded as credible by the Pakistan military. Although there have been CBM agreements concerning prenotification of missile tests, new hot lines, an inventory of nuclear facilities, and so forth; all have been unverifiable. Should there be another crisis, these agreements will probably be ignored as were earlier CBMs in times of great tension. India has failed to ensure Pakistan's adherence to a No First Use agreement.[21]

Given Pakistan's domestic political problems, India's nuclear pragmatists may have to revise their optimism about a "normal" relationship with Pakistan. If Pakistan should deteriorate further as a coherent state, India, more than any other country, will be faced with the problem of nuclear terrorism and rogue nuclear operations from Pakistan. The security of India vis-à-vis Pakistan is not determined by the quality of the Indian nuclear force, or the rationality of an Indian decisionmaking system, but upon the integrity of Pakistan's chain of command. Thus the lives of Indian citizens ultimately rest upon the calculations of the least reliable link: the least informed decisionmaker, the most extremist general, and the most rabidly anti-Indian politician in Pakistan's decisionmaking system. Deterrence must work with both rational and irrational foes. Thus states that begin by relying on a strategy of deterrence revert to strategies that include a component of defense, such as the antiballistic missile systems now deployed by the United States and Israel, and under consideration in India.

In contrast to Pakistan, China is a simpler proposition. India and China have a border dispute, involving a great deal of territory. The conflict has remained largely dormant, and both sides agree it should be solved peacefully. However, India knows it lags behind China, at least in nuclear and missile capability. Still, there is a slow evolution of India's China-oriented capability. One such new weapon is a missile that will reach high-value Chinese targets and could deliver the thermonuclear device claimed to have been tested in 1998. If India embarks on this course, Indian strategists will have to be assured that their own missile force and nuclear-capable aircraft are secure against a Chinese first strike. Even if there is little fear of a disarming first strike from Pakistan and considerable assurance that deterrence against Islamabad would be credible, there is uncertainty on both counts in the case of Beijing.

There is also the view that the Chinese threat can only be met by a sea-borne nuclear capability, preferably one mounted on a nuclear-powered, ballistic missile-capable submarine. The costs of such a system would be steep, but Indian strategists, especially those with ties to the navy, see this as the only way to secure second-strike capability vis-à-vis China, thus emulating American, British, Russian, Chinese and French arsenals. We discuss the newly floated *Arihant* nuclear-powered missile submarine in chapter 4, but note here that its expected operationalization, along with a tested and reliable warhead and missile, must be measured in decades, not years.[22]

In earlier years most of the discussion in India regarding tactical nuclear weapons was China-centered. As early as 1964 Indians discussed the use of nuclear weapons in the Himalayas to prevent another massive Chinese invasion. The introduction of tactical nuclear weapons along the Himalayas or in the disputed Aksai Chin area of Ladakh by either side could provide limited military advantage: a small nuclear weapon could have a significant military and psychological impact—and, in the case of a ground burst, a catastrophic environmental one. Besides air or ground bursts on military formations, either side could deploy nuclear land mines or use enhanced radiation weapons, which are thought to be in the Chinese inventory and may have been tested by India.[23] Such weapons blur the distinction between "tactical" and "strategic," if deployed on one's own territory—or territory claimed as one's own; they blur the distinction between the offensive and defensive use of weapons. As for Pakistan, its military writers have been thinking for several years about tactical (or battlefield) nuclear weapons, but Indian theorists consistently rejected them before Kargil. General Sundarji declared that India had no need for tactical nuclear weapons (against Pakistan), and a former Institute for Defence Studies and Analyses director, Jasjit Singh, derided tactical nuclear weapons as having "evolved" from cold war theologies.[24] He claimed that India must not place its confidence in tactical weapons, as "the artificial division of nuclear weapons into tactical and strategic is not only irrelevant for us, but carries with it the danger that a belief system could grow in a way that might justify the use and utility of such weapons for actual war-fighting."[25]

It remains to be seen whether the logic of nuclear weapons will be more powerful than the logic of restraint as far as India is concerned. The examples of recent crises seem to indicate that India and Pakistan have undergone nuclear learning, and are on the path toward a tacit nuclear restraint regime, perhaps limited more by technical capabilities than anything else.

Crisis Management

The many India-Pakistan crises have produced a debate over "red lines," shorthand for the limits of national tolerance and a signal to an adversary regarding the latter's plans to escalate. The problem is in determining what the actual limits are, and there have been several fiascos as one side or the other attempts to convey its national resolve or the precise parameters of its red lines. For example, in 2002 the director of Pakistan's Strategic Plans Division gave an interview to a group of Italian scientists in which he seemed to precisely identify Pakistani red lines; the interview had to be retracted, as Islamabad did not want to be too specific about these lest the Indians creep right up to them.[26] The Line of Control (LOC) is a particularly important red line. Never a permanent boundary, it was transmuted into one temporarily by the Kargil conflict. Crossing the international border or the LOC could be red lines, but this would depend on prevailing circumstances such as the physical presence of American military forces in the vicinity.[27]

India's and Pakistan's declarations of red lines may serve domestic ends but are of questionable strategic value, since full transparency on such operational issues could weaken rather than strengthen the fabric of deterrence. In any case, red lines may change depending upon particular circumstances. India has wisely declined to identify its red lines because any explicit description would indicate the limits of its tolerance, which, if crossed, would require a massive nuclear response. By identifying these red lines India would be bound to act if they were breached, thereby closing other options for responding to provocation. Defining red lines, therefore, is of greater value to the adversary for planning purposes; the adversary would then know the limits that could be reached, but not breached, with a relative sense of impunity.

As for stability, all new nuclear states tend to explore the limits imposed by possession of nuclear weapons. They push at the edges before backing off. This was the case in the U.S.-Soviet relationship until the Cuban Missile Crisis, and in the Sino-Soviet one until the Ussuri River episode. What does recent history tell us about the two main stability issues in South Asia, structural stability and crisis stability? Clearly, five major crises within a twenty-year period indicate a fundamental structural problem. Whether one attributes this primarily to the Kashmir dispute or to other causes such as India's rise as a major power, this region has not been stable and peaceful despite the common cultural and geopolitical heritage of its two dominant states.

As for crisis stability, South Asia's strategists differ sharply: some boast that relations are very stable (many Indians, some Pakistanis), and others that relations are dangerous (many Pakistanis and a few Indians). The "we are stable" school resents American or foreign interference, and also resents the implication that South Asians cannot manage their own affairs. The "we are unstable" school often exaggerates instability because it wishes to draw in outsiders into the region, or to blame the other side for dangerous instability. An interesting perspective is that India-Pakistan "crises do not progress linearly. The level of tension can move up and down, instead of constantly up, as many scenario-builders would have us believe."[28] The possibility also exists that either or both countries engage in assertive military action, assuming the other would be deterred from expanding the conflict into full-scale conventional war and nuclear exchange.[29]

After the India-Pakistan tests, there was hope for strategic stability in the subcontinent; stability did not prevail, however. The nuclearization of South Asia may have been expected to deter nuclear and large-scale conventional conflict between India and Pakistan. Nuclearization without normalization, however, moved the adversarial conduct into other channels, characterized by Pakistan's proxy war in Kashmir. Indeed, Pakistan's demonstration of its nuclear capability, in May 1998, emboldened it to undertake its Kargil adventure and simultaneously inhibited India from adopting a "hot pursuit" policy. India's frustration at its inability to convert nuclear capability into political or military advantage seems to have catalyzed thinking in military circles that limited war under the nuclear umbrella remains feasible. This is embodied in the development of Cold Start and other doctrines discussed in chapter 3. India has come to realize that while it sees nuclear weapons as political, not military, devices, it now gives careful consideration to the consequences of a nuclear war or even a nuclear incident. The task has been assigned to the new National Disaster Management Authority, which has a nuclear, biological, and chemical warfare section.[30]

Arsenal Management and Decisionmaking

One central feature of nuclear weapons is that decisions made in one state about control and deployment are of vital concern to other states. Issues seemingly internal to India fall into this category. The issues range from transparency about weapons security and safety, to developing a command and control structure that provides flexibility and does not tempt a take-out attack, to identifying the origin of a nuclear blast on India's own soil. India could be included in an international regime in which information about weapons radiochemistry is shared in times of crisis or catastrophe.

After the 1998 tests, Washington demanded that India and Pakistan develop a nuclear strategy with effective command-and-control arrangements. The request generated irritation in India, which had always prided itself on strong civilian control, and had kept its nuclear program entirely in civilian hands for many years. Above all, the question seemed to imply that India fell into the same category as military-dominated Pakistan.

The request was not frivolous even if it was patronizing. The United States and every other major power, including India's neighbors, now have a legitimate interest in the safety and security of Indian nuclear systems.

Further, beyond the technical difficulty of controlling nuclear weapons, special features affect India's command-and-control system, irrespective of whatever doctrine is developed. The integration of nuclear weapons into India's overall political and military strategy. These include the tight civilian control over the military and the consequences for India of even a "small" nuclear war or terrorist attack.

Civilian domination in India has important implications for nuclear doctrine and war fighting. As a matter of policy, the military has not played much of a role in developing nuclear doctrine or strategy. General Sundarji was one exception. Now, some serving officers and many retired ones speak out regularly about nuclear issues; all three armed services are jostling for control over nuclear assets now that the navy has embarked upon a ballistic missile nuclear submarine program.

The Indian government has allowed broader military participation in its nuclear deliberations, but it has not created a system in which the armed forces are in the position of making a decision to use nuclear weapons.[31]

India, like Pakistan, has created a Nuclear Command Authority (NCA) and a bureaucracy to service and supervise the development, deployment, and perhaps use of nuclear weapons. However, compared with Pakistan, India's nuclear operations are somewhat more shrouded in secrecy, and details are not always clear.[32]

In January 2003 the Indian Cabinet Committee on Security formalized an NCA and announced an eight-point Nuclear Doctrine that reiterated the commitment to No First Strike, a policy that was later clarified to exclude nuclear weapons states, and to keep the option of a nuclear retaliatory strike against a nation that attacked India with biological or chemical weapons. The NCA is composed of a Political Council chaired by the prime minister and an Executive Council chaired by the national security adviser. Policy guidance dictates that any decision regarding nuclear use is to be taken by the prime minister and implemented by the NSA.

On the military side, a Strategic Forces Command (SFC) was also established, reporting to the chairman of the Joint Staff Committee (the chairman of the Joint Staff is the senior-most of the three service chiefs). The first strategic forces commander was an air force officer; later commanders were both from the navy. The first served from 2006 to 2008 and the next from 2008 to the present. India's nuclear weapons are allocated to the air force and army; the navy has none at the moment, although there are long-range plans for a nuclear-powered submarine that would carry nuclear-tipped missiles.

India has moved steadily toward a full-fledged nuclear command-and-control system, but details are not known. Rumor has it that there are several secure sites in or near New Delhi, where the senior leadership can take refuge in a crisis, although given the openness of Indian society, these would be hard to conceal from a determined enemy. The military has its own fiber-optic communications system, which would presumably link both command authority and field formations. The NCA has a three-tiered structure: the Political Council replicates the Cabinet Committee on Security; the Executive Council is headed by the national security adviser; and the heads of the Department of Atomic Energy (DAE) and of DRDO and the service chiefs are members. The last tier comprises the NSA along with the service chiefs and the strategic force commanders. It is not clear whether the strategic force commanders will report directly to the NSA or to the head of the Integrated Defence Staff or the chairman, chiefs of staff, or their respective service chiefs. Given that India has just appointed a new NSA (the distinguished diplomat Shiv Shankar Menon), some changes in the structure may be expected. There is no evidence of how this cumbersome organizational arrangement will work in a crisis, and no drills have been held to validate the system structure.

According to one U.S.-based foundation that focuses on these matters, India's nuclear forces are not on a heightened state of alert; and nuclear-capable missiles, non-nuclear warhead assemblies, and fissile cores are maintained in a de-alerted state by the individual armed services, the DRDO, and the Department of Atomic Energy, respectively, with plans to reconstitute them rapidly during an emergency or national crisis.[33] The nuclear-capable missiles, bombers, non-nuclear warhead assemblies, and fissile cores are maintained in a de-alerted state by their respective custodians—the individual armed services, the DRDO, and the DAE — with plans to reconstitute them rapidly during an emergency or national crisis.[34]

The Indian government has entrusted operational control of India's nuclear missile force to the army. Although the air force flies at least two squadrons of nuclear-capable aircraft, the Nuclear Threat Initiative reports that it has lost the interorganizational battle with the army for custody of India's nuclear missile force.[35]

As for the hardware, there has been gradual improvement in the delivery systems and presumably in the weapons themselves. India has test-fired several liquid-fueled, medium-range missiles (the Prithvi II), capable of carrying a 500 kilogram warhead about 390 kilometers, with accuracy measured in meters, although the latter is unnecessary for a nuclear weapon of any consequence. The army has also raised several special battalions to man its Prithvi and Agni missiles.

This arrangement has been criticized. An early National Security Advisory Board recommended that India abandon its No First Strike Policy; this suggestion was rejected by the government and NSAB membership was subsequently changed. Others have argued that the National Command Authority needs more military participation, and that all three service chiefs should be added to the Political Council and serve on the Executive Council, even though the navy does not yet have operational command over any of India's nuclear weapons.[36]

Ironically, it is the weapons themselves that have created the greatest controversy in India, not over their existence or use, but whether they are in fact up to the standards claimed by government scientists. After the 1998 tests, India proclaimed that it had tested all the makings of a thermonuclear device, even though the yields were modest. This has now been contested by some of the lead scientists in the project, notably Dr. K. Santhanam, who has stated that India should retest to validate the design, and perhaps to assess new ones.[37] Only a few strategists and politicians support the prospect of a new round of testing, but the influence of Santhanam and others may make it impossible for the Indian government to sign the Comprehensive Nuclear-Test-Ban Treaty or a Fissile Material Cutoff Treaty; a more hawkish government may conduct more tests, certainly if another nuclear weapons state does so first.

Imponderables

The requirement of nuclear war, whether or not a state adopts a No First Use Policy, is that, at some level, the military will be put in charge of nuclear weapons, and decide how they will be used if communication with political authorities were disrupted or the chain of command broken. Further complications arise if a country adopts a policy of Launch under Warning or Launch under Attack without predelegation of launch authority. In that case India would require a widely dispersed civilian authority, with perhaps more than one civilian authorized to make a launch decision. Would such a civilian be fully briefed about possible choices? Would this authority include the president and prime minister? What if no senior civilians were able to communicate with force commanders? War-fighting doctrines and command structures are being worked out by India and Pakistan, but with short flight times, a multiplicity of targets, and a history of erroneous intelligence that has characterized all India-Pakistan crises, a measure of skepticism is justified regarding the confidence of some Indian strategists about the safety and security of the nuclear program, let alone the general feeling that nuclear weapons will never be used.

Every nuclear weapons state faces the same difficulties, but India's choices are more acute because of the high wall between the civilian establishment and the military. Nuclearization challenges this arrangement, not only because of the difficulty of communicating authoritatively during or after a nuclear war, but also because very few Indian prime ministers, and even fewer presidents, have had the kind of military or strategic background to make these decisions quickly. The experience of India's major strategic or military crises (Brasstacks and various border skirmishes with both China and Pakistan) indicate that on several occasions the Indian armed forces, despite civilian control, have exceeded their authority, or have misled civilians about the strategic situation. In one case (the Indian Peacekeeping Force in Sri Lanka), the military itself was misled by a civilian intelligence agency.

The task of arsenal management will be compounded by two other factors; although neither is unique to India, both may be more severe there than in most other nuclear weapons states. The first is establishing a balance between the requirements of secrecy and the requirements of deterrence. All nuclear weapons states must guard their vital national security secrets. To some extent, however, all must reveal how their systems operate, both to reassure the rest of the world that they are in safe hands, and to persuade opponents that they do have a deterrent capability. India's nuclear program has been shielded less from foreign eyes than from the Indian public, as was the case of India's chemical weapon capability, which had been kept secret from senior politicians and even the armed services for many years. The truth was revealed when India prepared to sign the Chemical Weapons Convention. In a crisis an insecure or uninformed opponent may conclude that New Delhi has plans, technologies, or capabilities, which have not been revealed, and consider a first-strike option.[38] Future Indian governments will have to strike a balance between keeping secrets and allowing outsiders a glimpse of their capabilities.

Command-and-control arrangements will be complicated by the difficulty of developing a system that will be "safe" against a variety of terrorist threats or false alarms. The reactors in Mumbai and in North India are within reach of Pakistani aircraft and missiles. Several have had safety problems. It may be difficult to tell the difference between a terrorist (either homegrown or foreign) attack on such a facility and a foreign military attack, or indeed a nuclear accident.

The security of nuclear weapons is also a concern. Not only are there widespread fears of theft of a nuclear device from the Pakistani arsenal (India presumably would be a prime target), the precarious security of India's own nuclear program was highlighted by the Mumbai terror attacks. One of India's reactors is sited on the water, just south of where the assault force landed in Mumbai. While the nuclear facilities appear to be hard targets, the ease with which the Mumbai and the parliament attacks were launched raises the question of their vulnerability.[39] While they are not nuclear weapons, some of these reactors will be producing weapons-grade fissile material or material to power India's new nuclear submarine and power reactors, and would thus be doubly attractive targets.

With a few exceptions, the actual costs of a nuclear war have not been the subject of public debate or government calculations. For thirty years those who dominated the Indian nuclear debate asserted that a nuclear war was unlikely as these occur when only one side has nuclear weapons (Hiroshima), or when nuclear adversaries foolishly compete with each other, recklessly deploying nuclear weapons and placing them in the hands of low-level officers or lending them to allies (the example most often cited is the United States, which allowed its allies to fly nuclear weapons on their aircraft, and once had large numbers of tactical weapons dispersed near potential battlefields).

A few studies do offer a rough picture of the effects of a nuclear war in South Asia. The most comprehensive—though it is the effort of a young

Indian scholar working with publicly available data—posits three levels of nuclear war and a range of outcomes. At the minimum, according to S. Rashid Naim, India and Pakistan would suffer casualties of half a million deaths each in a limited attack restricted to military facilities; at the maximum, Naim estimates about 17.5 million Pakistanis and 29.4 million Indians would be killed in a city-busting attack involving megaton-size weapons (these figures are for 1990 population projections; they also assume India and Pakistan have megaton-size weapons).[40]

India and Proliferation

Given its policy commitments and excellent past record, it is very unlikely that India will become an exporter of sensitive nuclear technology or nuclear weapons. However, this could change if global proliferation patterns were to alter. For many years India tried to become an arms exporter. Its defense industry was built with the expectation that surplus capacity would be diverted to foreign sales, thus earning valuable foreign exchange for the purchase of systems and parts not made in India. However, the overall impetus toward strategic restraint and caution, as well as the moral objection raised in India to such sales, inhibited this policy. Further, most of India's weapons (and nuclear programs) were dependent on foreign technology and operated at the pleasure of foreign suppliers.

Thus a policy of restraint on arms sales made necessity a virtue. This attitude seems to be changing, and the India civilian space industry has been actively pursuing customers. Several civilian systems, such as the Polar Space Launch Vehicle, have components, including solid propellant technology, with military applications.

Strategic benefits may also flow from nuclear exports, sales, or technology sharing. For years India has complained about Chinese nuclear and military assistance to Pakistan. The aid is believed to include missiles, missile and nuclear weapons designs, and even fissile material. North Korea has also sold advanced technologies to Pakistan. Although unlikely at present, a future Indian government, rather than condemn proliferation, may wish to share its own technology as counter-leverage to China. Covert assistance to Taiwan or to South Korea would make the point sharply, and while it now seems unlikely, India may help the Japanese move out from underneath the American nuclear umbrella. From the perspective of India's nuclear maximalists, arming such states would not threaten India, but would provide countervailing power along China's periphery, and would enhance Indian leverage vis-à-vis the United States.

To summarize, having declared itself a nuclear weapons state, India has to reconcile its own deeply held values and beliefs about nuclear weapons with the operational implications of being a nuclear weapons state. Morality and nuclear policy intersect in many ways.

One of the major reasons the BJP and many secular Indians supported a nuclear weapons program was to smash the image of India as a Gandhian or nonviolent country.[41] More practically, the BJP sought to undo Nehru's legacy with its emphasis on disarmament, peace talks, and opposition to nuclear weapons. By supporting the very weapons that the Congress Party of Nehru and Gandhi had for so long opposed, the BJP redefined India's national identity. The BJP and some members of the Indian security community have argued that even Gandhi would have approved of an Indian nuclear weapon on the grounds that it will be used to restrain the nuclear weapons of others.

Nevertheless, although India was never entirely Gandhian, it has not entirely rejected the Mahatma. Gandhi's political appeal rested upon his assertion of Indian pride and dignity. He argued that Indians had a special obligation to resist evil by nonviolent means if possible or by violent means if necessary. The greatest sin, for Gandhi, was to yield to evil or to collaborate with it by doing nothing.

If the development of Indian nuclear weapons fails to provide security for India against putative threats from Pakistan, China, the United States, or another quarter; then enthusiasm for their development and deployment will wane. The nuclear advocates will have to continually play up the external threat to win support for additions to the nuclear program, and argue that there is no other way to resist international "evil." Further, if non-nuclear threats continue—in the form of international instability, terrorism, or conventional conflict—Indians will have to examine the relevance of nuclear weapons to such threats that must be resisted. Indians may also find themselves in a situation where their own decisions have led to an accelerated development of nuclear weapons in their neighborhood. This scenario has not only practical implications, discussed above, but moral ones as well. For many years New Delhi had opposed treaties and regimes regarded as discriminatory, yet it now finds itself at the epicenter of nuclear proliferation. Should it ignore proliferation elsewhere? Should it join with other nuclear weapons states and signatories of the Non-Proliferation Treaty in a concerted effort to prevent further proliferation? In late 2009 Prime Minister Manmohan Singh announced India's support for a rene-gotiated NPT, a fanciful idea given the strong support for the treaty among major powers today.[42] Alternatively, should India accelerate the breakdown of the international nuclear and missile regimes? This would certainly generate active opposition from the major powers, and could endanger the special arrangements that India has achieved via the U.S.-India nuclear agreement. There is a tension between India's acquisition of nuclear weapons and its long-standing support of the international arms control and disarmament process.

There is a difference between the highly secretive, closed process of becoming a nuclear weapons state and the highly public implications of being a nuclear weapons state. The latter state will eventually become a subject of intense debate as the Indian public, especially in its major cities, becomes aware of the threats they live under, and the consequences of even a "small" nuclear war.[43] While the hawks were able to manipulate the debate in favor of "going nuclear," they may be unable to control the discussion after the first major Indian nuclear accident or nuclear crisis. Then other perspectives will re-emerge. India's anti-nuclear movement has actively opposed the siting of new civilian nuclear power plants; it has strong international support and is bolstered by the growth of global environmental movements.

India claims that it is a nuclear weapons state, but Indians have discovered that testing a nuclear weapon and declaring oneself to be a nuclear weapons state are technically and politically easy steps to take. India must decide whether it will be a major nuclear weapons state, whether it will maintain a very modest force, or whether it might some day eliminate its nuclear capability, like Brazil, Argentina, South Africa, and other states. Since all these options remain open, India's nuclear program continues to receive close attention by other countries. Whether this attention alone makes India a great or major power is doubtful. While nuclear weapons are clearly instruments of national prestige, India's trophy bomb will not impress other major powers with its military utility, nor does it seem to have much relevance to India's major security challenges, including those from China and Pakistan, its two nearest nuclear neighbors. India should be regarded as a great state, but in spite of, not because it has become a very modest nuclear power.

A nuclear state must make major changes in its military doctrine and reorient its strategy. These changes are not yet evident in India. The few Indian politicians with interest in such matters, and fewer still with expertise, are distracted by compelling domestic issues. India is likely to pursue a nuclear weapons policy similar to China's—a minimal deterrent, largely symbolic and political, with little interest in nuclear war fighting. Its new status as a nuclear weapons power has benefitted Indian diplomacy and enhanced national pride. However, it is clear that these weapons do not bring peace, that they provide new opportunities for low-level probes and conflict, and that should they be used in earnest, India as a modern state could be destroyed overnight. Although it may be too late to go back, it is evident that the trade-off between prestige and security remains an ambiguous one.

CHAPTER SIX

POLICE
MODERNIZATION

The main issues of military modernization center on the armed forces, but the most common threat to India's security manifests itself at home in the form of insurgency and terrorism. While tackling these problems is the primary responsibility of the police and India's huge paramilitary establishment—larger than the army itself—these insurgencies and terror attacks often draw in the military, notably the army, and increase the overall sense of unease and insecurity among Indians.

At the time of the partition and British departure from the subcontinent in 1947, several princely states were unwilling to join the Indian union and had to be forcibly integrated. Since then, the Indian Army has fought at least one major insurgency each decade. In the early 1990s, the army fought three separate counterinsurgency campaigns simultaneously in Punjab, Kashmir, and the northeast. Kashmir remains unsettled, but it is the rise of two new domestic threats that has increasingly exercised India's leaders. The first is a revolt across eleven states by marginalized tribal groups that is led by militant leftists, popularly known as the Naxalites. The second is the rise of Islamic terrorism in India outside of Kashmir, which government officials attribute primarily to Pakistan-based jihadi groups that have some support among alienated Indian Muslims. This chapter examines police and paramilitary modernization in response to insurgency and terrorist threats within the country. It is important to note that Kashmir, the most intractable of India's ongoing insurgencies, influences the issue of police modernization only marginally. The Kashmiri police have retooled organizationally over the last two decades.

Police and paramilitary, as compared to military, modernization has fared less favorably in resource allocation and technological upgrades. The persistence of the more recent threats could draw the army into yet another counterinsurgency campaign, potentially derailing its own plans of modernization, which require reduced internal security duty. Intelligence reform, a key component of the changes envisaged in the Kargil Review Committee Report, is predominantly dependent on police modernization, and India's intelligence services are staffed mainly by policemen. An internally focused police modernization is consistent with India's overall strategic restraint. However, to the extent that this effort is seen as eroding civil liberties, especially of Indian Muslims, there is the danger of inflaming extremist opinion in the country and among Pakistani jihadi groups who see another conspiracy against Muslims.

For several years Prime Minister Manmohan Singh has harped on the theme of internal security. In 2007 the Ministry of Defence acknowledged this concern for the first time when Defence Minister A. K. Anthony stated that the greatest security threats were the difficulties India faced in meeting the aspirations of all its citizens at a time of rapid modernization. Ironically, the Ministry of Home Affairs, not the Ministry of Defence, remains responsible for the problem.[1]

THE POLICING GAP

India has 142 policemen for every one hundred thousand citizens. The comparable figure for the United States is 315, the United Kingdom 200, and Australia 290.[2] Even the 40,000-strong Mumbai Police, one of the largest police departments in the country, is reported to be 15 percent short on manpower. Home Minister P. Chidambaram has stated that there are a quarter-of-a-million unfilled vacancies in the police.[3] There has been a low density of police in India since the colonial period. The British-run police system was thinly stretched, driven by crisis management, and known for its arbitrary use of power.[4] The police were backed by the colonial army, which was located in cantonments adjacent to every major city in the subcontinent by the end of the nineteenth century.

When the nationalist government of India decided to retain colonial institutions, it accepted the premise of how the state, including the police, functioned. The Indian Constitution gave state governments jurisdiction over their police, but the central government controlled most resources; subsequent developments have highlighted this mismatch. State police forces have languished while central police forces, especially the paramilitary, have grown. Central police forces and the Indian Army have repeatedly provided "aid to the civil" when state police have failed. Independence also exacerbated existing politicization. As policemen are appointed to key positions based on political loyalty, they are seen as serving partisan interests rather than the rule of law.[5] The criminal justice system, which provides the context of police operations, is widely seen as broken. Sixty years after independence, the police remain thinly spread across India, crisis-driven, and given to arbitrary action.

One response to inadequate police coverage has been the development of "special" task forces. The states of Tamil Nadu and Karnataka raised the first widely publicized special task force in the early 1980s against the infamous ivory poacher, Veerappan. The task force killed him twenty years later in 2004. In the late 1980s in Punjab, Central Reserve Police Force (CRPF) officers and troops seconded to the state police formed the core of special teams that targeted individual Sikh militants. Human rights and civil liberties groups have described these as India's death squads.[6] Eventually, the state police reconstituted and successfully suppressed the Sikh rebellion. In Jammu and Kashmir, the Special Operations Group (SOG), comprising select provincial constabulary and central paramilitary troops, has been effective in counterinsurgency.

The special teams phenomenon has spread to states such as Uttar Pradesh, Maharashtra, and Gujarat, which have used these teams to fight organized crime. Reliance on special teams reflects a choice to concentrate resources in a small, uncompromising team operating with some impunity. From time to time, the national government has provided resources for reorganizing the provincial constabularies on the condition that the reconstituted units— called India Reserve battalions—could be federalized on demand. The Tamil Nadu and Punjab armed police, for instance, have contingents in Jammu and Kashmir. One reason for SOG/STF (Special Task Force) success has been their access to critical local knowledge through a third tier of internal security organization of special police officers and village defense committees.

The institutional decay of the police has been accompanied by a more drastic reduction of resources than ever faced by the armed forces. Policemen are paid poorly, especially at the lower levels. On the other hand, the Indian Police Service (IPS), whose members hold leadership positions in the Indian police system, is a central civil service and has maintained a degree of parity with other administrative officers and the armed forces. Apocryphal accounts circulate of lack of petrol to transport prisoners to court or even shortage of stationery to register complaints. Station house officers receive small budgets and "raise" resources to run their offices. The state police forces do not have the resources to conduct investigations. When a serious crime captures political attention, investigative responsibility shifts to the Central Bureau of Investigation, a central government agency.

Most Indian policemen are unarmed. Officers above the rank of sergeant—subinspectors in Indian police parlance—may carry personal weapons. Most state police forces have an armed contingent organized on sections and battalions similar to the army's, though the rank structure of the police is different. These units are to this day equipped with the late nineteenth-century manual-loading .303 Lee-Enfield rifle.

There are also human rights problems. Uttar Pradesh's Provincial Armed Constabulary and Bihar's Armed Police have committed horrific human rights offenses, as did the Punjab police during the counterinsurgency years. Police throughout India are known to use torture, the accused routinely confess, and confessions are recanted in court. The conviction rate in the criminal justice system is woeful, though the judicial system shares blame for this particular failing.

The police in rebel states such as Kashmir and Punjab, in Delhi, and in the special task forces to fight organized crime and terrorism have been equipped with automatic rifles, but as the Ram Pradhan Committee Report on the Mumbai attacks shows, the antiterror squad of the Mumbai Police had no firing practice for a year before the attacks. Poorly equipped and trained policemen face highly committed terrorists wielding AK-47s, which can fire thirty bullets in a single automatic burst.

In instances of rebellion, the police themselves cannot function when they and their families must confront systematic attack by insurgents. In Punjab, Kashmir, and the Northeast, failure of the state police—and the state government—led to the induction of the Indian Army and central paramilitary forces. In all cases, but most visibly in Punjab, new leaders rebuilt the state police with central government resources. The latest incarnation of the police has emerged as a more militarized body. It has sought and received extraordinary powers, including shoot to kill, often on an informal basis but also at times formally.

Militancy in Punjab between 1983 and 1992 caused about 12,000 deaths, including 1,400 police, 300 paramilitary, and 50 army troops. During more than a decade of deployment in Punjab, the CRPF alone killed 2,551 rebels and captured 12,977.[7] Between 1990 and 1998, Indian security forces in Kashmir recovered around 18,000 AK series rifles, 7,000 pistols and revolvers, and 500 rocket launchers.[8] In Punjab, an estimated 10,000 AK series rifles were captured in the period 1988–94.[9]

Figure 6-1 captures war deaths in the eight counterrebellion operations in India between 1980 and 2004. While Punjab and Kashmir dominate the

Figure 6-1. *Casualties in Internal Conflicts, 1985–2008*

Number of deaths

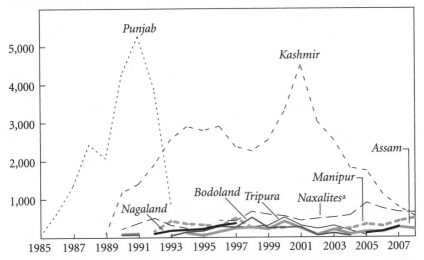

Source: Bethany Lacina and Nils Petter Gleditsch, "Monitoring Trends in Global Combat: A New Dataset of Battle Deaths," *European Journal of Population* 21, no. 2–3 (2005): 145–66.

a. The Naxalite violence is spread across a number of India's twenty-eight states. Geographically, the threat is concentrated in the states of Jharkhand and Chattisgarh, emanating outward to include West Bengal, Bihar, Orissa, Andhra Pradesh, Madhya Pradesh, Maharashtra, and a few others although to a much lesser extent.

counts, the sheer spread of political violence across India intensifies the country's general sense of insecurity (see table 6-1). Though the numbers are down, the violence in Kashmir remains. Between 1988 and 2000, for example, the Ministry of Home Affairs reported 45,500 incidents of political violence, including 16,800 attacks on security forces, 13,000 incidents of explosion and arson, and 10,000 attacks on civilians by rebels. As many as 8,300 civilians and 2,200 security personnel (most of them paramilitary) died, and 11,479 rebels were killed.

On average, the lifespan of India's insurgencies is significantly more than the average duration of civil wars globally—seven to ten years—since the end of World War II.[10] The Naga rebellion began in the mid-1950s and ended in the mid-1960s. The Mizo insurgency began in the 1960s and lasted into the 1980s. The United Liberation Front of Asom (ULFA) rebellion in Assam started in the 1980s and continues today. The Kashmir insurgency, which began in 1989, has now endured for over two decades. The Sikh rebellion in Punjab lasted for about fourteen years, from the late 1970s to the early

Table 6-1. *Violence in Jammu and Kashmir, 2003–07*

Year	Incidents	Security forces killed	Civilians killed	Terrorists killed
2003	3,401	314	795	1,494
2004	2,565	281	707	976
2005	1,990	189	557	917
2006	1,667	151	389	591
2007	887	82	131	358

Source: Ministry of Home Affairs, *Annual Report 2007–08*, p. 6 (www.mha.nic.in/pdfs/ar0708-Eng.pdf).

1990s. Dipankar Banerjee, the former Indian Army major-general who now heads a Delhi-based think tank, has opined that Indian insurgencies have a twenty-year lifecycle.

Though provincial rebels from Nagaland to Kashmir have long used terrorism as an instrument in their uprisings, the contemporary terrorist threat is a dramatically different construct.[11] The terrorism of provincial rebels was geographically contained to territory they claimed as their own. The government dealt with the old terrorism as part of a counterinsurgency strategy—isolated to rebel provinces and designed to secure popular support. Contemporary terrorism in India is more in line with terrorism prevalent in the West since the 1970s: decentralized, ideological, self-consciously symbolic, and a part of an international movement rather than a part of insurgency. The Indian government alleges that Islamic militancy, especially the Students Islamic Movement of India (SIMI) aided by foreign terrorist organizations, such as Pakistan's Lashkar-e-Taiba, are responsible for the spate of recent bombings in New Delhi, Bangalore, Hyderabad, and Ahmedabad.

No incident better marks the policing gap than the response to the Mumbai terrorist attacks on November 26, 2008. Ten extremists received training in Pakistan—the Indian government claims all were Pakistani citizens. They slipped into India's biggest metropolis and financial capital by boat and launched coordinated attacks on the Taj Mahal and Oberoi Trident luxury hotels; the main railway terminus in South Mumbai; the Leopold Café, a restaurant favored by tourists; the Metro Cinema; the Cama Hospital; and the Chabad House, the outpost of the Jewish Lubavitch sect in the city. Mumbai plunged into chaos and violence; the city police were unable to bring the attacks to an end. After three days the National Security Guard, an elite special operations force operating under the Ministry of Home Affairs, killed the remaining terrorists and rescued the last hostages. In all, 164 people were killed and 308 were injured.

POLICE MODERNIZATION PLANS

Historically, and naturally—given the resource distribution in the Indian federal system—police modernization efforts have focused on central police organizations. The first spurt of post-independence growth of central police forces occurred in the 1960s in response to external, rather than internal, threats. The threat from China led to the founding of the Indo-Tibetan Border Police (ITBP) in 1962. The force was intended for surveillance and special operations on the northern border and inside Chinese territory. The ITBP was recruited from acclimatized Himalayan communities and Tibetan refugees and received significant but short-lived U.S. assistance. Breaking from the past, the force came under the Ministry of Home Affairs, not the Indian Army, to facilitate coordination with the Intelligence Bureau (IB). India's largest paramilitary, the Border Security Force (BSF), was similarly raised after the 1965 war with Pakistan. The war had begun with Pakistani border incursions, and the BSF was set up to prevent future infiltration.

The BSF and the ITBP subsequently moved into internal security duty. The BSF's role expanded from border security to in-depth defense, which has meant counterinsurgency and counterterrorism service in the border states. In Jammu and Kashmir, the BSF served as the lead paramilitary agency until 2003. The majority of the ITBP has provided close protection to political leaders and government officials targeted by rebels. The ITBP's select recruitment has made it less susceptible to infiltration and a natural choice for this duty.

The Central Reserve Police Force expanded riot and crowd control and counterinsurgency capabilities through the 1980s and the 1990s, becoming a more mobile force and reconstituting riot control squads into a Rapid Action Force. In Punjab, the CRPF served as the lead paramilitary at the height of the Sikh rebellion. After the successful end of the insurgency in Punjab, the CRPF reverted to riot and crowd control, though it continued limited counterinsurgency in the Northeastern states. In 2003 the Indian government announced its intention to replace the BSF in Jammu and Kashmir with new CRPF units, returning the force to a more active counterinsurgency profile.

By 2002 the Central Paramilitary Forces included over half a million troops. The BSF at 191,000 was divided fairly evenly between border management and counterinsurgency. The force had gone from its initial 37 battalions to 56 in 1980, and to 157 in 2002. The CRPF, the second-largest, was 167,000, up from 15,000 in 1965. The ITBP went from the few battalions of special forces to 52,000 in 2002. The National Security Guard (NSG) in 2002 was 7,500. Taken together, the paramilitaries grew six times faster than the

Figure 6-2. *Number of Paramilitary and Army Troops, 1996–2010*

Number of personnel

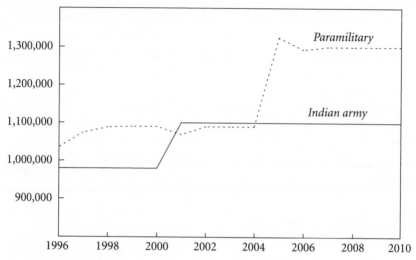

Source: Data from International Institute of Strategic Studies, *The Military Balance* (London, 1996–2009 [published annually]).

regular military between 1965 and 2002. Their budgets also increased dramatically: the BSF went from $246 million in 1987–88 to $330.3 million in 1996–97; the CRPF budget grew from $151.2 million in 1985–86 to $294.4 million in 1997–98.[12]

India's military participation ratio is still very low: 0.2 percent for the entire population and 0.6 percent for males ages 18 to 45. One report records a 71 percent increase between 1975 and 1996. In comparison, China grew 63 percent, Pakistan 64 percent, and Sri Lanka 81 percent.[13] However, India has seen one of the fastest expansions of paramilitary internal security forces in the world. Estimates are inconsistent because of variable definitions of the term, but India's paramilitary strength is widely believed to be over one million, representing 50 percent of the country's total men-in-arms and making India the second largest paramilitary force in the world.[14] In the last three decades, India has had the second highest increase in the ratio of security forces to the population in all of Asia; only civil war–torn Sri Lanka reported a higher growth rate.[15]

However, even this expansion has not been enough; the central police forces have been overstretched. A CRPF unit, for example, was ordered to move thirty-three times in 1987 and thirty-one times each in 1986 and 1985.

In the riot-prone city of Moradabad, Uttar Pradesh, a single deployment of the force lasted four years, from 1980 to 1984.[16] Between 1981 and 1992, the number of CRPF companies employed in the state of Uttar Pradesh alone rose from 50 to 208 (approximately twelve battalions or 12,000 troops to fifty battalions or 50,000 troops).[17] In the early 1990s, as much as 45 percent of the CRPF was deployed in Punjab alone. Though the CRPF was the worst hit, other paramilitary forces were also extended beyond their limits.

The Punjab Experience

Police expansion, especially as related to counterinsurgency, has been informed by the experience of managing the Sikh rebellion in Punjab. K. P. S. Gill, the Indian Police Service officer credited with overcoming the Sikh rebellion, has argued that effective internal security campaigns require a strong and independent police force and only a supporting role for the military. Gill has specifically criticized the army for its large deployments, which diffused the insurgency from the four border districts of Punjab into the rest of the state. In his second tenure as Punjab police chief, Gill subordinated the army and other security forces to his control. The primary task of the army in Operation Rakshak II, in 1992–93, was to seal the border so that rebels were cut off from outside money, weapons, and direction, and could not flee India for a foreign sanctuary.

While the Punjab police were greatly expanded in response to insurgency—indeed the expansion allowed the police to recruit and preempt young men from joining the insurgency—its numbers never reached the levels of the army and the paramilitary forces. Gill handpicked the best Punjab police officers and inducted a number of CRPF officers to create the superstructure for a new state police force. He added mobility, improved communication and firepower, introduced performance incentives, and created special task forces to target specific Sikh militants. Others have said that Gill inculcated a "killer instinct" in the police force.[18] These efforts paid off when the rebellion was finally quelled in the mid-1990s.

The experiences of Punjab led to elements of a new model of offensive counterinsurgency that was tried in Kashmir, not by the state police but by the army itself. Faced with the insurgency, the army was quick to separate internal and external formations in the state. Since the early 1990s, it has raised two corps (about 120,000 troops) of Rashtriya Rifles for counterinsurgency duty in the Kashmir Valley and the Jammu Hills. The army broke from the practice of border deployment to a grid system that assigned every inch of the state to a specific unit. Further, a new statewide unified command system brought all the agencies under a former army chief who was appointed state governor. Perhaps, the instrument that brought the army the greatest success was the Ikhwan militia, recruited from state-supporting ethnicities (the Gujjars) and later, reformed rebels. In particular local militias organized as village defense committees (VDCs) have been useful instruments of counterinsurgency. The committees are usually organized in sections of six to ten men, but larger and more organized militias exist as well. In 2006 there were 2,700 VDCs in Kashmir. Further, the government has authorized 30,000 special police officers (SPOs) in Kashmir.[19]

Naxalites and Maoists

While ethnic rebellions were self-limited to their nationalist groups, the Indian state has been challenged since the mid-1990s by a leftist insurgency called the Naxalites across eighteen of the country's twenty-eight states; a third of the country's administrative districts are affected by the violence. In the last few years there have been almost daily reports of attacks on policemen, government institutions, and political and administrative leaders. The worst-affected states are Jharkhand, Chattisgarh, Orissa, and Bihar, which account for 80 percent of the violence. The most notorious of these attacks occurred in April 2010, when seventy-five Central Reserve Police officers were slaughtered by Naxalites. This generated a public outcry close to that of the 2008 terror attack on Mumbai. Madhya Pradesh, Andhra Pradesh, and Maharashtra see some violence and Tamil Nadu and Karnataka have experienced sporadic attacks. The causes for the reemergence of leftist violence in the last two decades are contested, but it is clear that states that govern poorly have faced the brunt of the insurgency.

In response to the threats of insurgency, the Ministry of Home Affairs in 2000 set in motion a plan called the Modernisation of State Police Forces Scheme, which has focused on building physical infrastructure, improving mobility and communications, and upgrading weapons and training.[20] Apart from general improvements to the tenor and service of policing in India, the Modernisation of State Police Forces Scheme of 2000 sought to strengthen (1) counterinsurgency ability in rebel states, (2) policing on the Pakistan and Nepal borders, and (3) urban policing capacity in seven megacities including Mumbai and Delhi.[21]

In 2006 the Ministry of Home Affairs further constituted a special Naxal Division to coordinate state responses, a task force to bring together various union government agencies including intelligence and paramilitary forces and an interministerial group to direct and monitor increased development resources sent to the affected states.

The Mumbai Effect

As in the case of the Kargil War, the Mumbai attacks, especially the siege of the luxury hotels and the Chabad House, lasting three days, were televised in their entirety from the sidelines. The helicopter-borne rescue effort mounted by the National Security Guard on the Chabad House was shown on television. According to reports, the terrorists holed up in the Jewish center either saw the rescue effort on television or were informed about it on their cell phones by someone who saw it on television. All the hostages were killed, though we do not know whether this happened before or after the terrorists received information about the rescue effort. The Mumbai attacks rendered a shock to the Indian polity and policing system. The Congress government in New Delhi admitted to several lapses, replaced the minister of home affairs, and announced a series of reform measures, which are slowly making their way through the system.

The Mumbai attacks in 2008 produced an impact that the 1993 bomb blasts or the 2001 parliament assault did not. Whereas previous attacks in India had led to threats of retaliation against Pakistan, this time the initial reaction was one of disbelief and embarrassment. As the attacks played out on national and international television, the Indian police's inability to face a determined group of terrorists became painfully clear. The uproar that ensued caused the minister of home affairs, Shivraj Patil, to resign. Palaniappan Chidambaram, a political leader with a reputation for honesty and efficiency, replaced Patil. The Congress-led national government acknowledged the intelligence and policing failures and sought to overhaul the counterterrorism apparatus.

A number of intelligence and policing failures had contributed to the debacle in Mumbai. First, the terrorists had slipped into the country unnoticed using inflatable boats. According to the Ram Pradhan Committee Report, the Intelligence Bureau and the Research and Analysis Wing (RAW) had sent reports to the Maharashtra State police and the Mumbai police predicting a sea-borne attack aimed in particular at the Taj Mahal Hotel.[22] The Coast Guard and the Indian Navy acted on that intelligence, but were unable to find the vessels used by the attackers and gave up the search when there was no further follow-up to the initial intelligence report.[23] Investigations also revealed that a full five days before the attacks, the Kashmir Police had sent a list of thirty-five mobile telephone numbers to the Intelligence Bureau for monitoring, but there had been no follow-up. The attackers used at least three of the numbers.

Second, the Mumbai Police did not present a coordinated response to the attacks. The city had an antiterrorist squad, but did not have the command-and-control system in place to either synthesize information about the different attacks or to bring the right resources to the points targeted despite the modernization efforts of the last few years. In 2007 the city police had introduced a new incident command-and-control system created by a U.S. corporation.[24] The new system was supposed to quickly identify the location of landline emergency calls on a city map and direct the nearest police patrol vehicle to the incident. While individual policemen responded to the attacks, the police headquarters was unable to concentrate forces rapidly on appropriate targets.

Third, the Ram Pradhan Committee found that the Mumbai Police simply did not have the requisite guns or the ammunition to respond to the firefight unleashed by the fedeyeen-style terrorists. The report states that the city police modernization plan had been delayed by stringent procurement rules that required high-level authorization even for small and routine purchases of ammunition. The state and city police had created antiterrorist squads, but the committee reported that they were poorly equipped and that their members had received no firing practice for over a year due to an ammunition shortage. Certainly, they did not have the training to stop a terrorist attack. The procedure in place for the police stipulated firing practice every fourth day. The report showed that while state governments have remained on a shoestring, the central government has seen its coffers fill up in the last few years of growth. In Mumbai, the country's richest city, the police received its last supply of AK-47 rounds in 2005. After 2006 the city police received no ammunition.

Fifteen days after the Mumbai attacks, Minister of Home Affairs Chidambaram announced the creation of a national investigative agency and a coastal military command, an emergency response body called the Multi-Agency Centre. He also sought to expand the country's national intelligence agencies and equip them with advanced technology to enable improved surveillance and communication, and promised the establishment of twenty antiterrorism schools for retraining police and state-based police commando units to respond more quickly to attacks.[25]

The Mumbai attacks accelerated reforms, which were already in the pipeline such as the megacity and border policing initiatives. In the aftermath of the attacks, Chidambaram was able to secure significantly higher degrees of funding. In August 2009 at a meeting of chief ministers on internal security, he reported that the number of unfilled vacancies in the Indian policing system was down from almost a quarter million to 150,000. Rather than leave procurement to the states, Chidambaram has been looking at centralized procurement from New Delhi. Also in the pipeline are new intelligence schools to train state police in intelligence gathering and analysis. The central government also decided to extend the Modernisation of Police Forces Scheme of 2000 well into the future.

Technological Change

Since the 2001 parliament attack, central police organizations in particular have seen their budgets grow and their equipment upgraded. The modernization plan of 2000 provided central government assistance to the police forces in megacities such as Mumbai and Delhi to purchase night-vision goggles, global positioning and geographic information systems, surveillance camera systems, closed-circuit television systems, portable x-ray machines, vehicle scanners, and vehicle number plate identification systems. Mumbai Police had recently concluded the installation of the telephone-based integrated police response system that allowed patrol vehicle tracking and management.

In 2004 India also completed a fence to control infiltration from Pakistan across the Line of Control (LOC) in Kashmir. The fence, built in its later stages with Israeli technical help, has reduced cross-border movement.[26] The fencing was a physical challenge because of mountainous terrain and is technically complex: it includes sensors and electronic-monitoring devices for stretches of LOC that are not continuously guarded. The Indian Army's growing use of unmanned aerial vehicles is likely to spread to both the paramilitary and state police forces.

At sea, the Coast Guard is in line to buy drones for maritime surveillance, especially around Gujarat and Mumbai, where smuggling from Pakistan is common. A new head of the Coast Guard was appointed after Mumbai, an admiral on deputation from the Indian Navy, and pledges were made to give the Coast Guard new technology, planes, and surveillance devices, integrating them with the more off-shore capability of the Indian Navy.

Indian agencies have been particularly interested in improvised explosive device (IED) neutralization technology. The Indian armed forces were among the first in the world to be hit with IEDs. The initial response to the threat was to physically clear them from all travel routes. Every morning infantry squads would set out on foot with handheld metal detectors before vehicular traffic was allowed to move. Road opening parties still go out, but mainly to reestablish the outer perimeters of military encampments. By the late 1990s Indian forces had developed radio jammers to prevent the detonation of devices laid along its movement routes. The jammers did not always work, but combined with speed and good convoying practice, the threat of roadside bombs was reduced.

CHALLENGES TO POLICE REFORMS

The flexibility of India's federal system has allowed the country to manage internal unrest. The worst-affected states, Chattisgarh and Jharkhand, are new provinces created in the 1990s by partitioning larger states in an effort at greater political decentralization. The division of the administrative machinery and finances left the new states weak. These states had little in terms of industry and business except exploitation of natural resources such as coal and iron ore. The administration was weak because the best police officers and civil servants chose to remain with the older provinces rather than join the new state government. As it was, the pre-existing states of Bihar and Orissa were notorious for their poor governance. Although violence increased due to the reorganization of states, the insurgency was isolated, and the rising violence prompted the central government to support the greater mobilization effort in the affected states. However, police system reform has been elusive in India because it involves changes to the larger system and not just to counterterrorism and counterinsurgency capacity or police departments. Anand Mahindra, an Indian businessman from Mumbai, told an American television program, *The News Hour with Jim Lehrer,* that Mumbai should have a New York City–like mayor to put in place a modern security system.[27] Such a political reorganization is hard to imagine—the state government of Maharashtra, which administers the city of Mumbai as part of the larger provincial apparatus, is likely to fight any move to take away its biggest source of revenue.

Eight national police commissions met between 1947 and 1977. Their recommendations were repeated over three decades, implying that the government had ignored the commissions' recommendations repeatedly. The government even abandoned the pretense of reform after 1977. In 2000 the government constituted a new commission called the Malimath Committee to examine all aspects of the criminal justice system. The report of the committee lies ignored. It has not been released or even recognized as the new National Police Commission report. The last official report was released in 1977.

Though not publicly released, the Malimath Committee report has generated controversy. Civil servants and the human rights community have strongly opposed adoption of the report's recommendations. The human rights community has objected strenuously to the erosion of the rights of the accused, in particular to lengthening legal police custody, admitting confessions as evidence, and denying the right to silence and eventually the presumption of innocence. The report also raised the ire of constitutional specialists who think the committee's recommendations make the police too independent from the existing structure of governance and policing in India. The report recommended that a committee of mostly central government officials appoint the chief of police in states—a violation of the constitutional provision of full authority for the state government over law and order. An independent police force would reduce democratic accountability at the level of the state government. In a dissent, committee member and former civil servant Ashok Kapur argued that the recommendations of the committee raised serious constitutional questions.

For example, Chidambaram's proposed reforms attempt to centralize a variegated and state-based law-and-order mechanism, a prospect state governments have not yet weighed seriously. The national government's willingness to pay for the reforms will probably make cooperation more likely. However, states may react differently to the loss of authority. The reforms also demonstrated the problems that the central government has in pushing for change that is the domain of states. On the crucial issue of more police stations, Chidambaram can only recommend: "State Governments may augment the strength of police stations."

Civil Liberties

A central problem in internal security has been to create laws that promote counterinsurgency and counterterrorism efforts but do not compromise civil liberties. The opposition to the Malimath Committee Report from the human rights community is that the recommendations may be detrimental to civil liberties. India has a contested history of emergency laws. As early as 1958, the government passed the Armed Forces Special Powers Act to enable army personnel to operate freely in Nagaland. The act, ironically based on the emergency regulations used by the British to curb the Indian nationalist movement in 1942, authorized the army to shoot to kill, arrest, search, and destroy as part of their operations.[28] The act also shielded army personnel from prosecution for actions taken in the course of their duties. The act continues to be in force in various parts of northeastern India to this day.

When deploying the army, the national government has extended the law to other rebellion-hit states. The national constabulary forces in India such as the Central Reserve Police Force, the Border Security Force, and others are governed by their own particular laws, which give them a similar but lesser level of immunity. A series of "disturbed areas" laws further allow the national government to deploy security forces without the direct supervision of a magistrate, as is required for "aid to the civil" operations. In 2002 the BJP government pushed through the Prevention of Terrorism Act (POTA), which gave the police and security agencies broad authority to suspend civil liberties and due process. However, the Congress-led coalition did not reauthorize the law based on concerns of abuse, especially against Indian Muslims.

The failure to reauthorize POTA is a rare victory for civil liberties in India. In the past, Congress governments have passed several statutes curtailing individual rights. Indian courts have largely supported executive privilege, allowing all manner of special dispensations such as in camera courts and indefinite detentions. Many observers worry about the trend toward escalating state violence in India. Commenting on Indira Gandhi's terms in office, Kuldeep Mathur writes, "Her inability to get people to adopt the state's codes and norms led her to new responses—authoritarianism and harsh methods—that still ran headlong against the same brick wall. What is alarming is that this pattern of state response, in the face of its inability to enforce social control, is becoming more frequent. A vast state coercive apparatus has been built up and state power is linked to it through laws that may be authoritarian in character."[29]

Terrorist and Disruptive Activities Act (TADA), the predecessor to POTA, has been a source of constant contention. A news report in April 1992 reported 13,225 detentions under the law in the previous seven years, but only 78 convictions despite the easy rules of evidence. In 1993 state agencies detained as many as 65,000 persons, including opposition politicians, lawyers, and journalists under the law. From the perspective of the security agencies, moreover, the efficacy of the laws lies in their preventive potential rather than in their record of judicial effectiveness. While the militarization of Indian society is contested, it is apparent that the Indian security agencies are unable to effectively and quickly suppress rebellions in spite of the constitutional and legal framework.

The problem of preserving civil liberties is particularly important since erosion in personal rights, especially of Muslims, directly feeds into the cycle of alienation that has contributed to the problem of Islamic militancy in the subcontinent. Pakistani extremists see the Indian government as repressing Indian Muslims. The arrested Mumbai terrorist, Mohammed Ajmal Kasab, told his interrogators that his training highlighted Indian depredations against Muslims. More controversial is the collaboration of alienated Indian Muslims in the series of terrorist attacks that have occurred in India. The government has held the Students Islamic Movement of India as the main organization involved. However, there has been a problem of larger alienation of the community since the destruction of the Babri Masjid in Ayodhya in 1992. The Gujarat riots in 2002, which followed the torching of a train killing Hindu activists, strengthened the Muslim sense of vulnerability.

INTELLIGENCE REFORMS

The fate of intelligence reform hangs in the crucible of police modernization. Because police officers lead and staff India's intelligence agencies, the problems of policing in India also infect the intelligence function. Diverting resources to intelligence when basic policing tasks remain undone is difficult to justify.

India's intelligence agencies function under the Cabinet Secretariat, which was in the direct charge of the prime minister. The intelligence agencies have operated with considerable independence from the Ministries of Defence and Home Affairs, the frontline operational departments for suppressing rebellions. Real-time tactical intelligence is largely in the hands of the army, the paramilitary forces, and other police agencies. Most of the intelligence gathering, moreover, is from human sources, which can be of high value but is also often unreliable, especially under conditions where torture and intimidation occur. The focus of Indian intelligence organizations remains on collection rather than analysis. A key function of intelligence is to serve the cause of interagency coordination. The emphasis on collection over analysis means neglecting the coordination function. When sources and actual collection are the foremost concerns, there is greater tendency to protect those sources and possibly to see intelligence collected within that agency as more reliable and critical than that collected elsewhere. Greater emphasis on analysis allows counterinsurgency leaders to step back and see the overall situation more clearly. State-level intelligence is not priority. Maharashtra State's official Ram Pradhan Committee Report on the Mumbai attacks highlighted the dysfunction in the intelligence organization of the Maharashtra State police and the Mumbai police.[30]

The intelligence function also suffers from a lack of expertise as its work is not seen as a specialized function. The Intelligence Bureau is staffed entirely by policemen. The Research and Analysis Wing (RAW), India's external intelligence agency, has its own cadre of officers, but the agency itself is usually headed by generalist police officers from the Indian Police Service, the all-India civil service whose members fill practically every leadership position in policing across the country. Furthermore, there is no separation between collection and analysis, which may contribute to biased analysis of information.

The Intelligence Bureau, India's domestic intelligence agency, has been accused of partisan activity on behalf of the ruling party. There have even been allegations of illegal telephone tapping of opposition politicians by the Intelligence Bureau. Indira Gandhi is reported to have used the IB to support a radical Sikh leader, who went on to lead the Sikh separatist movement that cost her her life. When the army attacked the militants fortified in the

Golden Temple in 1984, neither the generals nor the IB had accurate information about whom they were fighting. In Sri Lanka, India's external intelligence agency, the Research and Analysis Wing, trained the Tamil Tigers, but could not provide the Indian Army with basic information about the training and motivation of the rebels during the Indian Peace Keeping Force campaign. The intelligence agencies could not even provide maps of Jaffna, despite almost a decade-long presence in northern Sri Lanka.

Post-Mumbai reforms have created a new National Investigative Agency, with some intelligence-gathering and analysis function. But more important a Multi-Agency Centre has been established to gather and disseminate information on a real-time basis. The center is designed to function as a "war room," that is, staffed and operating continuously. The government has also passed legislation that mandates the dissemination of information to state and local governments as part of the reform package. Lastly, the central government has encouraged states to set up separate intelligence wings within the police and to strengthen the Special Branch, which has historically been responsible for intelligence but has atrophied over the decades. In August 2009 Chidambaram also offered to open regional intelligence schools to train state police in intelligence collection and analysis.

Of all the police reforms, change in intelligence collection and analysis has the best prospects. It is a narrow and specialized function in which the government can train sufficient numbers in a short time. However, it is also true that no amount of intelligence is ever enough; the challenge lies in continuous reforms.

INTERNATIONAL COOPERATION

Finally, the new wave of terrorism, more than the rise of left-wing Naxalism, has catalyzed change in India's traditional reluctance toward international cooperation to meet internal security threats. The Indian government remains fervently committed to excluding foreign governments and nationals from "interfering" in its domestic affairs, and seeks no help or advice regarding its homegrown insurgencies. Yet for decades it has tried to marshal international support against Pakistan for its role in fomenting militant operations in India.

Until recently this has been difficult. Well-meaning outsiders have pointed to India's own shortcomings in Kashmir as it governs the larger part of that state. The Indian government has always taken the position that Kashmir is a settled matter and that the accession of the Maharaja in 1947 was irrevocable. This is not the position of the United Nations, the United States, or the United Kingdom, which regard Kashmir as formally and legally a conflict zone and refer to India's position there as that of the "administering" state.

India has worked closely with Israel, the United Kingdom, the United States, and others on intelligence cooperation. From Israel, India has sought new technology and training methods to improve the response of Indian agencies. With the United Kingdom and the United States, the relationship has involved exchange of information and slowly training Indian police and counterterrorism experts. Indian cooperation with the United Kingdom has been particularly significant in intelligence sharing on Pakistani militant groups.

The targeting of Western tourists and facilities in Mumbai was a breakthrough of sorts; nationals from twenty-five countries, including several Americans, were killed. While in the past America was wary of cooperation with Indian intelligence, Mumbai raised the level of cooperation significantly, as the FBI conducted field investigations in India and shared information with Indian counterparts. India itself is developing a high-technology interception capability and has provided data to Western services regarding Pakistani complicity in Mumbai. Although for years Indian officials have been highly suspicious of Western services that work closely with Pakistan, they understand that international counterterrorism cooperation is necessary when individuals such as David Headley, a Pakistani-born American citizen and agent for Pakistan-based Lashkar-e-Taiba, scouted out locations in Mumbai for the terrorists.

BEYOND MUMBAI AND CHATTISGARH

With the exception of Kashmir, the Indian government has generally viewed domestic threats as the domain of the police, and seen their solution in good governance and economic development. Whereas in the past the Indian Army was sent to quell rebellions, New Delhi has pointedly kept the military away from fighting the Naxalites and Islamic militants. The Indian Army supports training, logistics, and personnel. The hostage rescue team of the National Security Guard (the central police force used for SWAT and VIP protection) is comprised of soldiers rather than policemen. However, authority for the use of the force lies with the policing side of the government, primarily the states and secondarily the Ministry of Home Affairs in New Delhi.

The Mumbai attacks increased political attention to the problem of internal security and accelerated the process of intelligence sharing with foreign governments. The slaughter of seventy-five paramilitary soldiers and officers at Chattisgarh deepened public and official anxiety about this internal threat. Home Minister Chidambaram, who presented the great hope of internal security reform, has been burdened with balancing resources between the Islamic and leftist threats. Police modernization, with its implications for the larger criminal justice system and the Indian Constitution, appears to be troubled. Like military modernization, police modernization remains ensnared in a confusion of threats, strategy, and policy. Though state police forces are on the frontline of the fight against the Naxalites and Islamic militancy, state governments have not had the financial or professional resources to pursue police modernization with any degree of seriousness. In Punjab and Kashmir, the central government has led the creation of counterrebellion capacity after state governments failed. The Kashmir conflict continues, albeit with abated intensity. A solution to Kashmir may be critical to reversing the trend of police militarization in rebel states. Indeed, many police officers have also resisted the militarization of the police that accompanies counterterrorism and counterinsurgency capacity. They have argued instead for reforms that address fundamental gaps such as in the police-to-population ratio, functioning station houses, and investigation and forensic capabilities.

Can India devote massive efforts to domestic difficulties and project force overseas? We believe that the army is capable of both.[31] The institution is divided into an internal security army with a huge paramilitary auxiliary, and a potential expeditionary force suited for conventional ground armor warfare with Pakistan. However, we know that military multitasking reduces overall effectiveness. The quality of leadership required for each type of warfare is quite different. Past examples show that officers trained for conventional infantry and armor war who try to fight an insurgency are not generally successful.

The traditional Indian approach to insurgency and separatist movements has been to "hit them over the head, and teach them to play the piano," that is, a mixture of force and cooption. This takes time, but the method has repeatedly yielded results. Yet it is more difficult to apply this strategy because of the new links between the world and dissident castes, religious minorities, ethnic groups, ideological zealots, and tribes. These groups are now more successful in developing overseas and foreign ties (sometimes with neighbors, sometimes with a diaspora, and sometimes with human rights groups), making it more difficult for security forces to use unrestrained force. The Indian security leadership is acutely aware of these trends—it has some of the world's finest experts on insurgency—and of the prudent use of force and the overriding importance of economic development and political institutionalization. In a trend toward international cooperation, it now conducts intelligence sharing and permits foreign police and intelligence services to operate in India against specific, agreed-upon targets.

CHAPTER SEVEN

FIGHTING

CHANGE

In the larger historical and comparative context, India has managed its armed forces quite well. By promoting a relationship between the armed forces and the political community that was compatible with democratic politics, it avoided a takeover by the military—the fate of two neighbors, Pakistan and Bangladesh, and of many other Asian, Latin American, and African states. India is not a militocracy—a state ruled by the armed forces—nor are its policies highly militarized. There is little propensity to use force as an instrument of policy, and there have been regrets in cases when force was ill-used. India is not a culturally and socially militarized state: while the armed forces are praised and popular, they are not the fulcrum of Indian society. Yet it does maintain a huge military establishment—probably the largest volunteer army in history, and an air force and navy that rank in the world's top ten in size and perhaps quality. India's challenge is to shape the military to meet actual threats and to prioritize threats and opportunities, while making do with weak strategic guidance from political leaders. Our judgment is that the problem of India's military modernization, let alone transformation, is deep-seated. The defense acquisition system is in a state of dysfunction, which has been aggravated by the sheer magnitude of numbers involved.

The modernization effort is clearly led by the navy and the air force. The army's efforts are more problematic, as a massive ground war with Pakistan is ruled out by the presence of nuclear weapons. The navy appears to want one of each kind—a nuclear missile submarine, a modern aircraft carrier, a working cruise missile, but as service purchases move forward, little attention is paid to the question of jointness, or to the linking of weapons to strategic priorities—these weapons serve national interests mostly as defined by individual services. The navy also seeks a working cruise missile and eventually hopes to have a nuclear-armed submarine, but there is no discussion as to whether it can afford—or should have—samples of all kinds of systems.

MODERNIZATION AND ITS DISCONNECTS

Rapid economic growth has provided India with new resources to address its security problems. However, the effect of affluence is constrained by the institutional structure of its military system. New Delhi has been allocating more to defense since 2000, when its total military spending was $11.8 billion. In 2009 the proposed spending was $30 billion, a three-fold increase over the decade. It is remarkable that during most of the decade, Indian military spending actually fell as a percentage of its GDP, reaching a low point of 2 percent in 2007. The single biggest year-on-year increase of 34 percent in 2009 brought the figure back up to 3 percent of GDP. Still, the figure is lower than it was in the 1980s, the last round of military modernization. The quadrupling of the Indian economy allows the country to redress the problem that has plagued its security platform through post-independence history: the lack of resources.

The irony is that Indian military capacity does not seem to have increased in proportion to spending increases. Sushant K. Singh and Mukul Asher observe that the Indian armed forces, especially the army, have been exchanging numbers for better equipment without any accretion in capability.[1] "Policymakers tend to make only very broad and general statements on national defense goals that avoid future commitments. This is best illustrated in the ritualistic assurance by the finance minister during his budget speech every year that 'there will be no shortage of funds for defense, if the need arises.' [The] Defense budget is merely an allocation of funds with no clear relation to any national plan or strategy."[2] Certainly, India's military balance with Pakistan and China does not seem appreciably altered. At the strategic level, India may be entering a period of a missile gap with Pakistan.

There remains an imbalance among the services, and little or no serious integration of strategic planning, let alone operational coordination. The critical bottleneck, one unlikely to be remedied soon, is the lack of civilian expertise in defense and security matters, despite the proliferation of research centers and think tanks devoted to defense and security matters. Several of these organizations are tethered to one individual service, staffed by retired officers, and generally promulgate a narrow perspective. The venerated United Services Institution of India, more than a hundred years old, is not a modern research institute, and the government-run Institute for

Defence Studies and Analyses (IDSA) struggles to make itself relevant. As a former IDSA director noted, it is able to publish controversial research articles because senior officials in the government do not bother to read them.[3] Some of the most interesting and imaginative writing on Indian defense and security matters is web-based; much of it from the Indian diaspora.[4]

Though Indian power is growing each year, no single agency in the country combines military, diplomatic, economic, and intelligence capabilities into a coherent national strategy. There is no effective National Security Council. The National Security Advisory Board tries to shape the national security debate, but has no authority to assess progress; there is extreme competition among the services, and between them and External Affairs, the Defence and Finance Ministries, and the Prime Minister's office. As Teresita Schaffer notes, the Indian government rarely issues statements of grand strategy. Its national security policy has been based on dominating South Asia, countering any major threat that intrudes into this space, and deterring major threats from beyond.[5] The policy is vague, and strengthens the resolve to do as little as possible and as late as possible, with the hope that most seeming threats will melt away. As for parliament, its supervision and oversight were more effective in 1944 than they are today. Under the British, Indian members of the assembly could, and frequently did, force debates on defense and security issues. Today, only a handful of MPs take strategic issues seriously, and even fewer are interested in the military or the application of force.

The Indian emphasis on technology as the key to modernization and transformation reduces the incentive for organizational change. There is a glaring lack of expertise among political leaders and bureaucrats alike. The armed services approach organizational reform with great timidity; some deeply rooted cultural factors also seem to inhibit change, although Indian culture itself is not a barrier. After all, India has grown rapidly over the last ten to fifteen years, including growth in certain unanticipated sectors. However, the pace of modernization and access to technology will be the criteria that Indians will use to assess their new relationship with the United States. The underlying belief is that advanced technology is a shortcut to modernization, whether military or otherwise. Military modernization is not just new technology, but new thinking about strategy and security and the ability to implement good ideas; it also includes an attempt to meet an international standard of excellence, and a willingness to adapt foreign "best practices" to Indian circumstances. This attitude toward technology is notable within the scientific community, which has special privileges in the nuclear program and in defense research and development. It is also widespread among the Indian political elite, and makes up part of the Indian worldview—India lost its independence because of a technology deficit, so the story goes, and attempts by America and others to restrict access to technology resonate deeply. The 2005 India-U.S. nuclear deal was important in assuaging the sense of hurt and discrimination among the Indian political class brought on by a history of technology-denial, which had tainted the legacy of U.S.-Indian relations.

While there is new thinking about Indian strategic and defense modernization, there is still no framework through which to translate this thinking across the civilian-military boundary; among the services there will be more of the same. There will be incremental acquisitions, military unpreparedness, and a mismatch between threats and capabilities. Consolidation among the services will proceed very slowly. India also remains uncomfortable with seeking the means of strategic assertion. Although economic dynamism created a great boom in wealth, it is largely unconcerned with security and strategic policy.

India is not alone in this regard. Indian policy, like Japan's, is reactive, not strategic, unless one credits as a strategy the belief that India is fated to be one of four or five world powers. The Japanese, however, are fully covered by a formal American alliance. As we noted in the foreword, Japan and Saudi Arabia spend more than India on military modernization, but neither is in any sense strategically assertive, and both are shielded by arrangements with the United States; this is not the case with India.

India has not been able to set priorities in the strategic decisionmaking process. It lacks a strategy to deal with the most pressing external threat, Pakistan, and has not been able to determine whether it should develop the capacity to match China or accommodate it. Moreover, internal security, especially related to terrorism, will demand Indian attention and resources.

Above all, it is time for India to cease being an observer on the receiving end of security, and become a shaper of the international order. It does this now in limited ways through skilled diplomacy, powerful cultural influence, and increasingly economic power. But a modern military capability is part of the great-power repertoire. As Aseema Sinha and Jon Dorschner have written, "The path towards a major power role and status needs to be paved with more than good intentions and be accompanied by political will and institutional flexibilities that transform India's traditional emphasis on autonomy and self-reliance."[6] Nowhere is the need for will and reform greater than in India's defense and military sector, where there are three agreed-upon principles that inadvertently cripple any effort at military modernization.

First, there remains an emphasis on self-reliance and equipment autarky. The assumption is that self-reliance cuts costs in the long run, builds domestic

Indian capabilities, and, above all, frees India from potential arms cutoffs during crises, especially by the United States. This ensures that the Indian armed forces will be equipped with second-tier or untested equipment or, at best, the occasional off-the-shelf system purchased from abroad or by co-production arrangements, which are increasingly unattractive to foreign partners.

Second, the widespread assumption that the military can be praised but not trusted, coupled with the lack of civilian expertise in defense and strategic matters, means that high-quality military advice will not be available to political leaders. There may have been reasons for India's obsession with civilian dominance in the past, but it has come with a cost. As long as India defines "civilian control" as, in effect, civilian dominance over the armed forces, and allows the latter only a limited role in policymaking, it cannot expect to increase its efficiency in turning resources into power.

Third, one area where there is no conflict in military priorities is internal civil violence, although no coherent national (or even regional) strategy exists to deal with ethnic, linguistic, and now ideological movements pursuing separatism or greater autonomy. Thus the domestic law and order budget has escalated, and paramilitary forces have grown, although without a commensurate increase in effectiveness. Unsurprisingly, Indian politicians put domestic law and order ahead of the more conjectural threats from Pakistan or China, even after the 2008 terror assault on Mumbai and the April 2010 ambush of a battalion of paramilitary forces by Naxalites.

Keeping control, minimizing costs, building weapons at home, and prioritizing domestic security over international threats are all prudent choices, but they do not add up to a security and military policy that results in innovation, creative military thinking, or a nuanced understanding of the role of force in statecraft. Restraint was an acceptable strategy for an India that had no larger role and no corresponding ambitions, but Indian capabilities are slowly catching up with expanding Indian ambitions, and many states see India as a rising and therefore strategically more significant power.

Continuing Strategic Restraint

We believe that India will retain an approach of strategic restraint and caution, derived less from a shortage of resources than from a political culture stressing disengagement, avoidance of confrontation, and a defensive mindset. India is even unlikely to engage in UN Chapter 7–type peace-enforcement operations.

The overall thrust of strategic restraint is suitable for a country like India. The self-control of recent governments in the face of exceptional provocation is admirable. However, strategic restraint has critical drawbacks: it renders India unprepared to meet some threats, and it dampens reform efforts to better match threats and capabilities. The Indian system can be easily surprised because of its weak vertical and horizontal links, dispersed intelligence system, service rivalry, and lack of civilian expertise. These are the ingredients for future strategic surprises, complicated by the need for quick response, as in the 2008 Mumbai terrorist attacks.

At present, the critical issue for India's military capacity is less about the adequacy of resources than about their efficient allocation within a viable strategic framework. Can India have it both ways? Can it have a modern military establishment that meets genuine challenges without provoking neighbors and incurring ruinous cost? While there has been substantial (but still insufficient) public discussion about reforms that are necessary, we do not expect great changes. Although India is incrementally changing its military and defense posture, given the bureaucratic framework and lack of political comprehension of the problem, change is in fits and starts and outpaced by events. Recent reforms such as a move toward service cooperation or the creation of a system to provide integrated military advice to the political leadership have been only partially implemented.

Organizational Reform

At the bottom of India's modernization debate—conceptually and literally—and the most problematic to achieve, especially when it contemplates buying or building weapons, is the question of institutional and organizational reform. A whole slew of reform proposals have piled up over the last forty years. Decades ago the lament of Indian politicians was "implementation *hona chahiyee!*" [There must be implementation!]. This remains the mantra even today. Reform committees and the studies they produce are plentiful, beginning with the Henderson-Brooks Report after the 1962 defeat and continuing to the spate of studies in the 1990s, most of which were the product of just a few individuals. Many of these studies remain secret—and most remain only partially implemented. Even the official histories of several wars commissioned by the Ministry of Defence are unpublished. Only the Kargil Review Committee Report was made public, perhaps because India won that mini-war; but its recommendations have been only partially implemented. India remains reluctant to engage in serious official discussion of military reform.

Most countries divide and disperse military power to a range of agencies to achieve greater efficiency and control, but a national government coordinates the various parts to ensure effectiveness. In India there are two separate layers of authority in the armed services, and the political leadership has not prioritized the services or their particular functions. Interagency coordination is more difficult in India than in, say, China and Pakistan, where threats or domestic politics drive coordination. In this regard, India is much better off than failed states such as the Congo and Somalia, but closer to Indonesia and Mexico, where national governments also struggle with effective action.

The Ministry of Defence, the secretariat in which competing service visions of India's security and military modernization are supposedly coordinated, seems singularly incapable of fulfilling its functions. As one American official has noted, all but two of its eighteen joint secretaries deal mostly with procurement. Very few are interested in strategy, let alone reform, and even if this were their mandate, the Indian Administrative Services (IAS) officers seconded to the ministry lack expertise. Most of the best proposals for ministry reform have failed, including one to create a joint cadre of IAS and foreign service officials plus those in finance, who would remain in defense- and security-related positions for most of their careers. The Ministry of Finance has been notable for its lack of interest and expertise in defense and military economics for the last fifty years.

Coordination is left to the services themselves and depends a great deal on the issues, personalities, and ultimately budgets. From time to time crises have forced the Indian defense system to coordinate, but peacetime military change has been hard to prioritize and harder to accomplish. This ability of the Indian system to respond to challenges with a degree of coordinated effectiveness is a barrier against revolutionary action. Yet preparedness in expectation of crises is the essence of military modernization.

Given the early emphasis on technological modernization and defense autarky, Indian defense acquisitions are largely a by-product of India's strategic balancing act, as refracted through a process that emphasized reliability over quality. The most favored nations, the Soviet Union and Israel, provide good though not always great technology, but are viewed as reliable; and the military supply relationship has had an impact on strategic relations. France, another major provider, is also reliable, but is seldom, if ever, the cheapest or best supplier. India prefers to interact with these states largely because they are reliable suppliers, not necessarily because they provide the best technology or offer the best deal. In the case of the Soviet Union, links between Soviet manufacturers and Indian companies (and trade unions) are beneficial to the ruling Congress Party. This approach to defense acquisitions makes sense for a country that consistently falls short in its own weapons-development programs, even though the services are left in a position where they have to make do with what they were given.

The list of recent acquisitions is impressive, but obfuscates the degree to which they enable India's production of military power. There are considerable institutional constraints that must be overcome in order for true modernization to occur. First, India will have to procure these new weapons on a security-related time frame. Second, India's armed forces will have to overcome service parochialism and begin to work together. Third, the fragmented defense policymaking structure will have to be consolidated to bring all these elements together. The weak response to the terrorist attack on Mumbai is now the poster child of organizational incoherence—all of the personnel and equipment existed, but the system did not allow for timely deployment and coordinated use of force. India's systematic failure to anticipate and act beforehand is notable, but it is a price that the political leadership seems willing to pay.

The Armed Services

The Indian Army, with its size and budgetary heft, dominates the country's security policy. Though the Indian Air Force and the Indian Navy have grown in both numbers and budgets they are no comparison for the army's million-strong force. Though the army size has held for almost two decades, growth in the paramilitary internal security forces has raised the total number of Indian ground troops to two million. Moreover, the demand for troops is not on the decline. If the Indian military were to become directly involved against the leftist Naxalite insurgency, it would require even more troops. The troop requirements prevent military retrenchment, retraining, and the release of resources for capital purchases. In short, inability to resolve the identity crisis between constabulary duties at home and power projection abroad undermines the modernization program. The air force and the navy do not have the same problem, but the army's overwhelming size affects them as well: they too cannot grow beyond a point unless the army can retrench. Transformative change has to include the disproportionately large army and the patchwork of paramilitary forces built up in the infantry surge. A case in point is the notoriously inefficient promotion procedures across all the services; the navy and the air force cannot overhaul their policies without similar change in the army.

We were surprised their armed forces—professional pessimists—accepted the culture of strategic restraint, but they do accept it because it allows them considerable autonomy in how they organize themselves and prepare for war. A serving brigadier interviewed for this project, perfectly expresses the dominant view of most officers as: "Are we completely satisfied with what we have? No. Are we incompetent? No. Would we like more? Yes. Can we do the job? Yes."

In the meantime the services are basically on their own; they follow independent strategies and are ready to fight different wars. The Indian armed services have wish lists and not-to-do lists, and remain constrained by resources and politics. The three services and the paramilitary forces display strong institutional proclivities that have developed over years. This extends to the services promulgating war fighting and strategic doctrines independent of each other and without reference to any overarching national strategy. The profusion of doctrine has the potential for serious mismatches between the services as well as between specific service goals and national policy. The Indian Army's Cold Start doctrine proposes to undertake a short, sharp ground and close air–supported war against Pakistan that wins some bargaining capacity and increases the cost to Pakistan of its interference in Indian affairs. The Indian Air Force, however, is focused on strategic penetration, air dominance, and air defense. The navy, for its part, is searching for ventures as far as the Malacca and Hormuz Straits. The "seams" between the services are left unaddressed, notably the issue of air support for the army and naval reconnaissance, let alone a serious interventionary capability beyond the routine of UN peacekeeping. India has avoided peace-enforcement activities, especially after its misadventure in Sri Lanka. We discuss India's nonsupport of such operations in Iraq and Afghanistan in chapter 8.

As for service cooperation, the army demands jointness in ground operations, but resists the appointment of an official chairman of the Joint Chiefs of Staff who could come from the air force or navy. Future joint commands in India proper are likely to be headed by army generals, although those set up outside of mainland India may be led by one of the other services. India is some distance away from a Goldwater-Nichols transformation; the present Joint Staff is a token operation. In the absence of effective civilian leadership, the army will have to persuade the other services to adapt their own force structure and doctrines to an army-led doctrinal transformation.

These service innovations predate any overall, national assessment of doctrine and strategy—this is a case where attempts at innovation come from individuals, the armed services, or think tanks associated with them.[7] It was only in 2006 that the Ministry of Defence itself articulated a statement of joint operations. When the minister of defence, Pranab Mukherjee, said that the armed forces would be required in all future security operations to provide a full spectrum of security and an integrated response, his statement was more aspirational than operational. In press reports, Mukherjee was seen as "hinting" that India would set up more joint commands, and that the time had come for a "truly joint capability for the Indian armed forces." There were no further developments except the promulgation of a joint strategy to combat terrorism—which, in any case, has been deemed a police problem—and a joint amphibious doctrine.

In India the focus is on operational issues, not strategic ones. The air force, the army, and the navy separately implement national strategy. While their operational art is strong, the linkage to strategy is weak. This is complicated by a lack of direct communication between army, navy, and air force commands. They cannot talk to each other in the field; instead they must refer to headquarters. For example, Western Air Command covers the territory controlled by two different army commands; the navy and the air force had not agreed on strategy for the kind of maritime reconnaissance that might have prevented the seaborne attack on Mumbai.[8] After Mumbai, a dispute arose between the navy and the Ministry of Home Affairs as to who would control coastal defense and surveillance.

The army's response to domestic disorder is that it can modernize without reducing size. Extensive interviews with senior military officers reveal that the army has no choice but to fulfill both its internal and external commitments. The army's Prospective Planning Cell in New Delhi, which is supposed to generate and vet modernization ideas, firmly holds this view—partly because it does not possess the institutional authority to examine trade-offs between the different functions. In contrast, Gurmeet Kanwal, a retired Indian Army brigadier, made the dramatic proposal of retrenchment by bifurcating the army into internal and external security components. Kanwal's proposal is predicated on the idea that the Indian Army should evolve into smaller but technologically advanced ground forces integrated into combined arms and capable of offensive operations well into enemy territory. In the interwar period, the British Indian Army constituted internal and expeditionary elements, which also relegated the internal security force to secondary stature.

The prospect of bifurcation raises several questions. How would one divide the army? Who would go to which part? Why should those going to the internal security component agree to become a secondary force? Who will get the promotions? The internal security element will do more of the fighting and rightfully expect to be rewarded for its sacrifices, yet the external security force will be the premier service. In reality, the army already divides along these lines. An integrated command system actually holds the different parts together. Should this be broken into two, it would not be the same army. Moreover, India has already experimented with that option. The rise of paramilitary forces in the 1980s and 1990s in effect created a second army of a million men. Paramilitary growth has raised interservice rivalry issues with respect to deployment, intelligence, and credit-taking. The army raised its own counterinsurgency force, the Rashtriya Rifles, within its institutional structure but paid the price of "infantrizing" the entire force. Armor, artillery, and air defense soldiers are routinely assigned to Rashtriya Rifles, draining those departments of their cadres. Creating yet another force within the army would only result in more wrangling.

It is worth recalling that Samuel Huntington argued nearly five decades ago that no country could afford two military forces operating on the divergent logics of internal and external security.[9] Inevitably, one of the two logics will dominate, not least because the promotion system cannot accommodate both. This is true of the Indian Army: its ability to project power externally remains significantly lower than is suggested by its resources. On the other hand, the army has stayed the field against insurgencies for twenty years. The emphasis on internal over external security across several decades is not accidental, it is the outcome of political choice. India's political leadership has chosen to devote its energies primarily to internal security rather than to power projection. The modernization program therefore is not intended to take resources from existing functions but to add more resources from the growing economic pot.

The Indian Air Force, in contrast, appears to look at war fighting as a second-order objective. From all available indicators, it seems that the air force is at the forefront of the modernization effort, at least as reflected in the level of technology, the expenditure of money, and the diversity of imports. Its primary concern is acquiring visible technology leadership. This is reflected in its plans to buy large numbers of fighter aircraft—signing the biggest international arms sale agreement for a specific platform outside of active war. Not only are fighters the most expensive and complex weapons platforms in military history, but IAF's own doctrine emphasizes strategic strike (in which fighters play a secondary force protection role to bombers, which IAF has not sought) at the expense of ground support (in which fighters are vital in securing local air superiority).

The air force, created as an auxiliary to the army and tethered to an air support role, now sees itself in terms of "aerospace," a service that commands the skies and beyond. It pays token attention to its ground support role, but its primary goal is air dominance. The Indian Navy, meanwhile, has taken the most political view of its own role, emphasizing its presence in the Indian Ocean littoral. Its acquisitions are not driven by technology or the needs of war fighting, but rather, the ability to work with other navies, in particular the United States Navy (USN). These different approaches are present in modernization plans. The navy, never linked to the continent, is now freer than ever before to indulge in dreams of an Indian Ocean role, now in partnership with the world's leading naval power. While its role is limited regarding Pakistan, it sees itself as projecting power over vast distances via its visible fleet, as an adjunct to diplomacy, as a link to nonresident Indians or "persons of Indian origin" in the Indian Ocean Region (IOR), in its joint exercises with many navies around the world, and in an active "aid to the civil" role as disaster relief throughout the area. The new emphasis on energy needs has also enhanced the potential role of the Indian Navy. It can reach many critical sources in the Persian Gulf as it is widely projected to be a patrolling force (working alongside, but not necessarily in cooperation with others) for the sea lanes vital for its own energy requirements and those of many European and Asian states. In our view, and in the view of many who have studied India, the modernization process that rebalanced Indian armed services and reformed the national security system cannot be directed by the services—which understand the need more than anyone—it will depend on the government. But who in the government will take the lead?

Missing Leadership

In almost every interview conducted for this book, we asked our respondents to list contemporary political leaders and bureaucrats who they thought had a firm grasp of military organization and the linkage between force and strategy. Three or four names came up more regularly—previous defense ministers Y. B. Chavan, K. C. Pant, Arun Singh, and Jaswant Singh. Sometimes Pranab Mukherjee was mentioned, and occasionally a former or serving defense secretary was named. Invariably long-retired officials such as K. Subrahmanyam or P. R. Chari were noted. These two retired IAS officers have made enormous, albeit quite different contributions to the education of the Indian strategic community, but both remain concerned at the Indian Parliament's lack of interest regarding defense and military matters. Subrahmanyam has caustically noted that since parliament does not even debate the reports that have been tabled, other government entities or private groups cannot be expected to act more responsibly.

Without going into a detailed analysis of how a country of over a billion people has produced so few who understand the role of organized state force and its management, we believe that the very qualities that make India so attractive in the eyes of many foreign observers are also those qualities that subvert the Indian security and defense processes.[10] Samuel Huntington exaggerated when he contrasted the chaos and laxness of the American

"Main Street" with the discipline and rigor of West Point—arguing that the United States needed more of the latter and less of the former. There are parallels here with India. Can a state that is characterized by well-functioning anarchy ever acquire and deploy, let alone use, a modern military establishment in the service of a coherent national strategy? If strategic restraint and technology are the driving principles of the Indian state, then the answer must be no, especially if the system remains highly bureaucratized and permeated by the fear of reform.[11]

In a democratic state of enormous complexity, it is wrong to cast blame solely at the government for failing to reform itself. Reform will come when it has popular support, and it will be imposed on the government by a citizenry that recognizes the gaps and opportunities evident in the incomplete military modernization process.

While India is, if anything, a politically overdeveloped state, its politicians lack informed military and strategic expertise. The armed forces are highly professional and attuned to global developments, but they lack policy influence. The business community is acquiring expertise, and once it begins to produce weapons for the Indian military (and perhaps, for export), it can be expected to lobby heavily. It will be driven, however, as are all military-industrial establishments, more by the bottom line than a comprehensive assessment of national interests. Perhaps India's greatest strength is the greatest obstacle—a lack of seriousness regarding defense and military affairs and a strong belief opposed to military and defense spending, coupled with a tinge of nationalism.

A clutch of uncritical celebratory studies of India, its economy, and India-U.S. relations have not been helpful to sound analysis. If one were to heed such studies, there would be no question that India is the country of the future and that Asia's future resides in China and India. By implication, the United States must support democratic India in order to contain totalitarian China. The theme of "Chindia" has been belabored to the point where dragons and elephants rather than hard facts seem to dominate analysis.[12] Some of these studies have argued that it is the United States, in fact, that needs India to sustain its own economic growth rather than the reverse.

A major book by one of India's leading businessmen-thinkers, Nandan Nilekani, illustrates the gap between the India of the modern, advancing entrepreneurial class (Nilekani is one of the top figures of the IT industry) and a coherent vision of India in the world beyond the clichéd comparison with China. Nilekani offers a scathing indictment of governmental incompetence, demographic and environmental pressures, corrupt politicians, and bad educational systems as well as a visionary perspective on how sound management, science, and innovation can and should transform India. He does not, however, address any of the major security problems facing India or how the private sector might help.[13] China is discussed only in terms of "emerging superpower" comparison.[14] Senior Indian policymakers hold a more realistic estimate of India's potential, and the gap between India and China. As one former chief economic officer of the Indian government has written, the frequent lumping together of India and China makes sense only in that they are both very large, but this pervasive bracketing "too often masks critical differences between them and impedes a better understanding of the challenges posed to the world economic order by their economic expansion."[15]

Nandan Nilekani epitomizes the "techie" apathy toward foreign policy, security, and defense matters. These views are widely held in India's most modern sector. While the new class of modernizers do not underestimate the serious obstacles to Indian development, and may hold the key to faster and better growth; they are naïve about Indian strategic policy and how it handles complex domestic insurrectionist threats, international terror, the strategic rivalry with China and Pakistan, or the concerns of many states that would prefer India as a provider rather than a taker of security.

China and India are at present at different levels of development. China's fifteen-year lead is unlikely to change for some time, if ever. On current trends, India may match China's present economic scale in about fifteen years. Shankar Acharya writes that there is no reason that China will not itself triple. He observes that this differential may not be a bad thing in that the sequential, rather than the simultaneous rise of these two states makes things easier for the global economic community. It may also be a good thing from the perspective of strategic competition—the world has time to absorb China's emergence as a more-than-major power without worrying too much about a putative India-China rivalry, nor about the need to choose between them should their rivalry grow more intense.

Viewing India through the prism of advanced technology and emerging superpower status stems in part from defensive nationalist exuberance, and also the illogical assumption that if India has done well in one sector (software and business processing), then it can be assumed to do well in other sectors. Invariably, the example of the explosive spread of cell phones is cited as an example of the power of technology to transform India. However, we have yet to discover another example, except perhaps India's clever use of satellites for domestic purposes other than entertainment. For the most part, military (and social) modernization will have to rest on organizational reform, especially in the government itself. This has been the case in India's new and vibrant manufacturing sector, which was not transformed by technology alone but mostly by the adoption of modern organizational principles.

The technocentric approach to transforming India is misleading because India's talent and creativity is directed at the private sector, not the public sector; defense and security matters will be part of the latter for the foreseeable future. The view also contributes to the cycle of complacence, lack of preparedness, and surprise and shock after a crisis, with a subsequent post-crisis return to apathy and business as usual. India's lack of preparedness and interest in security and military threats can no longer be attributed to a lack of resources.

The expectation that private sector entry into India's defense industry will herald a different way of doing things is exaggerated at this point. There are a number of Indian companies eager to participate, some with foreign partners, but the government may not be ready to include them as full partners, nor to disband the state-owned monopolies and their powerful unions. Indian bureaucrats in particular are intensely suspicious of the private sector and its motives, and have stymied progress on this front.

The Nuclear Arsenal

India's most successful weapons project, even if it has taken fifty years, is notable for the organizational and doctrinal confusion that surrounds it. India has missed the opportunity to turn nuclear restraint to its own advantage. Its nuclear weapons policies are handled by a consortium of scientists and bureaucrats with some input from the services, which actually deliver the weapon. Its arms-control policies are made by a small number of Ministry of External Affairs officials. India is re-embracing the kinds of arms control and disarmament proposals that it once supported, notably Rajiv Gandhi's action plan, which moved beyond unrealistic proposals for global disarmament to the regional level, where India's greatest interest lies. But this thinking, plainly in response to new American initiatives, is unrelated to the fundamental question (for India and others) of "how much is enough": what the requisite minimum deterrent capability is for China or Pakistan, or the two together. Linking the two at the policy level would give India a clear diplomatic and political advantage, and might prevent the debacle of a nuclear Light Combat Aircraft (LCA), in the form of tentative plans to build an ocean-going strategic nuclear delivery system. Nuclear weapons continue to be regarded in symbolic terms; India neither embraces a hard calculation of deterrence nor has it adopted a strategy of reducing nuclear threats via diplomacy.

An unusual level of doctrinal confusion permeates the nuclear weapons program. The program is dominated by scientists, who have very little expertise in nuclear doctrine, let alone in planning to fight a nuclear war. This situation is accepted as nuclear weapons are regarded as instruments of deterrence, not as real weapons. How this view will match up with likely service demands for control over doctrine, as well as physical control over deployed weapons remains to be seen. Typically, the weapons are claimed to be undeployed and their warheads, in civilian hands, are not yet mated to delivery vehicles. It is only a matter of time before Pakistan declares that it has a truly deployed and dispersed nuclear weapons arsenal. India will then have to respond with a weapons architecture that involves the military in some way, unless it manages to achieve an agreement with Pakistan about continuing the present "nonmilitary" deployment of its most important weapon.

Meanwhile, the 1998 nuclear tests still fuel expectations of a dramatic break from strategic restraint. Hyperrealists such as Bharat Karnad and Brahma Chellaney and their service counterparts point to India's military weaknesses and advocate ambitious rearmament to secure India's status. The hyperrealist position finds practical resonance in the Indian Navy's modernization program, which includes aircraft carriers and nuclear submarines, as well as the ability to launch intermediate range ballistic missiles from the sea.

Intelligence

If the armed services are India's muscle, then its intelligence services should be the sensory organs that warn of impending dangers and report on how well current policy is working. However, in no other area is the stultifying colonial legacy more evident. In the past India's intelligence services were designed to gather information about threats to the Raj; today, by and large, the Indian agencies are still organized for reporting rather than analysis. Indeed, Indian intelligence agencies do not distinguish between the two functions, thus increasing the possibility that collection and analytical errors are mutually reinforcing.

While no intelligence apparatus in the world even approaches perfection, if one expects to prepare for the future without sound knowledge of others' plans and programs, the outcome will be very uncertain. Intelligence is primarily a predictive function that is bound to be imperfect. Few open-source analyses exist on the Indian intelligence system, but the Henderson-Brooks Report[16] on the 1962 debacle, the Kargil Commission Report on 1999, and the Group of Ministers (GoM) report of 2001, as well as writings by various retired government officials, suggest systemic flaws. There are no official studies of the role of intelligence in the Sri Lankan fiasco, where RAW was deeply involved in training the very force that the Indian Army was eventually sent to disarm.

The inability of Indian intelligence to adequately serve the political leadership affects the military planning and modernization processes. If judgments and prognostications of the future are flawed, no institution can plan well. It is here that the closed official culture debilitates the intelligence function. Given the nature of the problem, intelligence analysis, not collection or counterintelligence, must be conducted in an open system where the agencies benefit through osmosis from the general information that permeates the environment. Trends in stock markets, for example, have been used as a harbinger for a myriad of social phenomena. Whether Indian intelligence agencies study the Pakistani stock and bond markets in any serious fashion is doubtful. This is a double error because Indian analytical capabilities are among the best in the world and are one of India's great competitive advantages.

Advances in technology should provide a better system of sharing estimates and raw data, but fear of foreign penetration and disloyalty smothers such innovation. Additionally, the absence of a clearance system limits intelligence sharing; India needs both a system of clearances and graded intelligence access, with proper vetting for individuals and the inclusion of private or nongovernmental entities within the system. Such reforms, which have taken place in other democracies, now seem out of the question for India. Without them, intelligence sharing with foreign governments will be problematic. Yet, as Indian intelligence capabilities increase, notably in the multiplication of monitoring stations and the application of computers to data analysis, India will have more to offer. Still, India will not be able to move in this direction until it begins to draw more assistance and technology from the growing private technology sector; much new technology can be bought off the shelf and modified for government purposes.

A REFORM STRATEGY

Attempts to reform India's defense and security policies have led to the creation of new agencies, commands, and positions, which, when funded with new resources, are not controversial and quickly adopted.[17] However, there are other needed reforms that are not tackled and yet others that are addressed imperfectly. Coordination among the services and between the services and the government remains imperfectly realized while issues such as the creation of a joint defense chief for the three services are not seriously considered. That this state of affairs has existed over several decades suggests that the political leadership is not particularly concerned. This relaxed view of military matters comes from beliefs about the utility of force as an instrument of policy. If there is going to be change, it lies in the current massive increases in military spending and the new access India now enjoys to Western, particularly American, technology. But will change be characterized by the mere piling on of numbers or the blind emulation of what seems to work elsewhere? If so, then the system of strategic restraint, bulked up by new resources, will not predict or prevent new strategic surprises of the kind India has seen throughout its modern history, even in the last ten years.

India's rising self-confidence clearly contributes to the making of a new India, but advocates of military transformation articulate goals that place them at odds with political leaders who are largely satisfied with permissible additions to budgets, technology, and weaponry. India is changing in many spheres and in many ways, but military transformation may be too difficult.

Institutional continuity was part of the civil-military bargain that allowed the transformation of the colonial military—mainly the army—into a national armed force. What was good for civil-military relations, however, was counterproductive for the purpose of reforms. While the military as an institution found itself unable to generate political support for reforms—indeed there was not even the recognition for it—the political leadership stayed away from intrusion into military matters, particularly after the 1962 defeat.

The civil-military structure produces a number of second-order dilemmas. The military professionalism of India's armed forces preserves their institutional coherence and implies that reform can only come from the top—a prospect hostage to the vicissitudes of a flawed military promotion system. The economic boom has allowed the growth of defense budgets, which have remained unspent in the last few years and made India the biggest arms importer in the world. However, the present situation also masks grave institutional deficiencies, most of all in the indigenous defense research and development infrastructure.

The security debate manifests in military modernization in a limited way. Given that the debate focuses mainly on the choice of particular systems, budgets, and sequencing of purchases rather than the direction and character of military modernization, or rarely, significant organizational, doctrinal, or strategic change; most decisions are procurement choices. First, there is the choice to devote national resources to defense. In practice, this is a question of how much India's newfound affluence goes toward rearmament. Second, there is the choice to build at home or buy from abroad or work out some combination. The decision in this respect is heavily influenced by the place of prominence technology has held in Indian thinking about development. Third, corruption has slowed down and practically halted major systems of procurement in India. Other more far-reaching concerns about military reform remain unanswered. The debate is primarily a social one and produces a rebalancing of India's commitment to fighting internal and external security problems.

The direction of military modernization in present circumstances will not be determined by the demands of security but by civil-military relations, the pursuit of technology free of strategic content, budgetary politics, and procurement shenanigans. Put bluntly, the price of extraordinary civilian control of the military in India is military and strategic inefficiency; India has not struck the optimum balance between control and competence.

The peculiar Indian civil-military imbalance has rarely been criticized openly, but the Indian military is aware of its dysfunctional nature. One retired army officer, now a leading defense commentator, spoke for a number of his fellow officers when he wrote, "If India has to become a great power then Nehru's legacy of civilian supremacy in matters of national security must be abandoned. Just as the Indian economy was turned around by a group of technocratic professionals led by Manmohan Singh in 1990, at this dark hour, we need two cabinet ministers—one each for the ministry of defence and a new ministry of internal security—who understand what military options India can now exercise."[18]

What would a transformational project look like? It should deal with strategic modernization, organizational issues, procurement, and quality. As for strategic modernization, India must decide on the structure and purpose of its nuclear weapons arsenal, and craft an arms control policy that maximizes security and strategic influence. It may also re-examine earlier plans to develop a significant airlift-capable infantry force for rapid deployment to crisis regions in a peacemaking capacity, although the overall strategy of strategic restraint may prohibit this. It also may systematically examine the perennial question of dividing the army into counterinsurgency units and others designated for regular plains or mountain warfare.

Real organizational reform would involve the creation of an authentic joint staff and an effective chairman. It would rethink the traditional infantry structure that dates back to Lord Clive, and accelerate the officer training program to compensate for the huge shortfall, including the recruitment of women in larger numbers. It might also look at the cantonment system, which remains essentially unchanged since the British decamped. Again, this generalization is more pertinent to the army than to the other two services.[19] Most important, there is a need to educate civilian leaders—bureaucrats and politicians—about military matters, beyond the limited offerings of the National Defence College in New Delhi.

In terms of procurement and weapons development, above all, DRDO must be reformed so that it can compete with the private sector for defense production and research. The recent but belated attempt to improve DRDO operations was a major step in the right direction. All of the services would profit from force multipliers in the form of indigenously produced sensors and smart weapons in larger platforms, which engage the enemy from a stand-off position. The army and paramilitary forces certainly need body armor for infantry, and the air force could re-examine the model of aircraft procurement, which courts failure by pushing technology beyond India's capabilities. China may be an appropriate model, and Singapore as well, with their slow but systematic development of an aircraft-maintenance system that is integrated into the global aircraft industry.

Finally, India needs a stronger knowledge base. The top ranks of political parties, the intelligentsia, and certainly the business community remain deeply ignorant about defense and security matters. India vitally needs a core cadre of IAS, Indian Foreign Service (IFS), and Ministry of Finance officials who specialize in defense. It needs its MBAs and Indian Institute of Technology graduates to study defense and security matters and apply their professional skills where the bureaucracy comes up short—or even to be inducted in the bureaucracy itself—to produce a cadre of civilians who have direct familiarity with security and military matters. Another step would be the development of serious government planning and research institutions similar to those that now study economic policy, and as well a tighter linkage between universities and defense research. India also needs freer movement at the mid-level between "outsiders" and the bureaucracy, providing an infusion of new people and new ideas, lest the government fall further behind the transformed private sector. Women should be more fully included in the process, as is the case in other sectors, notably the new media and private industry. A greater openness toward women would improve the quality of the officer corps and the armed services as a whole.

A transformative military modernization would also have to rebalance relations between the civilian and military spheres, among the three services, between internal and external security, and between regional and global roles. No official document takes a long-term view of the balance between threats and capabilities, and how the latter should be shaped and directed over a long period. The mechanism for doing so is just now emerging in the shape of the National Security Council. While India's historical posture of strategic restraint makes threat prioritization less relevant, it need not make strategic surprise an inevitable occurrence. Military modernization is mainly the domain of the services. This is both good and bad. It is good to the degree that India maintains a Huntingtonian form of "objective" civilian control—each side has its own responsibilities and expertise, and the line between them is rarely if ever crossed. It is bad to the degree that while military advice is kept on tap and not on top, civilian lack of expertise permeates the system. Again, as long as India pursues a modest strategic policy, dominated by restraint and caution, this is tolerable, but if resources and capabilities grow rapidly, will expertise keep pace?

CHAPTER EIGHT

AMERICA
AND INDIAN
REARMAMENT

Over the last sixty years American attitudes toward the modernization of India's military and the idea of a strategically important India have waxed and waned. The Roosevelt administration at first sought early independence for India from the British, but later moderated this view in deference to its British ally. It did spend huge amounts of money to build up India's infrastructure, including airfields, modernizing the railways and the arsenals and the aircraft repair facility in Bangalore, then Asia's largest. Nehru chose not to build on this relationship.

Subsequent administrations (Truman, Eisenhower) valued Indian democracy and national integrity, and supported these with the largest of all foreign aid programs, but were irritated at Nehru's nonalignment and confounded by India's military stalemate with Pakistan, which had become a formal American ally. Very briefly during the Kennedy administration, a vision emerged of an India allied against the Communist (Chinese) threat, and New Delhi received large amounts of grant military assistance, sales, and some military production facilities. The Arthur D. Little Report, still classified, chronicled the effort. It was also in the Kennedy administration that the United States briefly considered encouraging an Indian nuclear weapons program. In the end, India's unwillingness to move very far, if at all, on Kashmir with Pakistan was frustrating; and after Nixon's opening to China, India was relegated to the strategic margins, and its special relationship with the Soviet Union confirmed that status.

The Carter administration zeroed in on India's sole military innovation and moved to actively oppose the Indian nuclear program. This policy continued through 1998. It was buttressed by the opinion that poverty-stricken India had no business rearming, let alone seeking a nuclear weapon. Why should the United States help one of the poorest countries (in per capita income) in the world to acquire modern weapons? India had been on the foreign aid dole for forty years. In the absence of a common strategic threat, there was no reason why the United States should encourage Indian military modernization. Doing so, administration after administration concluded, would also fuel an arms race with Pakistan.

Transforming the U.S.-India Relationship

In December 1990, Assistant Secretary of Defense Henry Rowen visited India, followed by a visit by the commander of the U.S. Pacific Command, Admiral Claude Kickleighter. Kickleighter prepared a proposal for expanded U.S.-Indian defense cooperation, including an annual exchange of visits, regular seminars and discussions, and joint training and participation in military exercises. A number of visits by senior Indian and American officers followed, and in May 1992, the two navies conducted their first joint exercise. These were efforts designed to help India modernize its armed forces, but they did not stem from a desire to see India evolve into a strategically more assertive state. The conflict with Pakistan still loomed large, and the United States was reluctant to once again arm both sides of an arms race. Nevertheless, the Indian interest in military-relevant technology was accommodated.

After India's 1998 nuclear tests, the Clinton administration engaged in the most extended strategic dialogue to date, a dialogue that took place before, during, and after the 1999 Kargil War.[1] We have discussed the 1999 Kargil crisis in chapters 1 and 2 in the context of Indian military reform efforts, but the crisis also had profound implications for U.S.-Indian relations. Until the 1990s the Indian services justified their requests for equipment as preparations for an American attack on India; almost all Indian strategists saw the United States as strategically hostile. The beginning of military-to-military cooperation in the latter days of the Clinton administration, plus Clinton's prompt, public, and strong support for the Indian position on Kargil, altered these perceptions. India found it helpful to have the United States in its corner; it was no longer risky to talk about emulating American military practices, even if suspicions remained regarding American policy.

The Singh-Talbott talks and America's forthright pro-India position on Kargil made room for an initiative by the Department of Defense, which proposed an increase in military-to-military relations, perhaps as a way of mending fences after sanctions had been imposed on India after the tests.

The George W. Bush administration eagerly picked up on these exchanges, although it saw India in the context of a larger strategic vision. Support for India was again strong in the Department of Defense, and Bush had come to appreciate India's strategic importance even before he became president. Defense officials such as Douglas J. Feith reiterated that the United States and India were "natural allies," picking up on the term coined by the BJP prime minister, Atal Bihari Vajpayee. Feith and others described the fundamental concordance of the two countries: the largest democracies, committed to political and economic freedom, protected by limited and representative government, with a common interest in the free flow of commerce, including the "vital lanes of the Indian Ocean."[2] With President George W. Bush at the forefront, American attention had also been caught by India's rise to prominence in the IT sector. There was an impressive growth in the Indian-American community, which many administration officials regarded as "naturally Republican." Finally, a shared interest in fighting terrorism and in creating a "strategically stable Asia" bound the two nations. Feith noted, as have subsequent Democratic leaders, that the relationship was somehow hampered by the cold war, but that India and the United States were now free to move much closer. Largely unfamiliar with Indian history and culture, many officials underestimated the core Indian concern with technology and autarky, and the still-powerful sentiment from colonial times that India should not be beholden to any outside power, especially one that provided military technology.

In 2001 President Bush sent a close adviser, Robert Blackwill, to India as the American ambassador. Blackwill's team, working with like-minded Indian counterparts, stitched together a vision of a truly strategic partnership between the United States and India.[3] Even the American rapprochement with the government in Islamabad after the 9/11 attacks did not alter the U.S.-Indian trajectory. In 2004 President Bush and Prime Minister Atal Bihari Vajpayee agreed to Next Steps in Strategic Partnership (NSSP), an agreement that formalized areas of bilateral cooperation and gave the relationship its bureaucratic legs.

The NSSP was a plan for cooperation between the United States and India on civilian nuclear activities, civilian space programs, high-technology trade, and missile defense.[4] Informally called the "glide path" by U.S. officials, it was formally unveiled on January 12, 2004, and led to expanded military-to-military training and exercises, and an agreement to look into missile defense (the only military components of the NSSP). During the first phase of the NSSP, the United States eased restrictions on the export of equipment and technology to India's space and nuclear programs, including the removal of the Indian Space Research Organisation (ISRO) from prohibition lists. After the initiation of the second phase in October 2004, both governments decided to accelerate the process, culminating in the U.S.-India nuclear agreement of July 18, 2005. This Washington accord between President Bush and Prime Minister Singh, which unveiled the nuclear agreement, also officially marked the end of the NSSP.

The NSSP was a breakthrough on many counts. It represented the first close military-to-military relationship between the United States and India since 1963–64; it did not end on a bitter note, as did the earlier cooperation; and it was explicitly intended to strengthen Indian technological capabilities in about fifteen areas, both military and nonmilitary. The Americans had by then learned some lessons on how to deal with India—not pressing New Delhi to act faster than the cumbersome Indian bureaucracy could move—while India understood the importance of occasionally accommodating American requests that went well beyond the demands of its relationship with other states, even the former Soviet Union. For both sides, the prospect of greater collaboration and cooperation was an incentive, not a threat, while the new economic relationship provided concrete evidence to both sides of the value of working together. For Americans, India was a new and welcome partner in a world that was increasingly hostile; for India, an opening to the United States had already paid dividends during the 1999 Kargil crisis, and the prospect of an easing or removal of barriers to technology transfer was enticing.

The 2005 agreement on civilian nuclear energy promised India access to nuclear technology while allowing it to preserve a military nuclear program. After ten years of sanctions, and decades of trying to pull India into a global nuclear nonproliferation regime, Washington accepted India as a de facto nuclear weapons state (NWS). Although New Delhi has agreed to prevent transfer of material between the military and civilian programs, technology diffusion through scientists and engineers will be hard to stop. The agreement liberates the weapons program from obstacles that prevented nuclear energy from becoming a major source of electricity in India. U.S willingness to rewrite the international nonproliferation regime in India's favor signaled a commitment from Washington to New Delhi that is unprecedented not only in U.S.-India relations but also in the history of arms control. The nuclear deal, therefore, is an extreme case of political pricing of a sensitive technology and has brought India closer to coveted nuclear technology than at any time since the NPT came into effect in 1968.

The nuclear agreement also led to optimistic assessments of the likely flow of dual-use technology to India's defense sector. In their anxiety over the slow pace of modernization, many Indians set aside their long-standing distrust of the United States and argued that the new relationship will clear the way for a flood of American technology into India. They decried the old Soviet arrangement as not having transferred any real technology, and looked to showpiece items such as a proposed theater-ballistic missile system to overcome resistance in the Departments of State, Commerce, and Defense bureaucracies to selling to India.[5]

Over an eight-year period there were four tests of the Bush administration proposition that India and the United States could be strategic partners and that India ought to be encouraged to be more strategically assertive, with American assistance. In three cases, one side or the other decided that cooperation was riskier or less important than going it alone, and the two countries took turns in saying no.

After 9/11 India was among the first countries to offer assistance to the United States in tracking down and eliminating the Taliban and their al Qaeda patrons. The Bush administration paid the offer scant attention, even though India had supported the Northern Alliance—the only force fighting the Taliban. Instead, Washington turned to Pakistan, judging it to be a more important ally than India against the Taliban and al Qaeda. Indeed, Bush policymakers privately warned India about its high-profile presence in Afghanistan.

Two years later India was invited to join the U.S.-led coalition invasion of Iraq. The outcome was inconclusive from an American perspective, but satisfactory from an Indian one. Americans described the relatively benign environment in which Indian forces would operate. India, some U.S. strategists argued, had a disciplined army, was a democracy, and had a long tradition—dating from the Raj—of working outside its borders.

On the Indian side, army headquarters was alerted for duty in northern Iraq; the figure of 18,000 to 20,000 troops was discussed.[6] However, no political decision was reached, and the cabinet and the foreign ministry did not give a definitive yes or no.[7] New Delhi was reluctant to place its forces under American command, and Washington never offered an alternative. There was also acute domestic sensitivity to the prospect of Indian forces killing Muslims in Iraq—this would have been used by the Left opposition and some Muslim groups as a stick to beat the BJP-led government. Pakistan's unwillingness to send troops to Iraq also figured in Indian calculations. If the generals in Rawalpindi were not enthusiastic about sending forces, why should India? If they did send forces, would India be bracketed with a longstanding cold war ally, like Pakistan, in a quasi-imperial operation against an old friend, Iraq? India had trained elements of the Iraqi Army and Air Force, and many Indians regarded Iraq as a fellow secular state, regardless of Saddam Hussein's behavior. In mid-2004, the Indian government, now under the helm of the Congress Party, reconsidered the decision. However, on July 7, 2004, Prime Minister Manmohan Singh denied in parliament that there had been any change in policy, and that his government remained committed to a parliamentary resolution against sending troops.[8]

A successful case of U.S.-India military cooperation took place immediately after the 2004 tsunami, when both sides joined in a massive rescue and relief operation that stretched from Indonesia to mainland India. However, it could hardly be called an act of Indian strategic assertion; it was perhaps a baby step in that direction. The cooperation was originally a four-power arrangement—involving the United States, Australia, Japan, and India—in part excluding China from a major role in relief operations. Tactically, the operation was a success, with India and the United States working together in a few instances (although not in India or in ocean territories that were part of India). For India, the most significant result of its cooperation with the U.S. was enhancing its own complex disaster relief operations. For example, Indian ships subsequently carried stockpiles of emergency rations, useful when the Indian Navy evacuated civilians from Lebanon in 2006. However, except for the initial exclusion of China from the relief process, cooperation between the United States and India was seen as a humanitarian, not a strategic, partnership. It did open the path, however, for similar operations in the future, and of course demonstrated Indian naval and administrative competence.

Finally, there was one major missed opportunity. In 2002 India could have been invited to join the Combined Task Force 150 (TF-150), originally a U.S. Navy task force, converted to a multinational effort with over a dozen navies to patrol the Persian Gulf and the Gulf of Aden. The original mission of TF-150 was to support counterterrorism operations in Iraq and Afghanistan, but it later expanded to counterpiracy. United States Central Command (CENTCOM) had wanted a moderate Muslim country in the operation, and turned down the idea of including India. Instead, India sent a single warship to the Gulf of Aden in 2008 in pursuit of a hijacked Thai vessel that had an Indian crew. This effort represents a major role-expansion for the Indian Navy, but it was trumped by the subsequent announcement that China was sending three ships to the region, and virtually forgotten when it was discovered that a terrorist group had sailed undetected from Karachi to Mumbai in November 2008.

India has shown consistency in saying no or maybe, but not yes to any major collaboration with the United States involving the use of force—or with any other power for that matter. The United States did not go out of its way to accommodate Indian political sensitivities regarding an Indian military presence in either Iraq or Afghanistan, and the Indian government found it far easier to pursue a separate policy in each case rather than to negotiate a satisfactory arrangement for both the United States and domestic critics.

The Bush years stand apart for the degree of American willingness to accommodate India's desire for advanced technology; however, there was little in the way of strategic reciprocity. Still, in a long-term context, much was accomplished. India received technology and some advanced weapons without having to make any major strategic concessions. As a senior American intelligence official noted, "On the global stage, Indian leaders will continue to follow an independent course characterized by economic and political pragmatism. New Delhi will not automatically support or oppose positions favored by the United States or any other major power."[9] India's caution should not be used to predict the future; these were the first efforts at cooperation between two states that had until recently regarded each other as hostile at worst and irrelevant at best.

An important study by the American consulting firm Booz Allen Hamilton notes limited progress in the Bush years in developing a "more robust strategic framework and a shared vision that is promoted by the senior leadership in both countries."[10] The report observed that both American and Indian interviewees proposed that "the relationship needs a strategic framework." Yet its content turns out to be a very long list of bilateral and multilateral issues, many dealing with the difficulties of communication between both sides. The "common strategic vision" is not focused on the China threat, nor do Americans and Indians agree that it is Pakistan. We regard as naïve the view that somehow the cold war was a barrier to good ties between the two countries—a notion embedded in the oft-heard software-derived metaphor that that period was version 1.0, whereas the Clinton-Bush years led to version 2.0. India and the United States were divided by more than the cold war; there were, and remain, differing visions of a just world order. Wide differences persist, notably in matters pertaining to the world economic order and global energy and environment, although these may have narrowed somewhat as Americans and Indians understand their need to cooperate on these issues.

On balance, the Bush administration's willingness to engage in technology transfer while pursuing strategic cooperation benefitted both India and

America. During those eight years, India was no longer subjected to American pressure on Kashmir or on global arms control issues. The former was assured by the American policy of "de-hyphenation," which separated the United States' India policy from its Pakistan policy; the latter was characterized by the Bush administration's distaste for arms control.

New Opportunities

What are the opportunities for the Obama administration in shaping its India policy, especially in relation to some of the insights about India's military modernization strategies that we have explored in this book? The tendency to assume a direct correlation between Indian economic success and a U.S.-Indian strategic alliance should be avoided, and steady assistance should be offered in India's military modernization.

It should not be assumed that India's stunning economic rise automatically implies a U.S.-India strategic alliance, let alone a technology alliance or the justification for an expanded transfer of military technology to India. This cheerleader approach to understanding Indian strategy assumes too much, most of it improbable. The steadying factor should be U.S. assistance for India's military modernization in those areas where likely Indian actions and interests match up or are compatible with known American ones. Enhancing India's peacekeeping capabilities, or even its ability to engage in peacemaking operations, strengthening its capabilities against domestic terrorism and separatist groups, and cooperating with India to deter terror attacks are actions that are in the United States' interests. Fostering an open-ended nuclear or conventional arms race between India and its neighbors is not. Improving the efficiency of the Indian defense policy process is a worthwhile—if difficult—goal; the question here is how amenable the system will be to reform.

The Obama administration must also change the transitive nature of American policy toward India. Obama came to office believing that Afghanistan was the central front in the struggle against radical Islamist terrorism; thus Pakistan was also critical. India was important to the degree that it influenced Pakistani policy. Obama administration spokesmen have frequently cited the need for India-Pakistan normalization so that Pakistan can devote its full energies to the fight in its western provinces and continue to support American efforts in Afghanistan. This approach has relegated India to a tertiary role, although a highly visible state visit and many encouraging statements have attempted to soften that message.

While there are many new opportunities for the United States, including some arenas opened up by the Bush administration, the Obama administration's major strategic tasks are to reintegrate India into an overall South Asian policy and persuade New Delhi to return to India's earlier commitment to larger arms control endeavors. However, in the words of an experienced South Asia observer, Ashley Tellis, after the White House visit of Prime Minister Manmohan Singh in November 2009, "India is viewed by the White House as mostly peripheral: Important in itself, no doubt, but no longer a pressing geopolitical priority."[11]

What, then, might be the best path forward for the Obama administration as it seeks to build upon the accomplishments of its predecessor yet pursue policies that are both realistic and in accord with its own different priorities in South Asia and the world? We see many areas of strategic cooperation beyond the long list of subjects that now form the core of the U.S.-Indian relationship.[12] First, the United States should move smartly ahead with the Bush administration's agenda of strengthening the Indian military through technology transfers and weapons sales. While a growing and increasingly confident India is in American interests, military modernization and strategic cooperation will not by themselves sustain a new relationship. Technology transfer as the main means of modernization will certainly fail to address India's deeper modernization problems, which are fundamentally organizational. It will require more statecraft than hardware to extricate the Indian military from the position of simultaneously fighting several small wars on the home front while preparing to fight two big ones against nuclear-armed neighbors. Additionally, power projection of a sort that might complement American interests in stabilizing adjacent regions has a low ranking on the Indian military agenda. Placing military modernization at the center of the relationship invites failure, as some technologies will not pan out, others are better met by non-U.S. sources, and reciprocity is very limited—it will be hard for offsets to rectify the imbalance between American high technology and the Indian economy.[13] That said, the United States should continue to accelerate the process of technology transfer; this is critically important from the Indian perspective (even if, in our view, overblown), and India should not be the last state among friendly countries to receive a specific technology.

Second, these programs should be structured so as to facilitate the reform of Indian defense structures and processes. India is too important a state to be regarded simply as a cash cow when it comes to arms sales and technology transfer. As the relationship grows closer, this will be easier to do. Thus the arms sales and technology transfer processes should not be driven solely by the needs of the American arms industry, although a profitable relationship, given India's overall arms requirements, is certainly possible.

Third, whether or not any single weapons system will create dangerous regional or global imbalances, the existence of a nuclear deterrent between India and two of its neighbors has made it difficult for India to use its conventional superiority to break out of the pattern of strategic restraint. While an enhanced Indian military capability will add to that nation's pride and confidence, and might increase its power-projection capability, it will not fundamentally change the regional balance of power. The United States should not attempt to "balance" (that is, treat equally) India and Pakistan, nor conversely should it take too seriously Indian complaints that Washington is arming a rogue Pakistan.

Fourth, modernizing India's defense and strategic organization is potentially more promising but also more difficult. What works in the United States has to be adapted to a different culture and society, one where the military has been segregated from society for many years. American patterns and models of defense production may not always be the best ones for India. That said, American military professional practices, especially the capacity for self-study and retrospective study of success and failure, could facilitate Indian military modernization. This is why International Military Education and Training (IMET) and other training programs are critical to the relationship: it is vital that Indian military personnel, but even more important, Indian bureaucrats and administrators and, if possible, politicians, gain firsthand familiarity with American defense and strategic planning. This is easier said than done: as long ago as 1987, attempts were made to have simple policy planning talks between the United States and India, but India's Ministry of External Affairs lacked the capacity to engage at this level. Apparently this is still true compared to, say, China, with which the United States has a far wider range of dialogues than India. A former U.S. official notes that "America's dialogue with India has been less global than with any other major power, even China, with whom the United States has held three rounds of dialogue on Africa, three on Central Asia, multiple rounds on South Asia, even a dialogue on Latin America. Not so with India, which last year declined a U.S. proposal for such regional dialogues. Nor do the United States and India coordinate their foreign aid, even though India has become a donor to Africa and elsewhere."[14]

Fifth, joint exercises between American and Indian services should be expanded.[15] While these cannot substitute for a shared strategic vision, they do serve a number of secondary goals. One, of course, is that Indians become familiar with U.S. equipment while Americans learn more about the operational characteristics of former Soviet/Russian equipment used by competent professionals. Further, exercises lay down a base for future cooperation. Officers come to know each other better, differences in implementation are worked out, and the limits and capabilities of each side are better understood. There may not be an immediate strategic payoff, but in an uncertain world these exercises would facilitate the armed services of both states to work together in some future contingency.

Sixth, the most promising areas will be cooperation between the navies, and the transfer of naval technology and navy-related skills. Navy-to-navy cooperation was notable in the joint operations during the tsunami rescue and relief operation. It not only familiarized both sides with each others' practices, it encouraged the Indian Navy to move toward multipurpose platforms, which could be used for disaster relief, off-shore power projection, and other tasks. In its first year as an Indian ship, the INS *Jalashwa* spent 200 days at sea, a remarkable accomplishment. There are plans afoot to sell India the newer version of this class of vessel, which would greatly strengthen India's power projection. This would also involve an important transfer of nonsensitive technology to India as new vessels are constructed along modular lines, whereas all Indian shipyards construct vessels in slipways. This is not cutting-edge shipbuilding technology—it is already used by South Korea and Japan, two American allies. Another example of naval cooperation has been in the training of Indian Navy pilots for carrier service. Both the United States and India use the British Hawk as an advanced jet trainer, and a number of Indian Navy pilots have become carrier-certified on American ships. Frustratingly, the pilots cannot fly off India's lone carrier because the only Hawks in the Indian inventory belong to the Indian Air Force and are not configured for carrier service.

At sea, naval cooperation is technically easy: the unit of cooperation, the ship, is tactically manageable (one ship, one signal), whereas army-to-army cooperation raises questions of hierarchy and coordination. The navy is also the most professional of the Indian services, and politically least sensitive in that most naval operations are carried out away from India. Specifically, Washington should move to join Indian, Chinese, and other navies in an effort that will also be a confidence-building measure.[16]

Finally, intelligence sharing was not a serious element in the U.S.-Indian relationship until after the Mumbai attacks. Whereas once the U.S. ambassador was called in and dressed down for suggesting publicly that the FBI might be able to offer assistance after a terror attack in India, following Mumbai there was intense and open FBI participation in the investigation, and India's dossier on the event drew liberally from information provided by American agencies.

However, America's own organizational idiosyncrasies obstruct attempts to work with India on military matters. The American global commands are divided geographically, so that there are a number of "seams" between them.[17] CENTCOM and United States Pacific Command (PACOM) have enormous vested interests in maintaining close ties with Pakistan and India, respectively, but find it difficult to work toward a common policy. CENTCOM, which has responsibility for the Middle East up to Pakistan, has vetoed efforts to get India into TF-150 (it preferred a moderate Muslim country such as Pakistan to join the flotilla, and it was assumed that the Indian and Pakistani Navies could not work together). While CENTCOM remains solely focused on gaining and expanding Pakistani cooperation, PACOM naturally sees India in a different light, and has sponsored regular joint U.S.-Indian exercises. The problem is further aggravated by the creation of United States African Command (AFRICOM), which has its own Afrocentric priorities, and where India has close ties to a number of African states, notably South Africa. Addressing these global command divisions to facilitate greater cooperation with the Indian Navy and other services should be a high priority.

While the Bush policy of de-hyphenation exacerbated the coordination problem, Obama's focus on the invented region of Af-Pak has diffused U.S. responsibility for India. As we have noted, the problem of a conventional arms race between India and Pakistan is less critical than the latter would claim, but there may be opportunity costs of not considering scenarios in which the United States worked with both militaries at the same time on the same project.

The other services offer less promise. The Indian Army is not yet ready for complex joint exercises or for exploring new strategic roles, though it has conducted some counterinsurgency interactions with the U.S. armed forces, and in April 2010 an Indian unit conducted a mock landing on America's West Coast. This is not surprising as the army is bogged down in domestic counterinsurgency, and still eager for an opportunity to attack Pakistan, while it must rebuild long-neglected infrastructure along the contested India-China border. Further, Indian Army leaders lack the long-term strategic thinking evident in the navy.

The Indian Air Force has engaged in numerous military exercises with the USAF. The greatest benefit for India has been to see, at close range, how its Soviet-designed aircraft match up against advanced American models, and what they can learn from the Americans in terms of tactics and technology.

There is little IAF interest in developing new roles and capabilities that enable it to work alongside the United States in other arenas—Pakistan remains the main focus. While it has one of the world's best airlift capabilities, this is useless unless there is planning and interservice cooperation. The most astonishing failure in this regard was the inability of the IAF to provide timely airlift for commandos to respond to the terror attacks in Mumbai. There is no practical planning regarding force projection, and the air force's theory of war fighting directly challenges the army's.

This brings us to the question of jointness, the ability of the armed services to work together in pursuit of strategic or military objectives. In this sphere, the United States can and should offer to share its own "lessons learned," but it is up to India to take advantage of American experience and that of other countries that are moving toward a functional reorganization of their armed services. The best way to share this experience would be to place Indian officers and civilians in positions where they can observe and participate in joint commands, as is done with formal allies.

American Reforms

While this book focuses on the problems of Indian military modernization, the India-U.S. relationship is complicated by the United States' own cumbersome administrative processes, some of which were designed to accommodate the complex web of laws that govern exchanges with foreign states and military establishments, and some of which are a function of bureaucratic rule-setting that ignores emerging strategic relationships, such as the one with India.

In the first case, the U.S.-India military relationship is only now acquiring a legal framework. India is not a formal ally. Until Secretary of State Hillary Clinton's visit to India in July 2009, there were no current agreements that provided overall guidance for arms and technology transfers, basing arrangements, logistic support, and end-use monitoring. Nor is there an information-protection agreement. At least twice in the past, there were such agreements, all providing for monitoring of India's use of American-supplied weapons and military technology. Such agreements are standard for states that purchase or use American military equipment and are congressionally mandated. Informed Indian sources report that India managed to strip away the most intrusive inspection clauses, and for this reason, the actual text of the agreement remains secret.[18] The problems in reaching the 2005 Bush-Singh agreement were not entirely congressional concerns. Other obstacles to expanded Indian-American military cooperation seem to be zealous Indian bureaucrats, who opposed expansion of American arms technology transfer to India, and French and Russian arms lobbies who blocked agreements that would have greatly increased the flow of dual-use and defense technology to India from the United States.[19] There is also the persistent problem of exceptionalism. Americans believe they need not accommodate others, or that American technology must be held very closely. Indians such as the general in the Booz Allen study, quoted here, have different expectations: "We expect the U.S. to create a third category for India that is characterized by an adult-to-adult relationship. The U.S. is accustomed to working with allies and subordinate countries. We want an equal relationship that allows us to maintain positions different from the U.S. It is important for India to have an independent foreign policy and to exercise its own options without being influenced by another country. Otherwise, it loses its independent standing in the region."[20] Everyone wants something for nothing, but for the relationship to work it is important to reiterate the commitment at the highest (presidential and prime ministerial) levels.

There is no doubt that India finds the United States very difficult to deal with in matters of technology and arms acquisitions. Corruption or political accommodation made the relationship with the Soviet Union, Israel, and some Western states relatively smooth. In the absence of a formal alliance or a strategic framework, Indians find they encounter inordinate delays and bureaucratic resistance in Washington. These complaints are echoed by American arms firms, who find the American system reluctant to facilitate their sales to India. India's new prosperity and prominence make it more attractive for American arms makers, but they also observe that India is overstretched in its military relations with other states. As one U.S. embassy official told us, "India has security and military relations with everyone from Chile to Central Asia," but they just do not have the manpower and expertise to manage all of these ties. Further, he complained that India's military relations are also shaped by political considerations. They seem to believe that "if you do something with the Americans you have to do it with the Russians; the same is true for the French and Japanese."

Dealing with India's Most Important Weapon

America has an opportunity to work with India to shape its nuclear arsenal and doctrine in such a way that it provides the maximum security for India with the minimum risk of accidental war, let alone the leakage of nuclear and missile technology to other states and regions. For this to occur several conditions must be met.

First, the agreement with India should eventually be folded into a policy that includes criteria that allow other states to enter such a nuclear halfway house. This halfway house would provide civilian nuclear assistance in exchange for an impeccable horizontal nonproliferation record. India now seems to meet most reasonable tests, as does Israel; but Pakistan and North Korea might not.

Second, the United States should work with India on an initiative to constrain vertical proliferation via a nuclear restraint regime in Asia—this initiative would include India, Pakistan, Russia, and China. Such a regime need not involve formal, negotiated limits, which would be very difficult to achieve, but could be based on a fissile material cutoff, continued restraint on testing, and limited deployment of weapons. The U.S.-India nuclear dialogue, rooted in the agreement to transfer technology to India's civilian program, partly covers this, but a wider, multilateral initiative may ward off an arms race between Pakistan and India. Of course, China's decision on renewing testing will be shaped by its response to the United States' nuclear plans, but the United States can continue its own ban on tests indefinitely without damaging nuclear preparedness.

Third, the United States should assist India in setting up a center to study "best practices," gleaned from the American and Russian/Soviet nuclear and missile experience, and from the experiences of other states. Such matters have been discussed in several Track II forums, but there should be an expectation that India will eventually join the process of nuclear arms reduction, which began with U.S. and Russian nuclear cuts. It is disappointing that such a long-term goal was not even mentioned in recent U.S.-Indian communiqués.

Fourth, it is in India's economic interest to be seen as a responsible global stakeholder; on the margins, this will shape the willingness of many important companies to invest in India (for many investors, its democratic politics and internationally moderate positions are part of its comparative advantage vis-à-vis China). The United States should continue to stress the importance of India's membership in such regimes, and link this to the argument that a globally engaged and responsible India is a good place for American investments. These investments could include civilian nuclear technology; the French and Russians may be less concerned about such matters, but Japan plans to invest in the Indian civilian nuclear industry.

Fifth, these agreements should be part of a larger process of crafting a diplomacy that addresses wider complex arms control and security concerns, not just meeting India's energy needs. The United States has such concerns in an area that stretches from Israel to China; this includes at least five states that have nuclear weapons and two that may be trying to acquire them. The 2005–07 U.S.-India Nuclear Deal did much to repair the torn U.S.-Indian strategic tie, and has a role in addressing India's massive energy shortfall, but it should be regarded as a beginning, not an end as far as American nonproliferation and strategic interests are concerned.

Washington was right to seek a new nuclear relationship with India; India should be treated as a de facto nuclear weapons state. India has demonstrated that it is responsible; it will receive no special advantage, but its fundamental status will change. The test should not be the safeguarding of reactors. India will have more reactors under safeguard than all the states designated by the NPT as "Nuclear Weapons States" put together. The United States should be more concerned about India's cooperation on nonproliferation and adherence to various regimes, including the Fissile Material Cutoff Treaty (FMCT) and its restraint in developing a nuclear arsenal so that it does not trigger an arms race with its neighbors. As one Indian analyst has suggested, India should pursue a regional nuclear restraint regime, developing either multilateral or bilateral agreements on force levels and targeting with its nuclear neighbors.[21] Instead, India has proposed the modification of the NPT, a near impossible task, implying an Indian seat at the nuclear high table, which excludes Islamabad. It is not a "shrewd move," and conjures memories of India's idealistic intransigence during and after the debates over the NPT and the CTBT in earlier years.[22] Washington should press, first, for de facto adherence to the letter and spirit of the NPT, but also support regional efforts to bring about an Asian nuclear restraint regime that would both give legitimacy to the Indian nuclear weapons program and place it in its proper regional deterrent context.

India is unlikely to build a very big arsenal (its nuclear policy is reactive, not based on some master plan to become a major nuclear superpower). The incentives of other states are region- and situation-specific. While New Delhi anticipated the rhetoric used by other states (notably Iran) to justify their nuclear programs, Iran has sought nuclear weapons very much for its own reasons, not to emulate India. The South Asian case may be met by active diplomacy, which would urge all states to act in their interest—and avoid an open-ended nuclear arms race. Here India should be encouraged to take the lead as a responsible state with nuclear weapons.

Sixth, as for testing, there may be circumstances when the United States would choose to overlook Indian tests (when they follow Chinese or Pakistani tests, or American ones), but at that point the least of our worries will be a small and still unproved Indian nuclear arsenal. American diplomacy should ensure that major (and minor) states do not regard nuclear testing as in their best national interest.

Finally, if India sought to become a major nuclear power, that is, develop forces larger than those of, say, China; and were it to build a nuclear-delivery system that would enable it to strike targets in Europe or the United States, then there would be legitimate concerns about India's contribution to regional stability and whether or not it was increasing or decreasing the risk of war and its own security. At the moment the Indian strategic and nuclear communities would not favor such a capability, but it would be alarming if circumstances were to lead in that direction. Confidence in the modesty of Indian plans rests on assumptions about India as a democratic, secular, and globally interconnected state; one that has historically avoided arms races with major strategic rivals. A very different India cannot be entirely ruled out: it was an authoritarian state for eighteen months during the period of the Emergency under Mrs. Gandhi, but such an India seems to be unlikely for the foreseeable future. Hence American recognition of India as a nuclear weapon state and support for its civilian nuclear program, if coupled with renewed arms control diplomacy, is to the United States' advantage, especially if India becomes a partner in such diplomacy. The historic U.S.-Indian nuclear deal, and present Indian plans to develop a modest but constrained nuclear arsenal, make such a partnership possible, but do not guarantee it.

Beyond Af-Pak

Washington must also transform de-hyphenation into a viable plan to recruit India to three critical strategic hotspots: Afghanistan, Iran, and Pakistan. These are the regional foreign policy priorities of the Obama administration. Indian and American relations with these countries, and with all of the Islamic world, have followed different trajectories. India's compulsions are both economic and domestic: Iran provides approximately 10 percent of India's oil, Indian refineries supply Iran with fuel, and it is estimated that after Iran, India has the second largest Shia population in the world. The North Indian city of Lucknow is a renowned center for Shia learning. Further, India and Iran work closely together in Afghanistan, where they share an interest in strengthening the Karzai regime against the extremist Taliban. This, of course, puts them both on the American side as far as Afghanistan is concerned. Washington should explore the possibility of expanding cooperation with India in Afghanistan—even if this implies working in parallel with Iran. After all, this was American policy in the period just before and during the overthrow of the Taliban, and an Indian partnership might advance several American interests, both in Afghanistan and with Iran itself.

India's presence in Afghanistan is also part of a long-term strategy to contain Pakistan. New Delhi has invested considerable resources in a new highway and electrical grid, plus many programs to strengthen Afghan infrastructure. India's official aid program to Afghanistan ($1.2 billion) is five times that of Pakistan. Indian-built roads link Iran and Afghanistan, bypass-ing Pakistan, thus reducing Afghan dependence on Pakistan. This policy strengthens a moderate neighbor (Afghanistan) that has been victimized by extremists; it balances Pakistani influence through the Taliban; it blocks Pakistani access to Central Asia; and it provides another way of delivering pinpricks to Pakistan via its intelligence services. When the Indian embassy in Kabul was bombed in July 2008, there was widespread agreement in India that New Delhi should not retreat from Afghanistan, and that vital Indian interests were at stake there.

But there is no sign that India will soon have a capability for independent operations in Afghanistan. While its initial offer to support the United States in Afghanistan was bold, New Delhi did not have the military or geographic assets to make it work. To operate at brigade- or even battalion-strength, it would have to construct a ground infrastructure and work closely with the United States, NATO, and Iran. It would probably insist on a separate UN mandate and a share in the control over operations. The most likely arrangement for the future would be that India provide limited support for allied forces in Afghanistan as it is doubtful that New Delhi will deploy its own soldiers there. However, India could help both the United States and Afghanistan by further training of Afghan security personnel. This will be resisted by Pakistan, but given the substantial economic and military assis-tance program it is receiving from the United States, there are opportunities for trade-offs.

U.S. policy must look beyond Af-Pak or Pak-Af (either way an execra-ble formulation) and realize that for the next five years or more Pakistan's own stability and viability as a state will be the acid test of any prospective U.S.-Indian strategic relationship. In both the Clinton and the second Bush administrations, the American position was that India and Pakistan were both friends (a major non-NATO ally in the case of Pakistan, an informal ally in India's case). However, the U.S. role was confined to soothing remarks about the importance of dialogue and a quick in-and-out intervention dur-ing moments of crisis. In the past the United States did what it could to de-link its India and Pakistan policies. For example, during the protracted negotiations with India over the breakthrough nuclear deal, there was no exploration of possible Indian concessions regarding Pakistan, or of using the same kinds of nuclear concessions for Pakistan to secure better compli-ance on nuclear issues or on Islamabad's stance vis-à-vis the Taliban.

American policymakers are discovering that it is impossible to treat Paki-stan and India separately when each sees the other as a real strategic threat.[23] Yet from an Indian perspective, this was acceptable—it meant that Indian policy toward Pakistan was not an issue, and that the Americans would not raise the Kashmir issue, where India remains vulnerable. This entire policy collapses under its own illogic whenever there is a terrorist attack or tensions rise in Kashmir, and Pakistan demands that the United States pressure India so that it can move its forces away from the borders with India and toward the west, where they are engaged in counterinsurgency.

The Obama administration is rapidly changing the United States' Pakistan policy in ways that benefit India, but also alarm it. The Peace Act (2009) has made American military assistance to Pakistan contingent upon the latter redirecting its armed forces toward insurgency and extremist threats in Balochistan, the North West Frontier Province, and even the Punjab. This will be of great benefit to Delhi, but prudent Indian policy will respond by making it easier for the Pakistan military to move in this direction. This does not require an agreement on Kashmir (improbable for many years, if ever), but it does require on-the-ground changes in deployment and doctrine that would make it possible for Pakistan to begin to retrain and redirect a significant portion of its ground forces. Focusing on Cold Start does not achieve this goal.

Indians remain divided in their attitudes toward Pakistan. They wait for others to compel Pakistani restraint. India has no long-term strategy that would ensure that its most problematic neighbor will not do it greater damage twenty years from now than it has done already.[24]

For the next few years Pakistan will be the biggest factor in American relations with India. China could be more important after that. The Bush administration saw India as a strategic player in Asia and a counterweight to China. The Obama administration seems to view China more as the first Bush administration and the Clinton administration did, less a potential problem than a potential partner. The goal seems to be to seek Chinese cooperation where possible—especially in Afghanistan and Pakistan, rather than to balance Chinese power with a resurgent India. While it is true, as Fareed Zakaria has written, that the rise of China upset the strategic balance in Asia, and that the new tie with India "will stand both countries in good stead no matter what the future balance of power in Asia looks like,"[25] it is also true that for the first few years of the Obama administration, seeking Chinese cooperation will be more important than balancing it. India may be Asia's third or fourth power—the weakest of its major powers. The overwhelming temptation for the United States will be to work with Asia's first major power.

This matches up with India's China policy. In Asia everyone is hedging against everyone else, including the hyperpower, the United States.

"Hedgemonism" is the byword as long as China remains a quiescent power. A continuing U.S.-India military and strategic arrangement would be reinsurance for both India and the United States in the event of a hostile China.

A Partnership with Fewer Illusions

Washington can and should assist India in modernizing its armed forces and defense structure, but this is unlikely to lead to a strategic alliance of consequence. The Indian elite, who view their country as emerging as one of the major power centers of the world, are eager for cooperation with many powers but reluctant to be placed in a subordinate position. Americans are accustomed to alliance relationships, which usually involve a degree of bargaining and often mutually acceptable outcomes. In this regard, India resembles France. France is the outstanding case of a democracy that has received considerable American technical and military assistance over the years, yet pursues a ruggedly independent foreign policy with the larger strategic objective of reducing America to "normal" proportions, while elevating France. India might evolve in such a direction—an English-speaking France of over a billion people. We would say that India only has to "be India"— a prospering and democratic state, to further many important American interests, a prospect that we noted in 2001.[26] An American under secretary of state, R. Nicholas Burns, had it right when he wrote that the United States must adjust to a friendship with India that will feature a wider margin of disagreement than the United States has known before.[27]

Further, while the rhetoric of democracy has been an important element of the relationship, democratic politics could derail the bold foreign policy transformation once envisioned in Washington and New Delhi. The Indian prospect of sending forces to assist the United States in Iraq was crushed by public skepticism. The problem is somewhat eased by the clear victory of Prime Minister Singh's Congress government in the May 2009 election, a victory that also reduced the power of parochial regional parties. Strategic thinking, which requires consensus across generations and across parties, will always be difficult. The default strategic option is restraint, minding India's business unless directly challenged, especially across land borders. Some Indian strategists have Israel-envy: they would like to emulate the Israelis, who are willing to retaliate across their borders, or copy the American global campaign against terrorist groups. However, India's external threats come from powerful states that have a nuclear retaliatory capability. With the legacy of the Sri Lankan fiasco (1987–90), few Indians can muster enthusiasm to send an expeditionary force anywhere. While some in the army would have loved to join the Americans in Iraq, declining the American invitation seems, in retrospect, to have been a shrewd decision.

Despite the rhetoric and the reality of a new economic relationship, we see little evidence for a long-term military or strategic commitment on the American side vis-à-vis India, and even less on the Indian side. India's democracy is appreciated as is its role as a major player in environmental and economic issues. However, these factors do not add up to a vision of a strategic, global, or even regional partnership, except to the degree that India might complicate American diplomacy in Afghanistan and Pakistan or that a new India-Pakistan crisis might occur. However, events could change the prospects for strategic cooperation very quickly (hence the need to expand the present level of military and defense cooperation). Consideration should be given to the longue durée view that India is only now beginning to develop the wherewithal to deal with the security threats that emerged after the cold war.

India is a strong society presided over by a weak state, but a state that is much stronger than its regional neighbors', some of which are disintegrating. India is rising as the state steps aside and allows the entrepreneurial talents of its population to fuel the economy. However, having done so, the state seems to be unwilling to raise resources for its military and security establishments and to persuade its population about the necessity of force—except when directly challenged as in Kargil.

The United States and India now have a complex, composite relationship, not a monotonal one. Although thirty years ago India was on the other side of almost all important world strategic issues, the situation has changed markedly, and India has accommodated many American concerns. In recent years, while the nuclear agreement dominated the headlines, and while it may make a marginal difference in India's energy shortage, its long-term importance was symbolic—after thirty-five years of sanctions, India was treated as an equal. The real transformations in the relationship are in the cultural and economic realms, the former through the presence of a large Indian-American community, which is rapidly and successfully assimilating; the growing cultural influence of India in the United States was symbolized by the Best Picture Oscar for *Slumdog Millionaire*.[28] The economic ties are self-evident; the ballast that was missing in 1998 now exists and is growing in both states. While India may have been oversold as a strategic partner, the potential is there, handicapped by the very slow pace of military modernization and even more so by Indian political leaders' lack of interest in foreign and defense policy. India is a potential strategic asset, although not one that is realized today. However, the United States can influence the pace and quality of Indian military capabilities and can look forward to the slow expansion of military and strategic cooperation in the areas noted above.

Solid and broad-based U.S.-Indian relations, including a military and security component, should be seen as a form of reinsurance for both sides. As a concept and as a policy framework, reinsurance should not be underestimated. Both India and the United States understand that they do not now have resources for a full-scale engagement on two fronts: with China on the one hand and Islamic extremism on the other. To move against Pakistan invites Chinese counterbalancing; to move against China provides still another reason for Beijing to strengthen its ties to Islamabad.[29] In terms of resources, the United States has dominance at sea, but this is only marginally relevant in Afghanistan and Iraq; India has a huge ground army but little naval power. India's vaunted strategic location is, ironically, too strategic— India is confronted by many kinds of external and internal threats, yet it is periodically stricken with indecision. Because there are so few resources available, the military solution is often difficult if not impossible to implement, and the cost of increasing military resources is exceeded only by the bureaucratic and political resistance to doing so.

It is in the United States' interest that India manage its response to such events as professionally and as carefully as possible. The widespread assumption that India beyond its borders is fundamentally a status quo power is correct—its government is responsive to checks and balances and popular opinion, and while its neighbors may not always agree, its behavior as a state has been largely responsible. These qualities make its rise welcome to many Asian leaders, who are quietly fearful of China's closed and more unpredictable leadership. These qualities are also compatible with long-term American interests, even though working with India—with no assurance of an identical strategic vision—may be trying at times. However, sufficient overlap exists in American and Indian visions to justify the effort in both countries to alleviate, if not remove, the persistent bureaucratic and perceptual obstacles that are so evident.

NOTES

PREFACE

1. George Tanham, *Indian Strategic Thought: An Interpretive Essay* (Santa Monica, Calif.: RAND, 1992).

2. Stephen P. Rosen, *Societies and Military Power: India and Its Armies* (Cornell University Press, 1996).

3. Rajesh M. Basrur, *Minimum Deterrence and India's Nuclear Security* (Stanford University Press, 2006).

4. For two lively rebuttals see Pranab Bardhan, "China, India Superpower? Not so Fast!" *Yale Global Online*, October 25, 2005 (http://yaleglobal.yale.edu/content/china-india-superpower-not-so-fast); and Minxin Pei, "Think Again: Asia's Rise," *Foreign Policy* (June 22, 2009) (www.foreignpolicy.com/articles/2009/06/22/think_again_asias_rise?p;irnt=yes&hidecomments=yes&page=full).

5. Ashley J. Tellis, "The United States and South Asia," Testimony before the House Committee on International Relations, June 14, 2004 (www.carnegieendowment.org/publications/index.cfm?fa=view&id=17070); Tellis, "India as a New Global Power: An Action Agenda for the United States," Carnegie Endowment for International Peace, July 2005 (www.carnegieendowment.org/files/CEIP_India_strategy_2006.FINAL.pdf); and Robert D. Blackwill, "The India Imperative," *National Interest*, no. 80 (Summer 2005): 9–17.

6. Tellis, "India as a New Global Power," pp. 33, 36.

7. Rodney W. Jones, "Conventional Military Imbalance and Strategic Stability in South Asia," Research Paper 1, South Asia Strategic Stability Unit (University of Bradford, March 2005).

8. See Paul Bracken, *Fire in the East: The Rise of Asian Military Power and the Second Nuclear Age* (New York: HarperCollins, 1999); Kishore Mahbubani, *The New*

Asian Hemisphere: The Irresistible Shift of Global Power to the East (New York: Public Affairs, 2008); and Fareed Zakaria, *The Post-American World* (New York: W. W. Norton, 2008).

9. Teresita Schaffer, *India and the United States in the 21st Century: Reinventing Partnership* (Washington: Center for Strategic and International Studies, 2009).

10. For a classic exposition, see Kenneth Waltz, *Theory of International Politics* (Reading, Mass.: Addison, 1977).

11. Juli A. Macdonald, "Indo-U.S. Military Relations: Expectations and Perceptions," Office of Net Assessment, October 2002. For a follow-up study see Booz Allen Hamilton's, Bethany N. Danyluk and Juli A. MacDonald, *The U.S.-India Defense Relationship: Reassessing Perceptions and Expectations*, report (unclassified) prepared for the Director, Net Assessment, Office of the Secretary of Defense (Washington, November 2008).

12. Amit Sisir Gupta, *Building an Arsenal: The Evolution of Regional Power Force Structures* (Westport, Conn., and London: Praeger, 1998).

13. Amitabh Mattoo, "Upgrading the Study of International Relations," *The Hindu*, April 21, 2009 (http://thehindu.com/2009/04/21/stories/2009042156680800.htm); Anit Mukherjee, "The Absent Dialogue," *Seminar* 599 (July 2009): 24–28, by a former Indian Army officer; and the American Daniel Markey, "Developing India's Foreign Policy 'Software,'" National Bureau of Asian Research, *Asia Policy*, no. 8 (July 2009): 73–96 (http://asiapolicy.nbr.org [July 8, 2009]). For a positive comment on Markey's argument by India's leading student of its foreign policy bureaucracy, see Kishan S. Rana, "MEA's Institutional Software—A US Prognosis," *Business Standard*, July 24, 2009 (www.business-standard.com/india/news/kishan-s-rana-mea%5Cs-institutional-softwareUS-prognosis/364646/ [August 1, 2009]).

14. Jaswant Singh, *Defending India* (New York: Palgrave Macmillan, 1999).

15. Harsh V. Pant, "A Rising India's Search for a Foreign Policy," *Orbis* 53, no. 2 (Spring 2009): 263. See also Pant, *Contemporary Debates in Indian Foreign and Security Policy: India Negotiates Its Rise in the International System* (New York: Palgrave Macmillan, 2008).

16. For an overview of Subrahmanyam's writings and career, see P. K. Kumaraswamy, ed., *Security beyond Survival: Essays for K. Subrahmanyam* (New Delhi: Sage, 2004).

17. The most persuasive case for India having the means and the interest to break with the past is presented by the distinguished Indian scholar-journalist C. Raja Mohan, in *Crossing the Rubicon* (New Delhi: Viking, 2003).

CHAPTER ONE

1. For a comprehensive discussion of Indian nationalist attitudes toward the armed forces and the use of military power, see Stephen P. Cohen, *The Indian Army: Its Contribution to the Development of a Nation*, 2nd ed. (Oxford University Press, 2001).

2. Lorne Kavic, *India's Quest for Security: Defence Policies, 1947–1965* (University of California Press, 1967), pp. 24–25.

3. For one of his final statements on Indian security policy, see K. M. Panikkar, *Problems of Indian Defence* (London: Asia Publishing House, 1960). Panikkar's work has been rediscovered by contemporary Indian realists. See an extract from Panikkar's address to the then new School of International Studies, February 13, 1961, reprinted in *Pragati: The Indian National Interest Review,* January 2010, republished as "Before the Enemies Reach Panipat" (http://pragati.nationalinterest.in/wp-content/uploads/2010/01/pragati-issue34-jan2010-communityed.pdf).

4. See Apurba Kundu, *Militarism in India: The Army and Civil Society in Consensus* (New York: St Martin's Press, 1998), pp. 76–80; and Raju G. C. Thomas, *Indian Security Policy* (Princeton University Press, 1986), pp. 119–34.

5. See Robert S. Anderson, "Patrick Blackett in India: Military Consultant and Scientific Intervenor, 1947–1972, Part I," *Notes and Records of the Royal Society of London* 53, no. 2 (May 1999), pp. 253–73; and Anderson, "Empire's Setting Sun? Patrick Blackett and Military and Scientific Development of India," *Economic and Political Weekly,* September 29, 2001, pp. 3703–20.

6. K. Subrahmanyam, "Indian Defence Expenditure in Global Perspective," *Economic and Political Weekly* 8, no. 26 (June 30, 1973), pp. 1155–58 (www.jstor.org/stable/4362796).

7. See Neville Maxwell, *India's China War* (London: Jonathan Cape, 1970). For Maxwell's more recent views on the war, see Maxwell, "How the East Was Lost," Rediff.com, April 29, 2004 (www.rediff.com/news/2001/may/23spec.htm).

8. Maxwell, "How the East Was Lost," Part II.

9. The official histories of this and two other wars, although written, remain unpublished. See Inder Malhotra's scathing discussion of bureaucratic timidity, "Babus and Their Top-Secret Fetish," *The Asian Age,* April 1, 2009 (www.asianage.com/presentation/leftnavigation/opinion/opinion/babus-and-their-top-secret-fetish.aspx [April 2009]).

10. As late as 1985 American officials incorrectly believed that the Soviets maintained a naval base in Vishakhapatnam, on India's east coast, and that the Soviet-built vessels that sailed in and out of the port were part of the Soviet Navy.

11. For a hard realist view of India's nuclear program, which emphasizes the China threat, see Bharat Karnad, *India's Nuclear Policy* (New York: Praeger Special Series, 2008). The editor of one of India's defense journals, Captain Bharat Varma has predicted that China will soon be compelled to go to war, attacking India. See "'Nervous' China May Attack India by 2012: Defense Expert," expressindia.com (www.expressindia.com/latest-news/nervous-China-may-attack-India-by-2012-defence-expert/488349).

12. China's defense modernization benefits from years of heavy investment on a scale unimaginable in India. As Richard A. Bitzinger observes, China is prepared for military breakout and is Asia's leading military producer—this could give it the means as well as the confidence to challenge other states in the Taiwan Straits, Southeast Asia, and westward—in the Indian Ocean. Richard A. Bitzinger, "China's Military-Industrial Complex: Is It (Finally) Turning a Corner?" *RSIS Commentaries* no.

121, S. Rajaratnam School of International Studies, Singapore, November 21, 2008 (http://dr.ntu.edu.sg/handle/10220/4533).

13. Chicago Council on Global Affairs, *The United States and the Rise of China and India: Result of a 2006 Multination Survey of Public Opinion* (Chicago, 2006).

14. Ibid., pp. 41–42.

15. See http://specials.indiatoday.com/petition_english/index.shtml (March 2010).

16. Jonathan Marcus, "India-Pakistan Military Balance," BBC News, May 9, 2009 (http://news.bbc.co.uk/2/hi/south_asia/1735912.stm).

17. Anthony H. Cordesman, "The India-Pakistan Military Balance" (Washington: Center for Strategic and International Studies, May 2002).

18. The figures for defense spending relative to GDP vary depending on how they are calculated. The 3 percent figure is taken from the World Development Indicators. There are other figures that put the number closer to 2.5 percent.

19. SIPRI offers competing figures of $72.7 billion for India, using the purchasing power parity, and $140 billion for China (www.sipri.org/yearbook/2008/files/SIPRIYB0805.pdf).

20. Ibid., p. 75. This is based upon 2007 data.

21. Rajat Pandit, "India to Acquire New Undersea Cruise Missiles," *Times of India*, August 4, 2008 (http://timesofindia.indiatimes.com/articleshow/msid-33223 88,prtpage-1.cms [January 2010]).

22. The nature of the growing India-Israel defense relationship has been widely commented upon. For a discussion of Indian concerns about corruption, see Yossi Melman, "Media Allege Corruption in Massive Israel-India Arms Deal," *Haaretz*, April 1, 2001 (www.haaretz.com/hasen/spages/1074540.html). On India-Russia weapons deals, see "Defense Contracts Expected to Dominate India-Russia Talks," CNN report October 2, 2000 (www.cnn.com/2000/ASIANOW/south/10/01/india.putin.advancer/ [September 2004]).

23. Instead, India has launched an indigenous program to develop an airborne early warning system. The program is far from delivering anything concrete.

24. See the FICCI press release, February 24, 2009 (http://ficcidrdoatac.com/press-release.pdf).

25. John Wilson Lewis and Xue Litai, "China's Search for a Modern Air Force," *International Security* 24, no. 1 (Summer 1999), pp. 64–94 (http://links.jstor.org/sici?sici =0162-2889%28199922%2924%3A1%3C64%3ACSFAMA%3E2.0.CO%3B2-R).

Chapter Two

1. Reforming the National Security System—Recommendations of the Group of Ministers, chap. 1, p. 1. The text of the declassified portions of the report is available at http://mod.nic.in/aboutus/body.htm#as1 (December 1, 2007).

2. For a brilliant analysis of the larger issues at stake see Admiral Verghese Koithara, *Society, State and Security: The Indian Experience* (New Delhi: Sage Publications, 1999).

3. For an authoritative account of the decision, see P. R. Chari, *Pokhran-I: Personal Recollections I,* Institute of Peace and Conflict Studies Special Report, August 2009, IPCS, New Delhi (www.ipcs.org [December 2009]).

4. Critics of India's nuclear program say that the Indian Atomic Energy Commission (AEC) did not do much research. Nuclear weapons technology had been widely available, and India did benefit from initial assistance from the West in constructing, fueling, and running nuclear reactors. Still, India's achievement in engineering nuclear weapons is a successful case of borrowing technology. The achievement is noteworthy when compared to India's larger industrial failures as well as to the inability of other third world countries to develop nuclear weapons (including overcoming international sanctions).

5. An excellent overview of DRDO appeared in a multipart series of articles in the *Indian Express* in January 2008; for a critique by a Singapore defense analyst, see Richard Bitzinger, "India's Once and Future Defence Industry," *RSIS Commentaries,* October 8, 2007 (www.rsis.edu.sg [December 26, 2009]).

6. Amitav Ranjan, "Arjun, Main Battle Tanked," *Indian Express,* November 27, 2006 (www.indianexpress.com/story_print.php?storyId=16589).

7. Manu Pubby, "What Went Wrong with LCA, Arjun Tank, Akash Missile," *Indian Express,* March 3, 2009 (www.indianexpress.com/news/what-went-wrong-with-lca-arjun-tank-akash/429935/).

8. One of the assumptions about Soviet weapons, cultivated by the now-defunct pro-Soviet lobby, was that the Soviet Union provided the best equipment available to India, whereas Western sources only sold second-rate technology. This was not true, and some of the Soviet equipment, designed for Soviet purposes, not Indian, was inappropriate for India, which often had no choice in the matter.

9. See the report of the Confederation of Indian Industries on defense production (http://64.233.169.104/search?q=cache:othn9-8Z3b4J:www.ciidefence.com/Main%2520Pages/About_US/About_US.htm+Vijay+Kelkar+Committee+defense&hl=en&ct=clnk&cd=2&gl=us&client=safari [December 1, 2007]).

10. Defence Procurement Procedure and Defence Procurement Manuals (New Delhi: Ministry of Defence (http://mod.nic.in/dpm/welcome.html).

11. Josy Joseph, "DRDO May Have Major Say in Defence Purchases," *DNA,* April 1, 2008 (www.dnaindia.com/dnaprint.asp?newsid=1158214 [December 21, 2009]).

12. Manu Pubby, "DRDO Revamp: Antony Appoints High-level Panel," *Indian Express,* June 12, 2009 (indianexpress.com/story-print/475162/ [December 21, 2009]).

13. Confederation of Indian Industry, "Opportunities in the Indian Defence Sector," report by KPMG, 2009 (www.in.kpmg.com/TL_Files/Pictures/Opportunities_in_the_Indian_Defence_Sector.pdf [March 2, 2010]).

14. Abhinaba Das and Kausik Datta, "L&T, EADS Revive JV plans; to Tweak Equity Structure to Clear FDI Hurdle," *The Economic Times*, February 5, 2010 (http://economic times.indiatimes.com/news/news-by-industry/indl-goods-/-svs/engineering/LT-EADS-revive-JV-plans-to-tweak-equity-structure-to-clear-FDI-hurdle/article show/5536473.cms).

15. Sandeep Unnithan, "Dent in the BRASS," *India Today International Edition*, January 4, 2010, pp. 38–44. For a thoughtful discussion of the military's image in light of these scandals, see Shekhar Gupta, "Our Harmed Forces," *Indian Express*, January 16, 2010 (www.indianexpress.com/story-print/567998/ [January 20, 2010]).

16. Matthew Porter, "More Indian Defense Corruption—But We Need the Weapons So What to Do?" (http://industry.bnet.com/government/10002027/more-indian-defense-corruption-but-we-need-the-weapons-so-what-to-do/ [March 1, 2010]).

17. Ibid.

18. Quoted in the blog of a former *Financial Times* correspondent in India, John Elliott, "Riding the Indian Elephant" (http://ridingtheelephnant.wordpress.com/2010/02/23/the-gun-that-has-crippled-the-equipping-of-India's-armed-forces-is-"innocent"/ [March 2, 2010]).

19. Ibid.

20. See Admiral Vishnu Bhagwat, *Betrayal of the Defence Forces* (New Delhi: Manas, 2001); and Gaurav C. Sawant, "Bhagwat Chronicles His Sacking, Book Release Today," *Indian Express*, February 16, 2001.

21. Report of the Kargil Review Committee, *From Surprise to Reckoning* (New Delhi: Sage Publications, 2000).

22. It is hard to see how the Kargil Review Committee reached its conclusions on avoidable casualties when nearly half (240) of the Indian deaths (527) were associated with the Battle of Tololing, the three-week assault on the first and the most strategic peak occupied by the Pakistanis. After almost three weeks of trying to scale the peak in the face of enemy fire, the Indian Army finally arrayed the Bofors 155mm artillery guns in a direct fire role on the hilltops. After suppressing the assault, Indian infantry units finally closed the gap. The delay in the use of the Bofors was as surprising as the problems with the use of air power.

23. The text of the declassified portions of the report is available at http://mod.nic.in/newadditions (December 1, 2007).

24. The most comprehensive of these is the *Indian Express* series published in January 2008.

25. See Admiral Arun Prakash, "Keynote Address," *Proceedings of a USI Seminar in Higher Defence Organisation* (New Delhi: United Services Institution of India, 2007), p. 9.

26. Anit Mukherjee, "Failing to Deliver: The Post Crises Defense Reforms in India, 1998–2008," unpublished manuscript.

27. Recent attempts at new procurement guidelines have not been inspiring. See Ajai Shukla, "Western Doctrine, Russian Arms," *Business Standard*, Aug 12, 2008.

Shukla writes that India's new Defence Procurement Procedure "is remarkable only for its lack of movement beyond an equally insipid predecessor."

28. The Centre for Joint Warfare Studies journal, *Purple Pages* (www.cenjows.in/home.php).

29. For a survey and critique of India's intelligence incoherence, and the recommendations of the Kashmir Review Committee and the Group of Ministers report, see Sunil Saini, "Intelligence Reforms," *Bharat Rakshak Monitor*, vol. 3, no. 4, (January-February 2001) (www.bharat-rakshak.com/MONITOR/Issue3-4/sainis.html [December 1, 2007]).

30. It mattered little that the officers were, until the 1930s, almost entirely British, and after that increasingly Indian—the great strength of the army was, and is, this body of professionals. For an overview of the officer corps see Stephen P. Cohen, *The Indian Army: Its Contribution to the Development of a Nation* (University of California Press, 1971).

31. The Centre for Land Warfare Studies (CLAWS), one of the more innovative of the service-funded think tanks, organized a rare seminar entitled "Military Sociology: Societal Changes and Impact on Armed Forces" on April 28, 2009 (www.claws.in/index.php?action=master&task=314&u_id=36).

32. The evidence here is anecdotal and drawn significantly from personal interviews. Also, the contention is not that the social origins of the officer class have remained unchanged. Rather, there has been a remarkable expansion of groups and communities entering the military, but the class differences still remain significant. The fact that there is a shortage of officers adds credence to the belief that the Indian Army is overly restrictive in its officer recruitment.

33. A retired junior commissioned officer, N. Kunju, has written extensively about the army's internal social tensions. See Kunju, *Indian Army* (New Delhi: Reliance Publishing, 1991). He has also won the 2006 *Indian Express* Citizens for Peace Prize for an essay on secularism in the army (http://dcubed.blogspot.com/2006/11/my-colleague-kadar.html [December 2009]).

34. Despite the claims that India's "youth bulge" is an asset, its military is aging, and except for women, it is difficult to attract young officer candidates. Older officers and *jawans* have not performed well in COIN and stressful situations. P. K. Gautam, "Why a Nation Needs a Young Military," CLAWS, pp. 250–56.

Chapter Three

1. India was not defeated decisively in the western portions of the India-China boundary, and in fact held its own, although this was the major area of the Chinese thrust. For an account of the war see the still unpublished official history on the Bharat Rakshak website (www.bharat-rakshak.com/ARMY/History/1962War/PDF/index.html [August 6, 2009]).

2. K. Subrahmanyam, "Indian Defence Expenditure in Global Perspective," *Economic and Political Weekly* 8, no. 26 (June 30, 1973), pp. 1155–58 (www.jstor.org/stable/4362796).

3. The army introduced helicopters and separated its aviation wing. The number of tanks increased from 2,120 to 3,150 between 1982 and 1990. Air force combat aircraft went from 614 to 836, and principal naval combat ships rose from 36 to 49 over the same period.

4. See Mandeep Bajwa and Ravi Rikhye, "Indian Army RAPIDS Divisions," February 11, 2001 (www.ordersofbattle.darkscape.net/site/toe/toe/india/rapids.html [December 26, 2009]). RAPIDS was a play on the American ROCIDS, Reorganization of Current Infantry Division, the "pentagonal" reorganization of American Army divisions in Europe of 1957.

5. A number of Sundarji's subordinates had doubts about the scope of his plans, and the army's ability to transform itself so quickly. After the crisis, Sundarji's successor, General V. N. Sharma, got rid of the high-tech command apparatus that had been installed, and the army reverted to ultracautious leadership.

6. For studies of these crises, see Sumit Ganguly and Devin Hagerty, *Fearful Symmetry: India-Pakistan Crises in the Shadow of Nuclear Weapons* (University of Washington Press, 2005); and P. R. Chari, P. I. Cheema, and Stephen P. Cohen, *Four Crises and a Peace Process: American Engagement in South Asia* (Brookings Institution Press, 2008).

7. In conversations with one of the authors, Sundarji observed that Brasstacks was the last time India could have expected to win a war against Pakistan. Once nuclear deterrence came into play in South Asia, the premise of Sundarji's reorganization fell apart. The Indian Army has since not had to fight a war with tanks, but still maintains a huge armored force.

8. K. Sundarji, *Blind Men of Hindoostan: Indo-Pak Nuclear War* (New Delhi: UBS Publishers, 1993).

9. Quoted in Sakat Datta, "War against Error," *Outlook*, February 28, 2005, p. 39 (www.outlookindia.com/full.asp?fname=Cover%20Story%20(F)&fodname=20050228& [May 2009]).

10. Prominent among those publicly discussing the problem was General Ved Malik, army chief during Kargil, who wrote and lectured extensively on fighting a limited war in a nuclear environment. See Malik, *Kargil: From Surprise to Victory* (New Delhi: HarperCollins, 2006); also Malik, "Limited War and Escalation Control," parts I and II, Institute of Peace and Conflict Studies, articles 1570–71, November 25, 2004 (www.ipcs.org/Military_articles2.jsp?action=showView&keyArticle=1018&status=artilcle&mod=a [May 7, 2007]).

11. The Kargil Review Committee was an unofficial body of inquiry, and was somewhat easy on the army's performance. See *From Surprise to Reckoning: The Kargil Review Committee Report* (New Delhi: Sage, 2000). A huge body of Indian literature emerged on Kargil, the most recent overview being an edited collection of papers by the army's Centre for Land Warfare Studies, CLAWS Journal, Summer 2009.

12. Firdaus Ahmed, "'No to Cold Start,'" Institute of Peace and Conflict Studies, article 1485, August 31, 2004 (www.ipcs.org/Military_articles2.jsp?actiojn=showView& kValue=1497&keyArticle=1018&status=article&mod=a [May 2007]).

13. Y. I. Patel, "Dig Vijay to Divya Astra—A Paradigm Shift in the Indian Army's Doctrine," *Bharat Rakshak Monitor*, vol. 6, no. 6 (May–July 2004), (www.bharat-rakshak.com/MONITOR/ISSUE6-6/patel.html [May 7, 2007]).

14. *Indian Army Doctrine*, Promulgated by Lieutenant-General K. Nagaraj, GOC Army Training Command, Simla, October 2004, p. 7 (http://indianarmy.nic. in.indianarmydoctrine.htm [July 2007]).

15. General Nirmal Chander Vij was the originator of Cold Start; for a discussion see Brigadier Rahul Bhonsle, "India's National Aspirations and Military Capabilities—2020 a Prognostic Survey," in *Army 2020: Shape, Size, Structure and General Doctrine for Emerging Challenges*, edited by Lieutenant-General Vijay Oberoi (New Delhi: Knowledge World, 2005).

16. Lieutenant-General Vijay Oberoi, "Approach Paper" in *Army 2020*, edited by Oberoi, p. 13.

17. We are grateful to Walter Ladwig III for sharing an early version of his study of Cold Start; see Ladwig, "A Cold Start for Hot Wars? The Indian Army's New Limited War Doctrine," *International Security*, vol. 32, no. 3 (Winter 2007–08), pp. 158–90.

18. Robert E. Osgood, *Limited War Revisited* (Boulder, Colo.: Westview Press, 1979), p. 3.

19. The NATO reference is by Subhas Kapila, "India's New 'Cold Start' War Doctrine Strategically Reviewed," *South Asia Analysis Group*, paper 991, May 4, 2004, pp. 3–4 (www.southasiaanalysisgroup.org/papers10/paper991.html [May 9, 2007]); Dr. Kapila, a former Indian Army brigadier, recollects that he was taught a similar course as a student in a British military educational institution. Brigadier Gurmeet Kanwal notes the similarity between the new organization and the division-sized integrated battle groups of Russia's "OMGs"—Operational Maneuver Groups. Kanwal, "Strike Fast and Hard: Army Doctrine Undergoes Change in Nuclear Era," Observer Research Foundation (http://orfonline.org/analysis/A607.htm), reprinted from *The Tribune* (Chandigarh), June 23, 2006.

20. Harbaksh Singh Nanda, "Analysis: Flaws Seen in India Military Doctrine," UPI, December 16, 2004.

21. See Ladwig, "A Cold Start for Hot Wars?" pp. 158–190.

22. Patel, p. 3.

23. Rahul Bedi, "India to Buy 330 T-90S Tanks from Russia," *The Hindustan Times*, October 26, 2006.

24. Madhusree Chatterjee, "Bids Received for Towed, Light Howitzers; Trials in February," *Indo-Asian News Service*, January 13, 2009. See also Ajai Shukla, "Catchovsky-22: The Scandal That Is the T-90," *Business Standard*, July 26, 2008.

25. Nevertheless, some senior Indian generals have shown remarkable distrust of the United States, and one former army commander has portrayed the United States

as an implacable enemy, which is eventually foiled by an India that resists pressure and mounts a global containment against it. See General S. Padmanabhan, *The Writing on the Wall: India Checkmates America* (New Delhi: Manas, 2003).

26. Kapila, "India's New 'Cold Start' War Doctrine Strategically Reviewed."

27. For a full exposition of his views see Malik, *Kargil.*

28. Ahmed, "No to 'Cold Start.'"

29. Kanwal, "Strike Fast and Hard: Army Doctrine Undergoes Change in Nuclear Era."

30. Arun Joshi, "Army Opposes Demilitarisation, Joint Management," *Hindustan Times,* January 8, 2007 (www.hindustantimes.com/News-Feed/nm21/Army-opposes-demilitarisation-of-J-K/Article1-198489.aspx).

31. "Commanding Heights," interview with Lieutenant-General V. K. Singh, GOC Eastern Command, in *Salute,* January 20, 2010 (SalutetoIndiansoldier.com [January 23, 2010]).

32. George Fernandes, "The Dynamics of Limited War," *Strategic Affairs,* October 16, 2000.

33. The concept of deterrence by punishment is explored in Glenn H. Snyder, *Deterrence and Defense: Toward a Theory of National Security* (Princeton University Press, 1961), pp. 9-16. For a discussion of why punishment is unlikely to succeed in this case, see Sumit Ganguly and Michael Ryan Kraig, "The 2001–2002 Indo-Pakistani Crisis: Exposing the Limits of Coercive Diplomacy," *Security Studies,* vol. 14, no. 2 (Winter 2004–05), pp. 316–17.

34. Edward N. Luttwak, "The Operational Level of War," *International Security,* vol. 5 (Winter 1980–81), p. 731; Carter Malkasian, "Toward a Better Understanding of Attrition: The Korean and Vietnam Wars," *Journal of Military History* 3 (2004), p. 940.

35. Luttwak, p. 65.

36. For a cynical view of Cold Start, arguing that neither the Indian nor the Pakistani Army has genuine risk takers, see Brigadier (retired) Shaukat Qadir, "India's Cold Start Strategy," *Daily Times,* May 8, 2004 (www.dailytimes.com.pk/default.asp?page=story_8-5-2004_pg3_3).

37. Terms such as "insane," "irresponsible," and "mad" were used to characterize Kapoor's banal observation that limited war was possible in South Asia underneath the nuclear umbrella—a position that Pakistani generals had discussed privately as early as 1982. For a more muted Pakistan Army response by the chairman of the Joint Chiefs of Staff Committee, General Tariq Majid, see Iftekhar A. Khan, "India Told to Beware of Strategic Mistake," *Dawn,* January 26, 2010 (www.dawn.com/wps/wcm/connect/dawn-content-library/dawn/news/pakistan/18-gen-kapoors-statement-outlandish-am-13 [January 3, 2010]).

38. Shekhar Gupta, "Our Harmed Forces," *Indian Express,* January 16, 2010 (http://Indianexpress.com/story-print/567998 [January 23, 2010]).

39. Tariq M. Ashraf, "Doctrinal Reawakening of the Indian Armed Forces," *Military Review,* November–December 2004, p. 59.

40. A recent reorganization of Pakistani ground forces into three commands does not change the situation on the ground.

41. Kidwai's red lines included an attack on Pakistan that seized a significant amount of territory, the destruction if Pakistan's land or air forces, the economic strangulation of Pakistan, or fomenting political destabilization or large-scale internal disorder. See Paolo Cotta-Ramusino and Maurizio Martellini, "Nuclear Safety, Nuclear Stability and Nuclear Strategy in Pakistan" (Como, Italy: Landau Network, 2001), p. 5. An influential retired Pakistan army general reformulated these red lines, and in the process made them less clear and more ambiguous. See Major-General (retired) Mahmud Ali Durrani, "Pakistan's Strategic Thinking and the Role of Nuclear Weapons," Cooperative Monitoring Center, Occasional Paper 37, Sandia National Laboratories, July 2004. For a discussion of the uncertainty surrounding Pakistan's red lines, see Rajesh M. Basrur and Stephen P. Cohen, "Bombs in Search of a Mission: India's Uncertain Nuclear Future," in *South Asia in 2020: Future Strategic Balances and Alliances*, edited by Michael R. Chambers (Carlisle, Pa.: Strategic Studies Institute, 2002), p. 130.

42. Ravi Rikhye, "A Short History of Indian Division Deployments against China," version 2.0, July 5, 2006 (http://orbat.com/site/history/volume4/448/deployments againstchina.pdf [July 1, 2007]). Rikhye is the online editor of the web-based *Orbat*, devoted to studies of the order of battle of various militaries.

43. See defense analysis website globalsecurity.org for "Indian Army Divisions," www.globalsecurity.org/military/world/india/divisions.htm.

44. See the authoritative Indian review of China's response by D. S. Rajan, "How China Views India's New Defence Doctrine," *Rediff*, January 7, 2010 (news.rediff. com/column/2010/jan/07/how-china-views-indias-new-defence-doctrine.htm).

45. Brigadier (retired) Arun Sahgal, "National Military Aspirations and Military Capabilities: An Approach," in *Army 2020*, edited by Oberoi.

46. Ibid.

CHAPTER FOUR

1. See Rahul Roy-Chaudhury, *The Indian Navy: Forces, Missions, and Engagement in the Indo-Pacific* (Singapore: Institute of Defence and Strategic Studies, 2005) (www.rsis.edu.sg/research/PDF/the_india_navy.pdf).

2. Rahul Roy-Chaudhury, *India's Maritime Security* (New Delhi: IDSA, 2000), p. 127.

3. Jasjit Singh, "Air Power and National Defence: the Strategic Force for Strategic Effect," in *Aerospace Power and India's Defence*, edited by Singh (New Delhi: Knowledge World, 2007), pp. 146–47.

4. P. V. S. Jagan Mohan and Samir Chopra, *The India-Pakistan Air War of 1965* (New Delhi: Manohar Books, 2005).

5. India claims to have brought down seven Pakistani F-86 Sabre jets, but Pakistan accedes to only three. One Gnat was forced to land in a Pakistani airfield and was

captured. Indians call the Gnat the "Sabre Slayer;" see www.warbirdalley.com/gnat. htm. The purchase of the Gnat, however, became a cautionary tale for the IAF because the aircraft turned out to be the deadliest fighter flown by the service. More Gnats were crashed by the IAF than any other aircraft. The aircraft did not go through the full development cycle of in-use testing since no other country's air force has bought the machine. See Group Captain Kapil Bhargava, "Quarter Century of the Jaguar in India" (http://bharat-rakshak.com/IAF/Aircraft/Current/607-Jaguar-25.html).

6. Rear Admiral (retired) Raja Menon, *The Indian Navy* (New Delhi: Naval Head-quarters, 2000), p. 52.

7. K. M. Panikkar, *India and the Indian Ocean* (London: Allen and Unwin, 1945).

8. K. M. Panikkar, *Problems of Indian Defence* (London: Asia Publishing House, 1960), p. 114.

9. See K. R. Singh, *Navies of South Asia* (New Delhi: Rupa and Company Books, 2002); and K. Subrahmanyam, "Naval Security Doctrine for India," in *Strategic Analysis*, February 1990, vol. 12, no. 11, p. 1144.

10. Jasjit Singh, "Some Reflections on the IAF," *Air Power Journal*, vol. 1, no. 1 (Monsoon), 2004, p. 166.

11. The IAF is wary of purchasing aircraft that are not in the inventory of the country that manufactures them. This was one reason why India refused in 1986 to consider the capable Northrop F-20, for which it could have obtained the tools and dies for manufacturing, it was not in the U.S. Air Force's inventory, although it was in service with a number of allied air forces.

12. In 1985 Pakistani officials confronted Americans with "evidence" that the Jag-uars were practicing toss-bombing, a way of delivering a nuclear weapon without the blast endangering the aircraft. The planes had gone missing from American recon-naissance satellites, and for a brief time the Pakistani statement seemed credible. However, India did not have a nuclear device at the time, and if the story had been true, then Indian pilots were either spooking the Pakistanis deliberately or simply practicing for the day when their aircraft would be armed with nuclear weapons.

13. George Tanham, *Indian Strategic Thought: An Interpretive Essay* (Santa Monica, Calif.: Rand, 1992).

14. Ibid., p. 62.

15. Tanham, pp. 45–46.

16. Rupak Chattopadhyay, "The Indian Air Force: Flying into the 21st Century," July 2, 2009 (http://bharat-rakshak.com/IAF/Today/Contemporary/327-Flying-21st-Century.html [December 4, 2009]).

17. Ibid.

18. Ibid. Chattopadhyay offers a subtle discussion of how these have been pursued by the IAF over the last decade.

19. Air Marshall A. K. Tiwary, *Aerospace Defence: A Holistic Approach* (New Delhi: Manas Publications, 2006), p. 180.

20. For a discussion, see T. D. Joseph, "Air Power in Limited Wars," in *Aerospace Power*, edited by Singh, pp. 165–67.

21. Ibid. See also Air Commodore (retired) R. V. Phadke, "Air Power and Escalation Control," 2007, the Stimson Center (www.stimson.org/pub.cfm?id=83 [August 14, 2007]). Earlier, Phadke had advocated for a sixty combat squadron air force with refueling capacity, AWACS, cruise missiles, and other high technology gear, observing that "in short, a modern high-tech air is unavailable if India wishes to face coercive threats in the future"; he adds, for good measure, the need to build a "robust aerospace industry capable of designing and developing state-of-the-art equipment and aircraft." R. V. Phadke, "Response Options: Future of India Air Power Vision 2020," *Strategic Analysis*, January 2001, vol. 24, no. 10, published by the Institute of Defence Studies and Analyses (www.ciaonet.org/olj/sa/sa_jan01phr01.html [August 23, 2007]).

22. This is exactly what one distinguished retired army officer has suggested, that the IAF only had two roles: air interdiction and ground support (plus the nuclear-delivery task). See Brigadier (retired) Gurmeet Kanwal, "Close Air Support to Land Forces: New Thinking Is Needed," *India Strategic* (New Delhi), vol. 4, no. 9 (September 2009), pp.12–15.

23. Sandeep Dikshit, " IAF Unhappy with War Doctrine," *The Hindu*, November 24, 2004 (www.thehindu.com/2004/11/25/stories/2004112503051200.htm), p. 200.

24. Tiwary, p. 55.

25. The Gulf War Air Power Survey (www.airforcehistory.hq.af.mil/Publications/ Annotations/gwaps.htm) and various studies of the war in Kosovo reveal that the initial optimism of the effects of the air war were misplaced. The air campaign did not do sufficient damage and what damage it did was irrelevant. Also see Stephen Biddle, "The New Way of War," *Foreign Affairs*, May–June 2002 (www.foreignaffairs. com/articles/58015/stephen-biddle/the-new-way-of-war).

26. Emily Wax, "India's Space Ambitions Taking Off," *Washington Post*, November 4, 2009, p. A–10.

27. K. K. Nair, *Space: The Frontiers of Modern Defence* (New Delhi: Knowledge World, 2006), p. 85.

28. The air force showed interest in the Hawkeye as soon as it was cleared for sale to the Indian Navy. Gulshan Luthra, "US Clears Hawkeye E-2D for India," *India Strategic* (New Delhi), vol. 4, no. 9 (September 2009), pp. 8–11.

29. George K. Tanham, *The Indian Air Force* (Santa Monica, Calif.: RAND, 1995), p. 65.

30. The subject of indigenous MiG quality and poor manufacturing techniques, as well as corruption in the defense-procurement sector, were the themes of a popular Bollywood film, *Rang de Basanti*.

31. For a useful history and critique of HAL by an Indian parliamentary committee, see the Seventh Report of the Standing Committee on Defence (2006–07), "Ministry of Defence: In-Depth Study and Critical Review of Hindustan Aeronautics Limited (HAL)," Lok Sabha Secretariat, New Delhi, May 2007. The report draws mostly on official statements, its main recommendation being that HAL be reorganized along more professional lines, perhaps modeled after the Indian Space Research

Organisation or the group that created the Brahmos missile, do more R&D, and include corporate representatives on its board.

32. For a narrative discussion, see K. Chatterjee, "Hindustan Fighter HF-24 Marut, Part I, Building India's Jet Fighter" (www.bharat-rakshak.com/IAF/History/Aircraft/Marut1.html [August 20, 2007]); and Amit Sisir Gupta, *Building an Arsenal: The Evolution of Regional Power Force Structures* (Westport, Conn., and London: Praeger, 1998), especially chapter 2, "The Indian Experience."

33. For a reliable overview of the IAF's problems and accomplishments, see Rupak Chattopadhyay, "The Indian Air Force: Flying into the 21st Century."

34. The LCA has acquired its own nomenclature: "Late Coming Aircraft," "Light Combat Arjun" (the Arjun is a tank), and "Last Chance for Arunachalam," a dig at the defense scientist who was a vigorous proponent of the LCA in the 1980s.

35. Vivek Raghuvanshi, "Home Stretch for LCA?" *Defense News,* April 26, 2009, p. 16.

36. For an American analysis see "All Fall Down," *Strategy Page* (www.strategypage.com/htmw/htatrit/20090603.aspx [July 9, 2009]).

37. The full story of the LCA has yet to be told, but some insightful articles include Air Marshall (retired) M. S. D. Wollen, "The Light Combat Aircraft Story," *Indian Aviation, Opening Show Report, Aero India,* 2001, reproduced in *Bharat Rakshak Monitor,* vol. 3, no. 5 (March–April 2001) (www.bharat-rakshak.com/MONITOR/ISSUE3-5/wollen.html [August 30, 2007]); and Sunil Saini and George Joseph, "LCA and Economics" (www.bharat-rakshak.com/MONITOR/ISSUE3-5/sainis.html [August 30, 2007]).

38. Tanham, p. 20.

39. For an overview, see Manu Pubby, "The MRCA," *Indian Express,* June 30, 2007.

40. Ibid.

41. Tanham, p. 95.

42. Ajai Shukla, "How Not to Do It . . . ," *Business Standard,* June 3, 2007 (http://ajaishukla.blogspot.com/2007/07/how-not-to-do-it.html).

43. Rupak Chattopadhyay, "The Indian Air Force: Flying into the 21st Century." Chattopadhyay is a formidable expert on the IAF and lives in Canada.

44. During the cold war, India based its Western-supplied ships in Bombay and Cochin on the west coast and its Soviet bloc ships in the east, mostly at Vizag, where they were sometimes mistaken for Soviet Navy vessels. India refused basing rights to all navies, and provided minimal refueling and ship-visit facilities to both NATO and WTO Navies. For an Indian perspective, see Onkar S. Marwah, "India's Strategic Perspective on the Indian Ocean," in *The Indian Ocean: Perspectives on a Strategic Arena,* edited by William L. Dowdy and Russell B. Trood (Duke University Press, 1985), pp. 301–17.

45. Roy-Chaudhury, *India's Maritime Security,* p. 125.

46. Ibid., pp. 127–31.

47. For a collection of the short writings of one of the navy's most distinguished admirals, Arun Prakash, see *Force Magazine,* New Delhi, March 2010 (www.forceindia.net/arunprakash.aspx [March 3, 2010]).

48. Indian Defence Reports (www.india-defence.com/reports-2594 [August 23, 2007]).

49. See Geoffrey Till, "Maritime Strategy in a Globalizing World," in Ruger Papers 2, *Economics and Maritime Strategy: Implications for the 21st Century,* edited by Richmond M. Lloyd (Newport, R.I.: Naval War College, 2007), pp. 19–24.

50. The 2004 Indian Maritime Doctrine refers to Corbett.

51. India's role in the greater Indian Ocean region has been noted by a number of Western writers. For two recent studies, see Walter C. Ladwig III, "Delhi's Pacific Ambition: Naval Power, 'Look East,' and India's Emerging Influence in the Asia-Pacific," *Asian Security,* vol. 5, no. 2, 2009, pp. 87–113; and David Scott, "India's 'Extended Neighborhood' Concept: Power Projection for a Rising Power," *India Review,* vol. 8, no 2 (April–June 2009), pp. 107–43.

52. See, for example, the extended comments of a recent navy chief, Admiral Sureesh Mehta, "India's National Security Challenges—An Armed Forces Overview," speech delivered to the India Habitat Centre, August 10, 2009 (www.outlookindia. com/article.aspx?261738 [August 2009]).

53. Harsh V. Pant, "India in the Indian Ocean: Growing Mismatch between Ambitions and Capabilities," *Pacific Affairs,* vol. 82, no. 2 (Summer 2009), pp. 279–97.

54. In 2001 India did not invite Pakistan when it hosted the International Fleet Review, so China refused to attend. Eight years later, in another International Fleet Review, China was the host and both India and Pakistan participated.

CHAPTER FIVE

1. Three books offer a comprehensive history of the Indian nuclear weapons program. George Perkovich, *India's Nuclear Bomb: The Impact on Global Proliferation* (University of California Press, 1999), is a careful account that draws upon an extensive interview with the Indian participants; Itty Abraham, *The Making of the Indian Atomic Bomb* (London: Zed Books, 1998), places the program in the context of India's search for a national identity; and Raj Chengappa, *Weapons of Peace: The Secret Story of India's Quest to Be a Nuclear Power* (New Delhi: HarperCollins, 2000), contains rich anecdotal information about the personalities involved in both the nuclear and missile programs.

2. One of the concerns of the nuclear establishment generated by the long delay between the first and second nuclear tests was that the weapons program would lose key people to retirement and that it would have a hard time recruiting a new generation of scientists who wanted to work for few rewards in a secret program with little public support.

3. The details of the American discussions only became public after the declassification of a set of Kennedy documents in the 1990s, and there are no reliable Indian records available. The U.S. Air Force position in 1961 was that India and other rivals of China should be allowed or encouraged to acquire nuclear weapons; the Department of State opposed any change in the policy of discouraging proliferation. During

the decade before the NPT was signed, American officials sought ways to accommodate India, which was itself interested in a joint U.S.-Soviet guarantee in the event of another confrontation with China. Nothing came of any of this. We are grateful to Ms. Tanvi Madan for tracking down the archival documents. For an Indian account that draws upon American records and familiarity with many of the participants, see A. G. Noorani, "The Nuclear Guarantee Episode," *Frontline* 18, no. 12 (June 9–22, 2001) (http://webcache.googleusercontent.com/search?q=cache:8Hdz-AHChdAJ:www.thehindu.com/fline/fl1812/18120940.htm+the+nuclear+guarantee +episode+frontline+the+hindu&cd=1&hl=en&ct=clnk&gl=us [cached version]).

4. Ibid.

5. An account by a participant in the decision makes this point. P. R. Chari, then an important official in the Ministry of Defence, observes that the decision to test the euphemistically named "peaceful nuclear explosion" was motivated less by any strategic compulsion or even a careful consideration of the pros and cons, and more because of Indira Gandhi's domestic political problems. Serendipity was also at play: the technology and the team were in place to test; not testing would mean that the whole effort was for naught. See P. R. Chari, *Pokhran-I: Personal Recollections I*, Institute of Peace and Conflict Studies Special Report (New Delhi: IPCS, August 2009), (www.ipcs.org [December 2009]).

6. The *locus classicus* for K. Sundarji's writings is the unpublished monograph, "Strategy in the Age of Nuclear Deterrence and Its Application to Developing Countries," written in 1984 when he was a lieutenant-general. This drew upon a number of unpublished, classified documents that Sundarji had prepared over the years. Later, he was to widen his audience with two important publications: one was a "mail seminar" that he ran while commandant of the College of Combat, Mhow; the other was a novel, *Blind Men of Hindoostan, Indo-Pak Nuclear War* (New Delhi: USBSPD Publishers, 1993), published after retirement. Sundarji frequently cited Kenneth Waltz's aphorism "More is not better if less is enough"; that has become the banner of the "pragmatists" in Pakistan as well as in India. For a systematic presentation of Sundarji's views about a year before he became army chief see Lieutenant-General K. Sundarji, *Strategy in the Age of Nuclear Deterrence and its Application to Developing Countries*, unpublished manuscript, Simla, India, June 21, 1984.

7. K. Subrahmanyam, "Indian Nuclear Policy—1964–98, A Recollection," in *Nuclear India*, edited by Jasjit Singh (New Delhi: Knowledge World, 1998), pp. 43–44. India's missile program, which formally began in 1983, also gained momentum from 1988 onward. The first Prithvi missile test took place in 1988 (with fifteen more Prithvi tests through 1997), and the first Agni missile test in 1989 (with subsequent tests in 1992 and 1994); these were coordinated with India's diplomatic efforts to resist American pressure.

8. For an authoritative statement of the proliferation problem from the perspective of a leading member of the American nonproliferation community, see Randy J. Rydell, "Giving Nonproliferation Norms Teeth: Sanctions and the NNPA," *The Nonproliferation Review* 6, no. 2 (Winter 1999): 1–19.

9. For views on these schools, or attitudinal clusters, see Kanti P. Bajpai, "War, Peace and International Order: India's View of World Politics," in Harvard Academy for International and Area Studies, Project on Conflict or Convergence: Global Perspectives on War, Peace, and International Order (Cambridge Mass.: Weatherhead Center, 1998), p. 2 and chapter 2; and "The World View of India's Strategic Elite," in Stephen P. Cohen, *India: Emerging Power* (Brookings Institution Press, 2001).

10. For a study of India's scientific community and its attitudes toward the West and nuclear weapons, see Abraham, *The Making of the Indian Atomic Bomb*; and for an excellent chronology, see the Nuclear Threat Institute, *India Profile*, Feb. 18, 2010 (www.nti.org/e_research/profiles/india/index.html).

11. Many of the same positions re-emerged during the 2005–07 debate over the U.S.-India nuclear deal.

12. The Deputy Secretary of State, Strobe Talbott, describes this in the opening of his book on negotiating post-test relations with India and Pakistan; see Talbott, *Engaging India: Diplomacy, Democracy, and the Bomb* (Brookings Institution Press, 2004). The deception effort deepened American suspicion of Indian motives.

13. "Draft Report of the NSAB on Indian Nuclear Doctrine," August 17, 1999 (www.acronym.org.uk/39draft.htm).

14. For an extended discussion, see P. R. Chari, Pervaiz Iqbal Cheema, and Stephen P. Cohen, *Four Crises and a Peace Process: American Engagement in South Asia* (Brookings Institution Press, 2008).

15. Of course, such a massive attack on Pakistan would result in enormous Indian casualties from fallout, even if Pakistan were unable to deliver its own nuclear weapon on India.

16. The proposed numbers of such a system vary considerably among authors, but most are in the range of 100 to 300 nuclear weapons. Some favor a thermonuclear capability; others believe that a first-generation fission bomb is adequate for deterrence.

17. Jaswant Singh, *Defending India* (New York: St. Martin's Press, 1999), p. 270.

18. Ibid., p. 128.

19. The *Kargil Review Committee Report* (New Delhi: Government of India, 2000). The three-member committee included a journalist, George Verghese; a former government official, K. Subrahmanyam (as chair); and a retired general, Lieutenant-General K. K. Hazari.

20. Ibid., chapter 10, "Nuclear Backdrop."

21. For a recent analytical overview, see Sumit Ganguly and Ted Greenwood, eds., *Mending Fences: Confidence- and Security-Building Measures in South Asia* (Boulder: Westview Press, 1996).

22. For an overview, see "Advanced Technology Vessel" in GlobalSecurity.org (www.globalsecurity.org/wmd/world/india/atv.htm [August 6, 2009]), p. 204.

23. For an overview of Chinese nuclear strategy in the context of the South Asia tests, see Ming Zhang, *China's Changing Nuclear Posture: Reactions to the South Asian Nuclear Tests* (Washington: Carnegie Endowment for International Peace, 1999).

24. Jasjit Singh, "A Nuclear Strategy for India," in *Nuclear India,* edited by Singh, p. 317. Generally, army officers who have served in the Himalayas have been more supportive of the idea of tactical nuclear weapons' use against China.

25. Ibid.

26. A more accurate description of Pakistani strategy is found in Major-General (retired) Mahmud Ali Durrani, "Pakistan's Strategic Thinking and the Role of Nuclear Weapons," Cooperative Monitoring Center Occasional Paper 37 (Sandia National Laboratories, July 2004), (www.cmc.sandia.gov/cmc-papers/sand2004-3375p.pdf [May 2, 2006]). Durrani briefly served as the Pakistani national security adviser in early 2009.

27. At the non-nuclear level India was inhibited from attacking Karachi during the 2009 crisis by the presence of ships that were part of the supply chain for American forces in Afghanistan.

28. Rajesh Rajagopalan, *Second Strike: Arguments about Nuclear War in South Asia,* (New Delhi: Penguin Books, 2005), p. 128.

29. See S. Paul Kapur, "India and Pakistan's Unstable Peace: Why Nuclear South Asia Is Not Like Cold War Europe," *International Security* 30, no. 2 (Fall 2005): 141.

30. See Colonel Anil Chauhan, "Consequence Management in the Aftermath of a Nuclear Strike" (report of a seminar sponsored by Centre for Land Warfare Studies [CLAWS], New Delhi, May 1, 2009). The report, compiled by a CLAWS research team, was essentially a rehash of a 1982 study done at an American university. During the heart surgery of Prime Minister Manmohan Singh in 2008, it was not quite clear who was the designated official responsible for nuclear decisions during Singh's incapacity.

31. For a survey of the doctrinal problems associated with India's delivery of a nuclear weapon, see Rahul Bedi, "India's Nuclear Doctrine Unclear," *Jane's Defence Weekly,* 34, no. 16 (October 18, 2000).

32. Pakistan moved quickly to create an NCA and a Strategic Plans Division in the Joint Staff headquarters in part because of the furor that arose in 2002 when it was revealed that Dr. A. Q. Khan had received and shared nuclear technology from a number of countries, indicating the possibility of lax government control over nuclear assets. Khan has recently replied that his actions were, indeed, approved by the civilian government of the day, then headed by Benazir Bhutto.

33. Report of the Nuclear Threat Initiative, *India Profile* (Washington, 2009), p. 81 (www.nti.org/e_research/profiles/India/Missile/index.html [November 15, 2009]).

34. Nuclear Threat Initiative, *India Profile* (www.nti.org/e_research/profiles/India/Nuclear/index.html).

35. Ibid.

36. For a discussion, see Ali Ahmed, "Re-visioning the Nuclear Command Authority" (New Delhi: Institute of Defence Studies and Analyses, September 9, 2009) (www.idsa.in/strategiccomments/RevisioningtheNuclearComandAutority_AliAhmed_090909).

37. "India Needs Two More Nuclear Tests," *Rediff News* (http://news.rediff.com/report/2009/sep/21/india-needs-2-more-nuke-tests1.htm [November 18, 2009]).

38. In every one of the recent India-Pakistan crises, including three that involved nuclear threats of one kind or another, one or both sides made a serious error of judgment or were the victims of faulty intelligence. This was also true of the United States in some of the crises. See Chari, Cheema, and Cohen, *Four Crises and a Peace Process: American Engagement in South Asia*.

39. For a comprehensive review of the problem of attacks on nuclear facilities and infrastructure, see Roddam Narasimha and others, eds., *Science and Technology to Counter Terrorism: Proceedings of an Indo-U.S. Workshop*, U.S. National Academy of Science, Committee on International Security and Arms Control and the National Institute of Advanced Science, Bangalore (Washington: National Academies Press, 2007).

40. This baseline study is by S. Rashid Naim, "Asia's Day After," in *The Security of South Asia: Asian and American Perspectives*, edited by Stephen P. Cohen (University of Illinois Press, 1987): a revised version appears in *Nuclear Proliferation in South Asia*, edited by Stephen P. Cohen (Boulder, Colo.: Westview Press, 1990); figures cited above are from the latter version, pp. 46–56. For a graphic depiction of a nuclear attack on a major Indian city, see M. V. Ramana, *Bombing Bombay? Effects of Nuclear Weapons and a Case Study of a Hypothetical Explosion* (Cambridge, Mass.: International Physicians for the Prevention of Nuclear War, 1999) (www.ippnw.org/PDF%20files/Bombay.pdf).

41. Lieutenant-General (retired) Eric Vas, "Nuclear Policy Options: The Satyagraha Approach," monograph, Indian Initiative for Peace, Arms Control, and Disarmament (Pune, India: INPAD, 1999) (www.inpad.com).

42. The Indian government did not further develop the idea, but for an advocate's position see M. Vidyasagar, "A Nuclear Power by Any Name," *Pragati* (January 2010): 15 (http://pragati.nationalinterest.in/wp-content/uploads/2010/01/pragati-issue34-jan2010-communityed.pdf [January 10, 2010]).

43. In a rare exception during the 2001–02 crisis, India's leading news magazine, *India Today*, carried a long feature story on the consequences for urban India of a nuclear exchange. Also see Ramana, *Bombing Bombay?*

CHAPTER SIX

1. Ajai Shukla, "Dysfunctional Defence," *Asian Wall Street Journal* (July 19, 2007) (http://ajaishukla.blogspot.com/2007/07/dysfunctional-defence.html), p. 206.

2. In March 2008 the Minister of State for Home Affairs, Sri Prakash Jaiswal, told the Rajya Sabha or the upper house of the Indian Parliament: "As per data compiled by the Bureau of Police Research and Development (BPR&D) the number of police personnel per 100,000 of population in India as of January 1, 2006, is 1:142.69 (142.69 police personnel for every 100,000 population)," (www.theindian.com/newsportal/uncategorized/only-142-policemen-for-every-100000-people-in-india_10024380.html#ixzz0XbY27aD8).

3. P. Chidambaram, "Concluding Statement of the Home Minister," at the Conference of Chief Ministers on Internal Security, New Delhi, August 17, 2009 (www.mha.nic.in/pdfs/HM-S-280809.pdf).

4. David H. Bayley, among others, has argued that policing even at its best in advanced industrial societies comprises those elements. However, the point made here still applies on a comparative basis. See Bayley, *Changing the Guard: Developing Democratic Police Abroad* (Oxford University Press, 2005).

5. See National Police Commission Report, 1977 (www.bprd.gov.in/images/pdf/research/police-commission-report/first-report.pdf).

6. Patricia Grossman, "India's Secret Armies," in *Death Squads in Global Perspective: Murder with Deniability,* edited by Bruce B. Campbell and Arthur D. Brenner (New York: St. Martin's Press, 2000), pp. 262–86.

7. Sanjay Kumar Jha, *Internal Security in a Third World Democracy: The Role of Paramilitary Force in India* (Ph.D. Diss., Jawaharlal Nehru University, Center for International Politics, Organization, and Disarmament, School of International Studies, 2000), p. 89.

8. B. V. P. Rao, "Small Weapons and National Security," *Seminar* 479 (July 1999): 38.

9. Bashyam Kasturi, "Review of Four Books," *Seminar* 479 (July 1999): 53.

10. James Fearon, "Why Do Some Civil Wars Last So Much Longer than Others?" *Journal of Peace Research* 41, no 3 (May 2004): 275–301.

11. For a good overview of Mumbai, see the *India Today* special issue on terrorism, "The Agenda for Action," January 19, 2009. For a detailed list of twenty-six organizational recommendations by a former Indian intelligence official, see B. Raman, "After Mumbai: Points for Action," *International Terrorism Monitor*, Paper 474, Global Intelligence News, December 2, 2008 (http://globalintel.net/wp/2008/12/02/after-mumbai-points-for-action/).

12. Jha, *Internal Security in a Third World Democracy,* p. 68.

13. Kit Collier, *The Armed Forces and Internal Security in Asia: Preventing the Abuse of Power,* Politics and Security Series Occasional Papers 2 (Honolulu: East-West Center, 1999), pp. 8–9.

14. Some estimates put the figure at 1.4 million, which would make India's paramilitary strength larger than that of China. See D. C. Arya and R. C. Sharma, eds., *Management Issues and Operational Planning for India's Borders* (New Delhi: Scholars Publishing Forum, 1991), p. 31.

15. Collier, pp. 8–9.

16. Officers of the CRPF jokingly (but not without some truth) say that "CRPF" stands for *Chalte raho pyare* (Keep on the move, my dear). See Shekhar Gupta, "The Tired Trouble Shooters," *India Today,* International ed., February 15, 1988, pp. 82–83.

17. Anjali Nirmal, *Role and Functioning of Central Police Organisations* (New Delhi: Uppal Publishing House, 1992), p. 14.

18. Chaman Lal, "Terrorism and Insurgency," *Seminar*, no. 483 (November 1999): 20.

19. Annual Report of the Ministry of Home Affairs, 2007–08, p. 7.

20. See Ministry of Home Affairs, "Scheme for Modernization of State Police Forces," New Delhi, 2000 (http://mha.nic.in/pdfs/MPF.pdf).

21. For an evaluation of the police modernization scheme, see Om Shankar Jha, "Impact of Modernisation of Police Forces Scheme on Combat Capability of the Police Forces in Naxal-Affected States: A Critical Evaluation," Institute of Defence Studies and Analyses (New Delhi: Institute of Defence Studies and Analyses, December 2009) (www.idsa.in/system/files/OccasionalPaper7_Naxal.pdf [March 7, 2010]).

22. See Harinder Baweja, "Why Can't You See the 26/11 Report," Tehelka, April 25, 2010 (www.tehelka.com/story_main42.asp?filename=Ne220809why_cant.asp).

23. Statement in parliament by Home Minister P. Chidambaram, December 11, 2008 (www.mha.nic.in/pdfs/HM-S-M-Atteck.pdf).

24. See Intergraph Corporation (a U.S.-based security training company), "Mumbai Police Implement Intergraph Public Information System," Huntsville, Ala., Feb. 14, 2007 (www.intergraph.com/assets/pressreleases/2007/47105.aspx).

25. Simon Montlake, "India Overhauls National Security after Mumbai Attacks." Christian Science Monitor (December 11, 2008) (www.csmonitor.com/2008/1211/p99s01-duts.html [February 17, 2009]).

26. See Defence Minister Pranab Mukherjee's statement in the Press Trust of India story, "LoC Fencing Completed: Mukherjee," Times of India, December 16, 2004 (http://timesofindia.indiatimes.com/articleshow/960859.cms). See also Joseph Josy, "India to Acquire High Tech Military Equipment," Rediff News (www.rediff.com/news/2002/jan/08josy.htm). The fence was one of the first manifestations of close Indian-Israeli cooperation on intelligence; it led to expanded cooperation between the two states on a range of matters, and the considerable sharing of Israeli high-tech–weapons technology, ranging from MiG-21 upgrades to aerial radar and command posts.

27. Jim Lehrer, "India's Government under Scrutiny after Mumbai Attacks," transcript, News Hour, December 2, 2008 (www.pbs.org/newshour/bb/asia/july-dec08/mumbaianger_12-02.html).

28. Human Rights Watch, "Getting Away with Murder: 50 Years of the Armed Forces Special Powers Act," August 2008 (http://hrw.org/backgrounder/2008/india 0808).

29. Kuldeep Mathur, "The State and the Use of Coercive Power in India," Asian Survey 33, no. 4 (April 1992): 337–48.

30. Baweja, "Why Can't You See the 26/11 Report?"

31. For an informed discussion see P. R. Chari, "Countering the Naxalites: Deploying the Armed Forces," Institute of Peace and Conflict Studies, Special Report 89, April, 2010, New Delhi (www.ipcs.org/pdf_file/issue/SR89-PR_Chari.pdf [May 3, 2010]).

CHAPTER SEVEN

1. Sushant K. Singh and Mukul Asher, "Making Defense Expenditure More Effective," Pragati, the Indian National Interest Review (February 2010): 19–22 (http://Pragati.com [February 2, 2010]).

2. Ibid.

3. K. Subrahmanyam, *IDSA—In Retrospect* (New Delhi: Institute for Defence Studies and Analyses, 2007), p. 14.

4. These include Bharat Rakshak and Pragati (Singapore), both web-based. From 1993 onward, tethered army, navy, and air force think tanks have been established in emulation of the American system. Today, each service has a counterpart in the think tank community: the army's Centre for Land and Warfare Studies (CLAWS), the IAF's Centre for Air Power Studies (CAPS), and the navy's National Maritime Foundation. The Ministry of Defence continues to fund the Institute for Defence Studies and Analyses, while the truly independent Institute of Peace and Conflict Studies offers informed perspectives on diverse military and security matters.

5. Teresita Schaffer, *India and the United States in the 21st Century: Reinventing Partnership* (Washington: Center for Strategic and International Studies, 2009), p. 66.

6. Aseema Sinha and Jon P. Dorschner, "India: Rising Power or Mere Revolution of Rising Expectations?" *Polity* 42, no. 1 (January 2010): 74.

7. For example, it was an army-funded think tank, CLAWS, that organized India's first-ever interservice workshop on "Firepower" in 2009. See http://claws.in/index.php?action=event&task=44. Other imaginative CLAWS projects have reviewed defense acquisition, interservice cooperation, and military sociology.

8. China has geographic commands, in which the PLA dominates other forces, the U.S. manages with vast regional commands, PACOM, CENTCOM, and the like, which, while creating a "seam" problem, manage the problem of interservice coordination within their respective geographic zones.

9. Samuel P. Huntington, "Patterns of Violence in World Politics," in *Changing Patterns of Military Politics,* edited by Huntington (Glencoe: Free Press, 1962), p. 22.

10. For two evaluations of the Indian foreign and security policy process see Dhruva Jaishankar, "Meta-Morphosis: the Role of Think Tanks and Independent Policy Analysts," *Pragati* (September 13, 2009) (http://polaris.nationalinterest.in/2009/09/13/meta-morphosis/); and Daniel Markey, "Developing India's Foreign Policy 'Software,'" *Asia Policy,* no 8, National Bureau of Asian Research, July 2009, pp. 73–96.

11. In his personal memoir *IDSA—In Retrospect,* Subrahmanyam has described the painful progress of the Institute for Defence Studies and Analyses (IDSA), one of India's few credible think tanks; he notes that the services refused to cooperate by sending serving officers to IDSA on detachment, and have recently developed their own think tanks.

12. We are grateful to Ms. Tara Chandra for her dutiful analysis of this mostly dreadful literature. Typically, one such book is titled *The Dragon and the Elephant,* another *The Elephant and the Dragon.*

13. Nandan Nilekani, *Imagining India: The Idea of a Renewed Nation* (New York: Penguin Press, 2009). For a similar view of India, see Jim O'Neil and Tushar Poddar, "Ten Things for India to Achieve Its 2050 Potential," Goldman Sachs, Global

Economic Paper 169, June 16, 2008. The paper notes that India ranks below the other "BRIC" countries (Brazil, Russia, China), in terms of Sachs' "Growth Environment Scores."

14. For a critique of this Asian superpower syndrome, see James Lamont, "India Prays for Rain as It Reaches for the Skies," *Financial Times,* July 16, 2009, p. 9. Also see Pranab Bardhan, "China, India Superpower? Not so Fast!" *Yale Global Online,* October 25, 2005 (http://yaleglobal.yale.edu/content/china-india-superpower-not-so-fast); and Minxin Pei, "Think Again: Asia's Rise," *Foreign Policy,* June 22, 2009 (www.foreignpolicy.com/articles/2009/06/22/think_again_asias_rise).

15. Shankar Acharya, "Rising India Labours in the Shadow of Asia's Real Giant," *Financial Times,* July 29, 2009, p. 9.

16. See Neville Maxwell, *Henderson-Brooks Report: An Introduction,* April 14–20, 2001 (www.claudearpi.net/maintenance/uploaded_pics/AnIntroductiontothe-HendersonBrooks.pdf [July 7, 2008]).

17. Anit Mukherjee, "Failing to Deliver: The Post Crises Defense Reforms in India, 1998–2008," January 2010, School of Advanced International Studies, Johns Hopkins University, unpublished manuscript.

18. Major (retired) Maroof Raza, "Serious Business of War," *Times of India,* December 11, 2008.

19. Some regimental training centers have been closed, often to allow regular units to move into the vacated center, but to the best of our knowledge, no Indian base has been closed down. A related reform might be to release military-held land to urban development. Indian armed forces own some of the most expensive property in the country. Yet there has been an unwillingness to move military bases to less expensive locations, to combine bases, and to rethink costs. Bases are traditionally the second most discussed subject in parliament—after railway stations—and at a time when every vote counts at the national and state level, no government is going to contemplate a major overhaul of basing policies.

CHAPTER EIGHT

1. The story is best told by then Deputy Secretary of State Strobe Talbott who engaged in over a dozen meetings with Jaswant Singh, successively Indian defense, foreign, and finance minister under the BJP government, which organized the nuclear tests. See Strobe Talbott, *Engaging India: Diplomacy, Democracy, and the Bomb* (Brookings Institution Press, 2004).

2. Under Secretary of Defense for Policy Douglas J. Feith at the U.S.-India Defense Industry Seminar (Washington, May 13, 2002) (www.defense.gov/speeches/speech.aspx?speechid=217).

3. See Ashley J. Tellis, "The Merits of Dehyphenation: Explaining U.S. Success in Engaging India and Pakistan," *Washington Quarterly* (Autumn, 2008): 21–42.

4. Tellis offers a fine-grained and authoritative account of changes in Indian missile and defense policy and how these became linked to American plans for missile defense. See Ashley J. Tellis, "The Evolution of U.S.-Indian Ties: Missile Defense in an Emerging Strategic Relationship," *International Security* 30, no. 4 (Spring 2006): 113–151.

5. Gurmeet Kanwal (Director of the Centre for Land Warfare Studies), "Defence R&D: What India Needs to Do," Feb. 12, 2009, Rediff.com (www.rediff.com/news/2009/feb/12-defence-rand-what-India-needs-to-do.htm [February 14, 2009]).

6. T. V. Parasuram, "Troops to Iraq: Sibal Meets Rice," *The Tribune* (Chandigarh), July 2, 2003.

7. In May 2003 the Cabinet Committee on Security (CCS) discussed the proposal but made no decision either to reject or accept it. Subsequently, the U.S. request was reportedly opposed by "non-BJP members of the CCS," which could only have meant Defence Minister George Fernandes.

8. "Troops to Iraq: Manmohan Clarifies Natwar's Remark," *The Hindu*, July 8, 2004.

9. Director of National Intelligence Dennis C. Blair, *Annual Threat Assessment of the Intelligence Community for the Senate Select Committee on Intelligence*, February 12, 2009, p. 24 (www.dni.gov/testimonies/20090212_testimony.pdf).

10. Bethany N. Danyluk and Juli A. MacDonald (Booz Allen Hamilton), *The U.S.-India Defense Relationship: Reassessing Perceptions and Expectations*, report prepared for the Director, Net Assessment, Office of the Secretary of Defense, November 2008, unclassified.

11. Ashley Tellis, "Mr. Singh Goes to Washington—Part I," *YaleGlobal Online*, November 30, 2009 (http://yaleglobal.yale.edu/print/6069 [December 21, 2009]).

12. These include the new trade and economic relationships, the growing cultural and social ties between India and the United States, and already-identified areas of cooperation such as Indian agricultural and educational reform. Energy policy, however, is proving to be more contentious than expected; it raises many of the same concerns in India as do military-technology transfers and sales, seemingly threatening Indian self-regard concerning autarky and independence. For an excellent overview of U.S.-Indian relations, see Teresita Schaffer, *India and the United States in the 21st Century: Reinventing Partnership* (Washington: Center for Strategic and International Studies, 2009).

13. Supplier countries do not like offsets, and the view of the supplier is generally that they are in the aircraft business, not the machine tool or agriculture business. These arrangements amount to barter, often unsatisfactory as the final agreement becomes very complex, and the trade-offs between different kinds of technologies very subjective.

14. Former Deputy Assistant Secretary of State for South Asia Evan Feigenbaum, "Clinton's Challenge in India," Council on Foreign Relations Expert Brief (www.cfr.org/publication/19852/ [August 2, 2009]).

15. An Indian assessment of these exercises expresses considerable skepticism, particularly the risk that they carry "major costs"—such as the United States gaining

insight into Indian capabilities, and even transferring information to Pakistan or China. Gurpreet S. Khurana, "India-U.S. Combined Defence Exercises: An Appraisal," *Strategic Analysis* 32, no. 6 (November 2008).

16. For a comprehensive American statement of the relevance of the Indian Ocean and the need to work with India in particular, see Robert Kaplan, "Center Stage for the 21st Century: Rivalry in the Indian Ocean," *Foreign Affairs* (March 16, 2009). The bottom line is that the United States needs to be the supreme coalition-builder.

17. For a discussion see the Booz Allen report, pp. 88ff.

18. See Ajay Shukla, "India Had Signed Two Earlier Agreements," *Business Standard*, July 29, 2009 (http://ajaishukla.blogspot.com/2009/07/india-had-signed-two-earlier-end-user.html). Also see Brahma Chellaney, "End-Use Monitoring Agreement (EUMA): A Backgrounder," July 31, 2009 (http://chellaney.spaces.live.com/blog/cns!4913C7C8A2EA4A30!1053.entry) for a sustained criticism of these agreements.

19. Indrani Bagchi, "End-User Travails," *Times of India* blog, May 25, 2009, "Counter-Terrorist Equipment High on India's Priority List after Mumbai Attack" (http://blogs.timesofIndia.indiatimes.com/globespotting/entry/end-user-travails). See also Danyluk and MacDonald, Booz Allen Hamilton, *The U.S.-India Defense Relationship*, pp. 92–96.

20. Ibid.

21. Suba Chandran, "Exploring Regional Zero: An Alternative Indian Nuclear Disarmament Strategy?" South Asia Brief 16 (New Delhi: Institute of Peace and Conflict Studies, October 2009).

22. K. P. Nayar, "Singh's Nuke Gamble II," *The Telegraph*, December 1, 2009 (http://telegraphindia.com/1091201/jsp/frontpage/story_11806763.jsp [December 26, 2009]). For a positive interpretation of the gambit, see David P. Fidler and Sumit Ganguly, "Singh's Shrewd Policy Move: A Shift on India's Nuclear Policy," *Newsweek*, December 4, 2009 (www.newsweek.com/2009/12/03/singh-s-shrewd-move.htm [December 21, 2009]).

23. From Islamabad's vantage point, the new U.S.-India relationship demonstrated that Washington was an unreliable ally. In the words of one senior Pakistani general, the new U.S.-India "alliance" would show Indians how untrustworthy America can be, and America would learn about India's treachery.

24. For an analysis of India's paralysis, see Stephen P. Cohen, "India and Pakistan: If You Don't Know Where You Are Going, Any Road Will Take You There," in *Pakistan—Consequences of Deteriorating Security in Afghanistan,* edited by Kristina Zetterlund (Stockholm: Swedish Defense Research Agency, 2009), pp.131–45.

25. Fareed Zakaria, "What Bush Got Right," *Newsweek*, August 9, 2008 (www.newsweek.com/2008/08/08/what-bush-got-right.html [February 2009]).

26. See Stephen P. Cohen, *India: Emerging Power* (Brookings Institution Press, 2001).

27. R. Nicholas Burns, "America's Strategic Opportunity with India," *Foreign Affairs* (November/December 2007) (www.foreignaffairs.com/articles/63016/r-nicholas-burns/americas-strategic-opportunity-with-india).

28. *Slumdog* was technically brilliant but also misrepresented a great deal. A better characterization of the Indian-U.S. encounter, albeit in pastel colors, is the film *Outsourced*.

29. For many years, Pakistan has been China's largest recipient of arms aid, and then of highly sensitive nuclear technology; it was also China that assisted the North Korean nuclear program.

INDEX

BROOKINGS The Brookings Institution is a private nonprofit organization devoted to research, education, and publication on important issues of domestic and foreign policy. Its principal purpose is to bring the highest quality independent research and analysis to bear on current and emerging policy problems. The Institution was founded on December 8, 1927, to merge the activities of the Institute for Government Research, founded in 1916, the Institute of Economics, founded in 1922, and the Robert Brookings Graduate School of Economics and Government, founded in 1924. Interpretations or conclusions in Brookings publications should be understood to be solely those of the authors.